With the Guns

With the Guns

Two First Hand Accounts of
British Gunners at War in Europe
During World War 1

Three Years in France with the Guns

by C. A. Rose

With the British Guns in Italy

by Hugh Dalton

LEONAUR

With the Guns: Two First Hand Accounts of British Gunners
at War in Europe During World War 1
by Hugh Dalton and C. A. Rose

originall published in 1919 under the titles
Three Years in France with the Guns
With the British Guns in Italy and

Published by Leonaur Ltd

Text in this form copyright © 2007 Leonaur Ltd

ISBN: 978-1-84677-269-6 (hardcover)
ISBN: 978-1-84677-270-2 (softcover)

http://www.leonaur.com

Publisher's Note

Contents

Three Years in France
With the Guns

Introduction

These brief notes of experiences with the guns for thirty-eight months in France were primarily penned for my own satisfaction. Friends who read the manuscript expressed much interest in it, and added the hope that it might be given a more permanent form. Hence it is that it is now printed for private circulation.

The story is a simple record of the fortunes of my own Battery and Brigade, and is intended as a tribute to the good comradeship which existed, under all conditions, among all ranks.

C. A. R.
Edinburgh
January 1919

CHAPTER 1

Breaking Us In

On a morning early in August, 1915, the Brigade disembarked at Havre without mishap to man, horse, or material, and proceeded to a Rest Camp on the outskirts of the town. We were in France at last! The same evening the Batteries started to entrain, and every two hours a complete unit was despatched up the line—to an unknown destination. The men received refreshments at various halts, and the horses were duly watered and fed, but the journey was, on the whole, long and tedious. On one occasion only was the monotony broken, and that unwittingly, by the humour of one of the officers. In the course of the evening, the train stopped at a small station, and the compartment in which the officers were settled drew up in front of the Buffet. Some one asked where we were, and a subaltern, anxious to display his newly-acquired knowledge of French, replied, *"Bouvette,"* which called forth no response. Shortly afterwards the train proceeded on its way, and the occupants of the carriage settled themselves down to sleep. All passed quietly for the next couple of hours—then the train stopped once more, and, as luck would have it, again our carriage came to a standstill directly opposite the buffet of the station. At once a question was asked as to our whereabouts. The same subaltern, shaking himself out of a deep slumber, stretched, roused himself, and, peering out of the window, exclaimed, "Good Lor', still at this beastly hole, 'Bouvette'!" He expressed much surprise at the "unseemly mirth," as he described it, which followed!!

After detraining, the Battery marched through beautiful country, which reminded one of the Borders, as it was not unlike the valley of the Tweed, and we were at once taken to the hearts of the inhabitants of the good village of Seningham, which place was destined to be our home for the next few days. The officers were afforded spacious accommodation in the house of the Maire, whilst the men had comfortable billets in the neighbourhood. Time was spent making our unit shipshape after its travels by land and sea, and the "hairies" obtained as much grazing as possible, to make them fit for what was in store for them. It was wonderful how quickly the men adapted themselves to French ways, and much amusement was caused by their eager, if somewhat unsuccessful, attempts to master the language of our Allies.

When it became known that the officers were anxious to increase their knowledge of the language of the country, the maidens of the village vied with one another to obtain posts as instructresses, and there was nearly a free fight amongst them for the possession of our worthy Senior Subaltern, whose taking ways did not fail to catch their attention!

But, alas! our peaceful warfare was not to be for long! One morning sudden orders came through to prepare for the line in a couple of days' time. All was instant bustle, extra grooming was given to the horses, and finishing touches were put to the howitzers and vehicles. We were to be given a trial in action to show how we would comport ourselves before joining the "Feet" of our own Division, the Guards, who at that time were out at rest. For this purpose we were to be placed under the orders of the C.R.A. of an Indian Division, to reinforce the Batteries already in positions and receive instruction from them.

At last the morning arrived to move off, the column, skirting the town of St. Omer, took the main road to Hazebrouck, and, as we passed through the village of Arques, we caught a first glimpse of our future infantry. They appeared equally keen on seeing their new artillery, and inspected us with a critical eye. The march was made in easy stages, and on the morning of the third day the Brigade arrived at Merville, a quaint old town in Flemish Flanders. After a hasty lunch, the officers rode ahead, in order to get into touch with the unit we were to support in the line, and another amusing incident happened *en route*. One of the Junior Officers owned a sturdy mare, whose reputation as a charger was apt to be ridiculed by his companions, as she was notorious for her slow gait. When the party had proceeded some distance at the trot, "Halting Hilda" was observed, to the astonishment of everyone, to be gradually taking the lead. This fact called forth the remark from her master, "By Jove, she is pulling extraordinarily hard to day: what can be the matter with the animal?" It was then discovered that the rider had been at her mercy for the last couple of miles, the bit clanking merrily from side to side under her great jaw. In the hurry and excitement of departure, after lunch, the bit had not been replaced in her mouth!

The afternoon was spent in reconnoitring the gun positions allotted to us, which were the alternative positions of the units already in line. As a rule, each battery makes a second or alternative gun position, in case it should be shelled out of its existing one, so that no delay takes place in getting into action again. When night fell there was subdued excitement in the wagon line as the time drew near to take the guns "in." This was actually the beginning of our first venture—would we have the luck to get there without being caught in the enemy's harassing fire? How would we behave under shell-fire: would we be steady or otherwise? All these and many other questions flashed through our minds, for a great deal depends, more than one would believe, on how a new and inexperienced unit receives its baptism of fire.

At length a start was made, and the Battery moved off, and soon turned down the long, straight main road leading to La Bassée, the trees on either side showing signs of shrapnel scars, and even in the darkness it could be seen that the cottages were,

13

for the most part, in ruins. It felt distinctly eerie as the small column proceeded silently on its way without showing lights of any description; the stillness and darkness broken now and again by the barking of a gun as we drew nearer the battery zone, and by an occasional Verey Light, which seemed to reveal us in all our nakedness. That long stretch of road seemed interminable—were we never going to reach our destination? However, all remained quiet throughout our progress, and at last we arrived at the entrance to the gun position, which was to be our home for the next fortnight. The guns were speedily unlimbered and man-handled into the pits awaiting their reception, the ammunition was unloaded from the vehicles, and the teams were returned to the wagon line.

The following morning the pieces were "laid out" on our particular zone, and we had time to look round and take stock of our new abode, which was a farmhouse standing in the centre of an orchard adjoining the main road. The building itself was by no means intact, although, as yet, habitable. It gave us enough shelter of a kind, and we soon adjusted ourselves to the prevailing conditions, and the outhouses surrounding it afforded ample accommodation for the detachments. The gun pits were cunningly concealed in the front portion of the orchard, special care having been taken against the prying eyes of hostile aeroplanes. We were fortunate in the choice of position made for our first time in the line, for two reasons, firstly, it was an interesting zone—including the village of Neuve Chapelle now immediately behind our front line—and, secondly, it was quiet. The country there is extremely flat, with the exception of Aubers Ridge, which, occupied by the enemy, overlooked us to a certain extent, although the many trees and woods prevented his having an uninterrupted view. Our tuition began at once, and we were conducted to the front line through innumerable communication trenches, which, at first, reminded one of a maze at an exhibition, the only difference being that numerous notice-boards directed our movements.

There we were welcomed, with smiling faces, by men of a Ghurka battalion, their white teeth and flashing eyes showing up their brown skins. Now and then they would stop sharpening their deadly-looking kukris, their dearest possession, to allow us to pass along the trench. Nothing delighted these brave little men more than to be permitted to go on a silent raid at night, when they wormed themselves through the wire in "No Man's Land," and did as much damage on the other side as possible. They have been known to enter the enemy trenches without a sound, killing everyone within reach, and to return radiant, quite unscathed. When questioned as to why they had not brought in any prisoners for identification purposes, they would merely roll their eyes, shrug their shoulders, and say, "Enemy all quiet, he asleep," and calmly remove the still warm gore from their knives! Continuing on our way, we next struck a Highland regiment, the necessary complement of the one of stout little men just left behind. It was most interesting, as one had heard so much about the traditional good comradeship existing, in India, between Ghurka and Highlander, and here they were still side by side in France. Their mutual admiration is boundless and unconcealed, and it was most amusing to watch the little men aping the ways of the big Highlanders, who look huge in comparison with them. The Ghurka regiments have their own pipe bands, and play them as if they, too, had been born and bred in the mountains and glens of Scotland.

Soon we came to a fire bay, specially well placed to obtain a good view of the enemy trenches, which had been converted into what is known as an O.P., i.e., an artillery observation post. These O.P.'s are manned during daylight by the F.O.O. (Forward Observation Officer) and his signaller assistants. Their job is to keep a close watch on hostile trenches, watching for any unusual movement or for the appearance of new constructive works, such as machine gun emplacements or new saps. The O.P. has numerous wires leading into it, and these come from all the batteries in immediate support of that part of the line, which are jointly responsible for its defence. Our own signallers had been out early, and a wire had already been carefully laid and labelled from our gun position to the O.P., so we were now ready to register our howitzers on some definite object behind the enemy lines. A house, or some such landmark which is shown on our trench maps, is usually chosen to calibrate upon. There is little trouble in effecting this, but, at first, there is some difficulty in following the rounds as they fall, through a periscope, owing to its small field of vision. It was, however, imperative to make use of that instrument, in this case, as an enemy sniper, watchful and on the alert, had already seen the top of it, and from time to time a bullet passed overhead unpleasantly close. This served to remind us to be discreet and to run no risks by exposing ourselves in the slightest degree above the parapet. Sometimes it is very difficult to restrain one's enthusiasm when there is an interesting shoot taking place.

The pieces being duly registered, the Battery is now ready for any emergency, and theoretically we can engage any target in our arc of fire. It is then essential to learn the country in hostile territory, and one looks out for likely targets and for points at which one can inconvenience the enemy by keeping him under constant harassing fire. This work must necessarily be done from a point of vantage where a good wide view can be obtained, and, in most cases, a house, tree, or high piece of ground well behind the lines, is selected for a Rear O.P.

In an incredibly short space of time every officer learns the country off by heart, and can bring any gun to bear on a particular target at short notice. At first Junior Officers are allowed practice shoots on targets well behind the enemy lines, and as they gain confidence and experience, are entrusted with "close shoots," i.e., firing on hostile emplacements, etc., in the front line, a job which requires extreme caution and accuracy, as "No Man's Land" averages not more than 200 yards in width in most places. Batteries can always communicate with Battalion Headquarters in the line, a wire, usually buried, leading from there to our Brigade Headquarters, and each Battery has its own private wire to the latter place. In the same way one can be linked up with nearly every unit in a Division by means of an Exchange run by the Royal Engineers.

A few days sufficed us to make ourselves quite at home, and officers went freely about "seeking whom they might devour," visited old established O.P.'s, and searched for new or better ones. It is a curious fact that the average subaltern is never fully satisfied with an O.P., and is always bent on discovering "something better," although in few cases is his ambition realised! One officer favours this O.P., another that, and on this occasion the one which our worthy Battery Commander had a preference for was a most unpleasant place, commonly known as "The Doll's House," though why so called no one could tell. At any rate, it was an abode to be avoided on all possible occasions, and the subalterns were quite convinced it was the registering place of all the hostile batteries within range and vision. At any rate, we daily found less and less of the building, until one day the staircase was blown away as well as the perch on top which afforded us our view. Great was the relief when the B.C. at last declared the O.P. "out of action" until further notice.

Nearly every O.P. has an appropriate name given to it, and so we repaired to "Stink Farm" after abandoning our old love! We put in most useful days of practice there, and the knowledge and experience gained was invaluable. Our thanks were due to the enemy for his consideration in allowing us to conduct our daily tasks almost unmolested: he showed himself to be most lethargic and sleepy, and did not waken up unless we were unusually energetic. Perhaps his chief reason for remaining so inactive was the absence of any heavy guns on our side. Our largest piece was a 60 pdr., and he may have thought mere Field Artillery beneath his consideration. Nor was he more active in the air; his planes rarely passed over our lines, and when they did, it was at so great a height that it was quite impossible for them to gather information. However, one day, we were extremely fortunate in seeing a hostile plane, that had ventured to cross over our lines at a lower altitude, brought down in flames by a direct hit from an "Archie" battery lying in wait close behind our own position. It is a rare sight, for, to tell the truth, anti-aircraft batteries are not held in particularly high respect by anyone except by those of their own ilk, and on only two other occasions did we ever see the like again.

Our fortnight soon sped by, and we were quite reluctant when the time came to go "out." We left our neighbours, who had befriended us so well, with the sincere hope that we would have the good fortune to meet and lie alongside of them again in the future. This hope, however, was not destined to be fulfilled. We retraced our steps through Merville and Aire to the same area from whence we came, to a village called Nielles, in order to concentrate as a Division, which, when formed, was designated the Guards Division.

The inhabitants, as usual, extended a warm welcome to us and showed us every consideration, and we settled down to enjoy the peaceful surroundings bathed in the warm and pleasant September sunshine, while the Senior Subaltern availed himself of the opportunity of again laying siege to the hearts of his former conquests at Seningham close by. Our own C.R.A. came to visit us here, and the officers were severally introduced to him. He expressed satisfaction at the report which came to him from the line, concerning our conduct in action, and added that the high opinion formed of us at home had in no wise been diminished, and that our reputation merited the distinction conferred on us of being selected as the Artillery of the Guards from among the many units of the new Army.

Thus we waited, confident in the belief that, whatever we were in the future called upon to do, we would at least put up a good show, and determined to be a credit to the Division of which we now formed a part. We had not long to wait, whispers passed round that we would be up and doing at no distant date, and these rumours proved to be well founded.

CHAPTER 2

Our First Battle

Our marching orders came within the next few days. Each unit was provided with portable bridges, which were carried under the wagon bodies, and this, and several other preparations, gave us a good indication that we were out for business. A couple of days trekking brought us to the village of Nedonchel, which proved to be another place of happy memory to our Senior Subaltern. Here we were given a rough idea of the part we were to play in the coming proceedings. Two army corps were to attack, on a six mile front, in the neighbourhood of Loos and, if the assault was successful, the corps in reserve, which included our Division, was to go through and exploit the victory to its fullest advantage. We were to take no part in the initial attack.

Large masses of troops were being moved up behind the battle area, and, in order to screen our movements from hostile aircraft, the latter stages of the journey were to be made under cover of darkness, so the whole of the next day was spent in resting. At nightfall a diversion was caused by a Cavalry Division passing through the village on its way up, and a splendid sight it presented, as one famous regiment followed swiftly on another. It was now almost time for us to make a start, and the good lady of the house had remained out of bed to brew us hot coffee and see us off the premises. As we were about to depart she told us that her old mother, aged 88, who was in the next room, had expressed the desire to see us for a moment, and so we were conducted to the old lady's bedside. She was lying telling her beads, but sat up as we approached and beckoned to each officer in turn, who advanced, knelt, and received a blessing.

The inhabitants knew well that a big battle was to be fought quite soon, as the little village had been the scene of great activity during the past few days and, although it was a considerable distance from the line, the preliminary bombardment could be distinctly heard. The low muffled rumble was incessant, and, to-night, seemed, if anything, more intense. Shortly after midnight we set off and disappeared into the darkness, followed by words of good cheer from the villagers and shouts of *"Bon chance, messieurs, bon chance."*

Passing through Bruay we arrived a few miles behind the battle front on the morning of the assault, which was delivered at an early hour, and soon the news came back that, so far, everything was going well; the village of Loos had already fallen into our hands. As the day wore on, however, and the expected orders to advance were not forthcoming, we suspected that all was not as it should be and our fears were confirmed soon afterwards by instructions being given to prepare to bivouac overnight on the ground close by. What actually happened was this:

The initial attack was successful in capturing and overrunning the enemy's front line trenches over the whole area, but, on advancing to the second trench system a great deal of wire was found to have been left unbroken or untouched by our artillery, and this held the infantry up at vital places. The attack, however, was pressed with great courage and determination, and in some places the flood of men swept on, but, unfortunately, in others, little or no progress was made. The line, consequently, soon presented a crooked, irregular shape, which made the situation difficult and obscure. The enemy, moreover, had anticipated the attack and had large reinforcements at hand which were at once thrown in, and after a ding-dong struggle throughout the day the advance

20

came to an abrupt standstill. Two Divisions from the Reserve Corps were then sent in, and, on the following afternoon, the Guards attacked and helped to a large extent in straightening out a considerable portion of the line.

It was not until nightfall of the third day that we entered the battle and took up a position immediately north of Vermelles Station in the back garden of a row of damaged villas. On our way "in," a couple of cavalry regiments, which had been holding Loos for the last two days and which had just been relieved, passed us. There passed also the remnant of one of the Scottish Divisions which had fought so valiantly and paid so heavy a price. Footsore, weary, and caked with mud from top to toe, with every sign of what they had been through upon them, and heavily laden with "souvenirs" in addition to their full kit, the men could scarcely crawl along. However, just as one battalion came abreast of us, in such condition, the pipes tuned up and at once every head was erect and not a man was out of step as they swung past us; such is the moral force of the bagpipes. It was one of those moments in which a lump rises in the throat and a thrill runs down the spine.

In our new position we speedily learnt what we could do and what we could not do. For instance, the signallers were able to introduce electric light into our abode by tapping a live wire which ran outside, from one fosse to the next, for we were now in the Lens coal district with mines dotted about here and there. On the other hand, we soon learnt to refrain from sleeping or showing lights in the second storey of our billet which was evidently under direct observation by the enemy, who did not take long to acquaint us with the fact.

There was always a good deal of firing to be done each day, for, although the battle may be said to have finished after four or five days, there were several side-shows before the line was adjusted to our liking, and the enemy's fire was almost continuous. This bothered the F.O.O. parties considerably, and communication was difficult to maintain for more than a short time between the front line and Battery. The wire was frequently broken in numerous places, and this kept signallers and linesmen working at high pressure to repair the damage. The O.P.'s were moderately good, with the exception of one in "Gun Trench," where our men held a portion, then came a sand bagged wall occupied on the other side by our opponents which they were able to enter by a T-shaped communication trench, then another sand-bagged wall with our infantry beyond.

Neither side could shell this trench for fear of injury to their own party, but this did not prevent a lively exchange of bombs, intermingled with various forms and sizes of "Minnies," which were hurled at frequent intervals. Sniping was also rampant, and periscopes, no matter how small, survived not longer than a few minutes.

It was from this delightful spot that one of the subalterns arrived at the Battery one evening with his head swathed in bandages like a Sultan's turban. He had been trying conclusions with a "Minnie," and, as this was in the days before the introduction of the steel helmet, the latter had easily come out on top. When the wound was ascertained to be nothing like as serious as the size of the bandage seemed to indicate, he was removed to the wagon line amid jeers from his brother officers, and a few days' rest sufficed to bring him back to duty again.

Now, in one portion of the zone which we were covering, "No Man's Land" extended some 1500 yards in depth, and midway, lying in the valley, were what appeared to be two derelict enemy guns partially camouflaged This aroused the curiosity of the Staff, who called for volunteers to go out and make an investigation and report as to the condition of the sights, etc. Our B.C. gallantly offered his services, in spite of the fact that he was over six feet in height, and presented a most conspicuous figure, and would not be deterred. He set off crawling through the long grass on his perilous journey, and there was a huge grin on his face when he returned. After his report went in we ascertained that the two pieces were nothing more than cleverly constructed dummies formed from cart wheels, telegraph poles and trunks of trees, but it was not until he almost came up to them that he made the discovery.

The detachments meanwhile had settled down, making improvements to their billets and strengthening the gun pits, and were already proving themselves seasoned warriors. On one occasion a nasty accident happened, due to the explosion of a howitzer, caused, as was afterwards proved, by a faulty shell. The complete gun crew, with the exception of the No. 1 in charge, was wounded. Three of their number were temporarily buried by the earth thrown up by the explosion, and it was probably due to that fact that no one was killed. The pit naturally fell to bits and the debris was indescribable, but the Sergeant managed to disentangle himself, and, standing stiffly to attention, reported to the officer on duty, "No. 2 gun out of action, sir!"

No time was lost in digging out the injured men, and it was only found necessary to evacuate three of the number to the nearest dressing station—the remainder flatly refusing to go. The layer, in particular, deserved great credit for his grit, for, in spite of having been buried, and having scarcely a hair left on his head and devoid of eyebrows, not to mention the shock to his nervous system, he was again serving his gun 24 hours later, on the arrival of the new piece. Some idea of the force of the explosion can be gathered from the fact that the barrel was found, in two pieces, some 150 yards away, having been blown over a railway embankment, while the breech block, which weighs about a cwt., was discovered, after a 12 hours' search, embedded in the ground six feet below the pit. At this period a considerable number of "prematures" were taking place, and, on one occasion, we ascribed this wounding of two gunners to this cause, but afterwards found out our mistake.

An S.O.S. went up after dark, and, at the time of firing No. 3 gun, the layer and another gunner were both badly hit by what appeared to be a "premature" just outside the bore of the piece. Throughout this period we were firing nothing but high explosive shells. Great therefore was our surprise when, three weeks later, letters arrived from both men, who were in hospital, to say that in each case shrapnel bullets had been extracted from them! What had actually occurred was this: At the same time that the trigger was pulled and the shell discharged, a "pip squeak" must have burst in front of the mouth of the gun pit, driving the bullets through the entrance.

Day after day passed in much the same way, neither side attempting to make an attack on any large scale, but on the morning of the 8th October, it was observed that the hostile shelling was not normal, and had increased in extent along the whole recently captured area. Preparations were therefore rapidly made to meet any eventuality, and, as the day advanced and his bombardment gained in strength, it was apparent to everyone that the enemy contemplated an attack. At noon orders were received to be ready, at any time, to lay down a destructive barrage on a certain zone. The Staff had happily anticipated the point of attack accurately, and, by the time the enemy concentrated his final burst of fire on his objectives, every gun in the neighbourhood which could bear, was trained on the vital spot ready to open out. When at last the time arrived, the bombardment ceased abruptly, and the enemy's infantry advanced to the assault wave upon wave, for the most part in mass formation and with arms linked together.

Emerging from a wood, they had a considerable distance to cover across open ground before approaching our trenches, so both our infantry and artillery fire was at first withheld. This gave encouragement to the enemy, and, as his bombardment had been pretty severe, he expected more or less of a "walk over," and did not reckon on what was to follow. When he had advanced to within 200 yards of our lines, suddenly rapid fire spurted out from our rifles and machine guns, and guns of every description spat H.E. and shrapnel, and his ranks were

literally mown down. Then a curtain was put down behind—
a solid wall of fire—which made it practically impossible for
the troops to retire, and their plight was beyond all hope.

While they were cogitating whether to come on or go
back, they were slaughtered in heaps—raked by the deadly
machine guns. Very few indeed survived to tell the tale, but
one prisoner claimed to be most indignant with the whole
proceedings, and expressed his opinion that we did not "play
the game" by withholding our fire, and that they imagined
they had only to walk into our trenches and take possession
of them. This proved to be the last big hostile counter-attack attempted, and indeed both sides were content to remain in their own trenches. We made a smaller attack the next
week, but it was also unsuccessful, and little or no ground was
gained. The enemy artillery devoted themselves principally
to counter battery work, and several British batteries, which
were ill concealed, had a most unpleasant time. Free use was
made of lachrymatory shell, our first taste of it. One clear,
moonlight night the battery was firing at a slow rate, and apparently the enemy saw our flashes, for he speedily turned a
4.2 battery on to us, his shells landing just short of each gun
pit. No casualties resulted, but a shell entered the window of
one detachment's billet and exploded, completely wrecking
the room and destroying the men's equipment. Soon afterwards instructions were issued to change positions, and this
was effected without loss or mishap.

The new position was more favourably placed, some
little way in front of the Fosse at Annequin, and had been
constructed by the French. We were now covering the
Hohenzollern Redoubt of evil memory. Another O.P. was
constructed on the railway embankment on the La Bassée-
Vermelles line, which lent itself favourably to the construction of a shaft for protection, the soil, for the most part,
being chalk, as indeed it was in all the surrounding neighbourhood. It was our misfortune at this position to say
farewell to our Battery Commander, who left us to take up

a Staff appointment with the Mediterranean Expeditionary Force, and all ranks were sorry to lose a leader who had thus far shared all their joys and sorrows. At the same time we were fortunate in securing in his successor one who quickly and tactfully took up the reins of office, and the Battery continued to run on equally smooth lines.

It now became quite evident that operations would not resume the nature of a battle, and it was no surprise to receive intimation that the Division would shortly retire from the conflict. Nobody was sorry at the prospect of going out, although useful lessons had been learnt and considerable experience had undoubtedly been gained.

The weather was beginning to break, and towards the end of the first week in November we withdrew to the village of Sailly, preparatory to marching into the nest area for which we were bound.

CHAPTER 3

"Peace Warfare"

When it became known that our destination was to be the sector immediately adjoining the one we had already been in, facing Aubers Ridge, our delight knew no bounds, for all were well aware that that locality was considered a "cushy" spot which augured well for the coming winter.

No delay was made in leaving Sailly, and, proceeding by way of Bethune and St. Venant, we arrived at a small hamlet midway between the latter town and Merville. The Battery remained in rest for a few days, while a couple of "subs." with a working party commenced construction on the new position selected by the B.C. This entailed a considerable amount of labour, for timber and all other material had to be carted from the R.E. dump at La Gorgue some distance away. With an eye to comfort as well as concealment, it was decided to dig the pits in an orchard, along some old assembly trenches which had been used by troops before the battle of Neuve Chapelle. Close by was a cluster of cottages and outhouses in a wonderful state of preservation.

By the end of the week the guns were pulled in, although there still remained a lot to do on the position. The house in which the officers quartered themselves was intact, with the exception of a few slates on the roof and several broken window panes. Moreover, there was a little furniture left and there were some fine open fireplaces, so we had every reason to be satisfied. Within a short space of time the gun pits were completed and camouflaged in keeping with the nature of the ground, and great assistance was rendered us during this undertaking by an airman who flew over the position from time to time and pointed out the various deficiencies.

At last when he reported that the position could not be seen from a height of 2000 feet we concluded, rightly, that nothing was to be feared in that direction. Thus we settled down to a period commonly known as "Peace Warfare." This may be summed up as a time when one experiences the maximum amount of pleasure that is possible under war conditions, with the minimum amount of discomfort.

The enemy were completely deceived as to our whereabouts, and took us to be in another vacant position some way down the road, which was liberally shelled by them whenever fire was opened by us, and we used to encourage this procedure by occasionally ceasing in order to lead him into the belief that he was doing us damage. At all events, the position was never shelled the whole time we were in possession of it—a somewhat unique experience for a battery in France.

The infantry were also kept busy at the commencement of this period, as we had relieved another Indian Division, and on this sector the parapet had been built for the most part by Ghurkas, who, however stout fellows they may be at heart, have not the stature of Guardsmen. The result was the latter found their heads and shoulders showing well above the parapet, and this necessitated the immediate heightening of the same some two to three feet.

The O.P. duties were divided equally between the subalterns, each doing a third daily. The wagon lines were situated east of La Gorgue within easy reach, and frequent visits were paid to them, although no officer remained there permanently.

During our stay here the Battery came under the direct orders of the C.R.A. and was attached to no group in particular. Various tasks were allotted to us, and these were, as a rule, most interesting and instructive. To further increase our knowledge the B.C. gave the majority of these shoots to the

Junior Officers, briefly explaining the orders and then leaving us to our own devices by departing for the rest of the day to the wagon lines on the pretext that he had a birthday to celebrate. He had many of them. This plan was much to our liking, and tremendous keenness was displayed by all. Great pains were taken to carry out everything to the letter, and the signallers also carried out their part with equal spirit. The gun detachments at this time rose to a high pitch of proficiency and could get 10 rounds a minute out of the howitzers, which, considering the double load and triple movement, was by no means a bad performance.

A fine level field ran alongside of the position, and it was speedily made use of as a recreation ground. Goal posts were erected, and often a hot contest at football would be interrupted by the shrill blast of a whistle summoning the men hastily to action. Their task completed, they would calmly return and finish the game.

All kinds of mutual understandings existed between the opposing sides in this area, which we soon learnt and respected. For instance, the village of Aubers lay behind the enemy lines approximately at the same distance that Laventie did on our side. Both were used as Brigade Headquarters and filled with troops. Neither town was shelled unless the enemy accidentally dropped a shell into it, when instant retaliation was forthcoming. On one occasion the placid calm of Laventie was rudely shaken through the instrumentality of a young officer in one of our sister brigades who, unconscious of what he was doing, planted several shells into Aubers. The consequence was the following conversation took place over the telephone between Headquarters and the offending subaltern.

"Hullo! Is that Ack Battery?"

"Yes, sir. Just a moment, sir. I'll put you through to the mess, sir."

"Right you are, but look sharp about it, please. Yes. Hullo! Is that an officer? Well, I say, have you been firing just now?"

"Yes, sir. So-and-so is doing a practice shoot from the O.P."

"Put me on to him at once."

"Yes, sir."

A brief interval follows, in which various mutterings are overheard by the signaller in the exchange, who smiles to himself as he continues to listen.

"Hullo! hullo!! Damn these young officers! Will they never learn to answer quickly? Slow, slow is not the word for it. Will have to go round and shake them up a bit. This is absurd. Hullo! there. Hullo! Is he never going to come? Exchange, can't you get him?"

"Just a moment, sir."

"Hullo! hullo!!"

"Yes, sir. So-and-so speaking."

"What the devil are you firing at, young sir?"

"Well, sir, I was given permission to fire a few rounds—"

"Where?"

"At the cross roads, sir."

"Seen any of them fall?"

"Not as yet, sir."

"Well, for God's sake stop firing at once, sir. Why, man, your shells are dropping in Aubers, and they are retaliating like the very devil. There goes another, just outside."

"Very sorry, sir. Couldn't make out where the shells were falling."

"Well, report to me as soon as you get back, remember. Have no time to listen to an explanation now."

"Very good, sir. Good-bye, sir."

An animated discussion now takes place in the telephone exchange, and the unanimous opinion is that poor So-and-so is "for it" and will perhaps even get the sack, and who will succeed to the Right Section if he leaves the Battery?

In these days a walk along the front line was a delight, and nothing gave the F.O.O. greater pleasure than to take his morning constitutional from one end of our area to the other and to peer over the side at frequent intervals by means of a periscope. Sniping was sometimes indulged in, but a target rarely presented itself for the simple reason that the enemy was hardly ever in his front line trenches during daylight. From one O.P. we could often see one or two men running along the trenches with lighted torches kindling fires and causing smoke in order to lead us into the belief that the trenches were powerfully manned.

Now, about this time, a number of hostile batteries, whose positions could not be located, gave us a certain amount of trouble, but a successful ruse was carried out which enabled us to discover them. Operations were undertaken in order to force the enemy to show his hand, and every indication was made by us that we were about to institute a raid. Wire cutting was done by one battery, and others registered strong points in rear behind the prescribed area. Then at dusk, known as flesh time, when batteries are most likely to give their positions away, all the O.P.'s were manned, spotting apparatus made ready, and our barrage was put down on this sector. The infantry had been provided with dummy figures, which they held aloft on poles, and in the semi-darkness this gave the impression that they were preparing to quit the trenches and go over the top, while high overhead hovered a number of our aeroplanes waiting to assist. The plan worked admirably, and in a few minutes the enemy's counter preparation commenced. As the result of our efforts his positions were pin-pointed and dealt with by our 60-pdrs. the next day, after which we were not bothered by them to such a great extent.

Soon after this episode there came upon the scene what were commonly known as "Cook's Tourists." These were officers whose units were still at home, and who were sent out to gain experience by being attached to batteries for a short period. At times the tourist laid himself open to being the victim of many practical jokes, and this certainly contributed to the liveliness of the mess. A certain officer was escorted down to the front line trenches one day, and, as usual, the party was armed with periscopes. All of a sudden he emitted a cry of delight, as, gazing through the instrument, he told us of how crowds of the enemy were walking along a road. Could we not get our guns on to them quickly?

This seemed an incredible occurrence, as, in this sector, not a single German had been seen for days on end. The mystery was speedily solved, however. By some means or other, he had been holding the periscope so that it faced the opposite direction, and what he actually saw was a party of our own men walking leisurely along the road some way behind our lines. Needless to say, this officer came in for a considerable amount of chaff, and, in course of time, was solemnly presented with a paper medal, suitably inscribed, on which reversed periscopes figured prominently.

The festive season was now drawing near, which necessitated the gathering of provisions, for the men were to celebrate the 25th of December by having a special dinner, and presently leave was opened to our unit and the first lucky ones departed for "Blighty." Some sort of gift was due the enemy on this occasion, and it took the shape of a sharp five minutes' bombardment, from every gun in the area, on the stroke of midnight on Xmas Eve. In spite of this gruelling, the enemy next morning showed signs of wishing to fraternise with our men in the front line, but strict orders had been issued in advance that this was not to be countenanced.

The Germans showed themselves freely above the parapet, and one could see that they had been dressed up smartly for the occasion, probably in order to impress us with their appearance. However, there was "nothing doing." Little or no sniping took place, but the artillery went through their usual routine, in fact rather increased their fire that day.

The men's dinner was a great success, and all seemed pleased with their fare—pork and potatoes, vegetables, plum pudding and fruit, with plenty of beer or stout to wash it down. The Officers' Mess was lively also, and our first Xmas, under war conditions, was voted most successful. Next day the Padre turned up, and a service was held in one of the barns, but, in the middle of the address, on "Peace on earth,

goodwill towards men," there was a sudden call for "action."
A rush was made to the guns, and, after a few minutes' argument with the enemy, we returned and finished listening to the discourse. Somehow or other one could not help feeling that the two happenings were incongruous!

We had a notion that perhaps the enemy would make an attempt to retaliate on us at New Year for our little joke on 'Xmas Eve, and this proved to be correct. He made rather a feeble demonstration, and it was speedily squashed, as we were awaiting it. It was an extraordinary thing, but we always found our foe very slow in the uptake: it generally took him quite a week to think out some measure of retaliation, and when it came, it consisted, as a rule, in copying what we had done to him. We could usually count on that and consequently guard against it.

One day instructions came through calling for a report on a new charge, for reducing the flashes when night firing, which was supposed to be in our possession. Our worthy Senior Subaltern was at that time in command, so he decided to have the trial the same evening and put in his report at once. The remaining officers were to "stand by" at the guns and first fire a salvo with the ordinary charge and then one with the new one, while he stood some distance in front to wait the results. All went well and the salvoes were duly fired, although, at the battery end, there did not appear to be any difference between them, which fact was unanimously agreed upon.

However, that was not the opinion of the Senior Subaltern, who waxed eloquent on the "soft, velvety colour" of the new charge. This was all set down presently, in a lengthy dispatch covering, at least, two columns of "foolscap," and sent to the Brigade. Nothing further was heard for several days, then a telephone message came through which brought a smile to the face of everyone in the mess except the officer concerned. It ran as follows—"Reference my B214 of the 9th inst. Report on flash reducing charges is herewith cancelled. The production of same has not yet been issued to batteries in the field A.A.A." Both salvoes had been of the same nature!

Our Right Section Commander had a mania for spy hunting, and it was true that spies were known to infest the neighbourhood and had sometimes actually been caught. On every available occasion this officer would set out to scour the countryside in quest of a suspect. One day this led to the waste of much energy on his part. Having followed hard on the scent of a suspicious character, from one end of our area to the other, the quarry suddenly doubled back along the La Bassée road and disappeared into a house. Our friend entered also, and found himself in a Brigade Head-quarters, confronted by the "spy," who greeted him warmly, and asked him what service he could render him, at the same time calling for tea. He had shadowed none other than the chief Intelligence Officer of the Division the whole af-ternoon! There was nothing for it but to own up and apolo-gise as best he could, to the vast amusement of the Staff Of-ficer. After this incident, we were spared further wild-goose chases by this enthusiast, and the keenness hitherto shown by him for these quests somewhat abated.

A good deal of excitement was caused, at this time, by the arrival of some heavy artillery in our neighbourhood, so much talk had come to our ears concerning them. The guns were duly placed in position, and on the afternoon on which they were to open fire a large turn out of F.O.O.'s collected in the O.P.'s to watch the enemy get a surprise. They did consid-erable damage, but, at the same time, were largely responsible for stirring up a veritable wasp's nest of hostile heavies which had been lying dormant for ages, and consequently our front again became active.

While our F.O.O. was proceeding one day from the O.P. to the front line, he was caught in one of those bursts of hate and separated from the telephonists who accompanied him. On the conclusion of the shoot, a search was made for him, but he was nowhere to be found. They returned to the Battery and reported the circumstance to the B.C., who, much con-cerned, speedily organised a search-party, and set out for the scene of action. After a couple of hours weary tramping, they came upon a Company Headquarters in the front line, and there, comfortably ensconced in an easy-chair, with a large whisky-and-soda by his side and a cigarette in his mouth, sat the missing officer. Much indignation was expressed and explanations followed, but, in future, it was only in the last extremity that search parties were instituted!

Thus the days sped by, until it came to the minds of those in authority that the Division had vegetated quite long enough in this area, and, at the beginning of February, we were pulled out and transferred to another sphere of activity.

Everyone regretted leaving this peaceful spot, and the period we spent there was always looked back upon as the brightest and happiest time of our sojourn in France.

CHAPTER 4

In "The Salient"

It soon became known that we were bound for Ypres. This town will, without doubt, be the Mecca in France of the British soldier for all time. This place, above all others, was always mentioned with a voice of reverence and awe, and is hallowed by the presence of the gallant dead who helped in its defence. It was truly the most ill-favoured sector on the whole of the front held by our armies.

Proceeding by way of Hazebrouck and Cassel, we entered the area immediately behind the Salient and took up our quarters near the village of Arneke, for we were not yet due for our spell of duty in the line. At this time the weather was most unpropitious, and rendered training in any shape or form out of the question. The ground was covered with snow to the depth of several inches, and the roads were, for the most part, frost-bound. A Divisional Artillery Horse Show was organised, however, and great keenness was displayed by all the batteries, who spent most of their time horse coping until the day of the event, which was held at Zeggers Capelle. Our Right Section Commander, with a team of fine little blacks, managed to secure the second prize in the principal event.

Several days afterwards we relieved the Division who were holding the left centre of the Salient, and took up our position on the northern extremity of Ypres itself, close to the Dead End of the Canal, a short distance from "Salvation Corner." Here a short description of the position is imperative, in order to give some idea of the awkward nature of this sector and of the conditions attaching thereto. The distance between the jaws of the Salient was some five miles across—from the banks of the Yser Canal at Boesinghe on the north to the neighbourhood of St. Eloi on the south, while the ground held by us extended about two-and-a half miles east of Ypres in a semi-circle. Nearly everywhere the enemy was established on rising ground and overlooked our territory, and, with few exceptions, all that was visible to us was his first line system. The enemy was thus enabled to detect any movement behind our line, while we were more or less "blind."

Owing to the confined space through which an entrance into the Salient could be effected, great difficulty was experienced in the matter of transport, as there was only one main artery, namely, the Ypres-Poperinghe road. Every evening at dusk this thoroughfare was crowded with all manner of vehicles, an endless stream, coming and going throughout the night, and from Vlamertinghe onwards the road was subjected to constant shelling, and was enfiladed from either side. Piles of wreckage were always to be seen on the following morning, which told the tale of the previous night's work, and this long, straight piece of road holds more sentiment for the British soldier than any other.

It was soon quite evident that the enemy was acquainted with our location, and it was imperative to prepare an alternative position. A site was chosen across the road, in the garden of a private villa, well sheltered by shrubs and trees. As soon as the work was completed and a communication trench constructed, covered with turf and plants, we commenced moving the guns. This was done without interference from the enemy until the last gun was in the act of being placed in position, when, as luck would have it, a shrapnel shell burst in front of the party, mortally wounding one layer and injuring another. Our B.C., also, who was assisting, received a bullet through his arm, and was forced to leave us. This was the second mishap we had suffered during the course of the first few days, as the Right Section Commander had already been lost to us. Having an insatiable thirst for knowledge, this Officer had left the O.P. with his telephonist in order to explore the front line, which, as everyone who knows the Salient will readily own, was somewhat difficult to recognise in places, especially by a newcomer. Suffering as he did from acute absent-mindedness, it was not surprising that this zealous officer awakened suddenly from his day-dreams to discover that something was wrong, and found himself standing with his companion waist high in a shallow disused trench, which, on further investigation, appeared uncommonly like "No Man's Land!"

After a brief consultation, they decided to retrace their steps. Alas! all too late: a hostile sniper, reserving his fire in the hope that they would continue to walk into the enemy trenches, on seeing them turn about, and thus being baulked of his prize and the prospect of a fortnight's leave in his own country, fired a bullet which passed through the thighs of both men one after the other. A party of our infantry, unable to attract their attention and put them right in time, had witnessed this little drama, and proceeded, at great personal risk and at the expense of at least one of their number being wounded, to extricate the two unfortunates and convey them to the nearest dressing station.

It was not until a late hour that night that word came to us at the Mess that the missing party had been passed through the prison at Ypres, on their way to a C.C.S. Now, our Battery Commander, after great trouble, had lately gained possession of an improved type of periscope, which he had been persuaded to lend the F.O.O. on that day, and, on receipt of this news, his first thought was for the safety of his precious instrument. The fact that two valuable casualties had resulted did not seem to weigh with him in the least compared with its loss, and he was not to be consoled until it was ascertained that the periscope was in safe keeping. Only then could he be persuaded to make enquiries as to the nature of their wounds and express his sorrow at their misfortune.

The Infantry found the trenches in an appalling state, and forthwith proceeded to repair them, but the enemy would not allow this to go on long, and, after a few days' work had been spent on them, a couple of hours' bombardment would suffice to demolish anything that had been done. As it was a case of labour lost, all attempts at building on a large scale were soon abandoned.

Many interesting excursions were made in and around the town. There was a certain amount of splendour about the ruined place. The high battered remains of the Cloth Hall Tower stood up in proud defiance in the centre of the stricken city, while the ancient ramparts surrounding it gloried in their battle scars and showed a dauntless front to the enemy.

A good deal of annoyance was caused in getting about from place to place through the uncongenial presence of a couple of hostile high velocity guns which were commonly known as "Quick Dick" and "Silent Sue," his consort. They were so named on account of the rapidity with which the shells arrived, and there was little or no warning of their coming. Their chief object was to harass the neighbourhood, for they appeared to have no definite target but just dropped a shell here and there, trapping the unwary and doing considerable damage, as well as effectively raising a certain amount of "wind"!

As conditions suited the enemy admirably, many raids were made by him, and, on one occasion, he launched four simultaneously, one on each sector of the Salient, after a sharp and heavy bombardment. He attacked us between Wieltje and Potijge, but was unsuccessful in his endeavour to obtain an identification. The attempt was frustrated, and the only result was that he left a number of prisoners in our hands.

About the middle of May, the Division came out and returned to the area behind Poperinghe. There was an unexpected treat in store for the Brigade, for it was shortly sent down to the coast for a change of air. A two days' march brought the Battery to Cap Gris Nez, while the other batteries were distributed along the small villages between Calais

39

and Boulogne. It was a real holiday for us, and a better part of the year could not have been chosen. All that was expected of us was to exercise the "hairies," which we did by taking the guns a walk along the hard sand in the early mornings.

A large field was secured, and for several hours daily the horses were put out to grass, and, if ever animals showed signs of joy, they certainly did, and their antics were most amusing to witness. It was expected that some difficulty would be experienced in catching them again, but, after the first day, a trumpet call was all that was required. On hearing the sound, they would throw up their heads, and then slowly wander towards the entrance, where the drivers awaited and secured them.

The main feature of the day was, undoubtedly, the bathing parade, enjoyed equally by man and beast. The horses knew at once what was in store for them when they were led down to the beach. The men stripped, and, mounting the eager horses, a wild dash was made for the water, and quite a number of the animals proved themselves excellent swimmers, many remaining a considerable time in deep water. On leaving the sea, they would gallop along the sands, showing every sign of contentment, and we were glad that, at last, they were receiving some reward for their patient devotion and faithful service, for we were all fond of our four-legged comrades.

Amusements were instituted for the men—all manner of sports by day and concerts in the evenings. The officers lived out of doors, attracted by the cliffs, from which Dover was visible on most clear days, and everyone voted this peaceful place the next best thing to home leave.

It was, therefore, with much regret that, at the end of twelve days, we retraced our steps to Arneke, where we were to remain for the latter portion of the rest.

We had no sooner arrived at this place than the enemy started making himself unpleasant in the southern portion of the Salient, and, attacking the Canadians from Hooge as far as St. Eloi, succeeded in driving them back some distance before he was finally held up. It was quite imperative to retake the ground lost, as he had captured important points of observation overlooking the Salient. A counter attack was set on foot, and we were suddenly called upon to help in the preliminary bombardment and cover the assaulting troops, which included a Brigade of Guards. Just before setting off, our B.C. rejoined us once more, and at two hours' notice we made a beeline for the scene of our future activity. At dusk we entered the ruins of Ypres, and, without delay, proceeded to dig ourselves "in," behind a convent, not far from the south side of the Cloth Hall.

Owing to the number of extra batteries assembled for the operations, we found ourselves without a billet until the genial Commander of a Pioneer Battalion, affectionately known to the entire Dominion Forces as "Big Jim," and credited with innumerable deeds of "daring do," took pity upon us, and invited us to share his hearth and home. This offer we gratefully accepted, and accommodation was also provided for the detachment, and all were made most comfortable.

The bombardment continued for three days, and it became clear, from the enemy's counter preparations, that he was not going to give up his newly acquired gains without a struggle. A most stubborn resistance was offered, and the infantry were forced to fight hard for every foot of ground that was eventually recovered. The bombardment grew in intensity as the zero hour approached. Shortly after midnight, the men went over, and, by breakfast time, had gained all that was required of them, except at one or two points, which were taken without much trouble later.

By the time affairs had settled down normally again, the Division was due in the line, so the Battery pulled out for one night, before transferring to our new zone, which was in the most northerly sector, adjoining the one in which we had already been, and which had an even worse reputation for unpleasantness.

After crossing the Yser Canal, the ground gradually rises towards Pilkem Ridge, and the enemy was ensconced thereon in a kind of stronghold known as the High Command Redoubt. Our trenches lay beneath them, which gave us the feeling of being in a cup encircled round the brim by our foes. During this particular tour, the Battery was split up for the purpose of forming two forward sections, and the greater part of the firing was done by the left section, whose position was well inside the Salient. Its chief object was to harass a certain portion of a hostile trench which was taken in enfilade by it! In order to accomplish this successfully, the guns were placed in an old disused position in a field, near La Brique, on the backward slope of a hill, and the low gun-pits were completely covered with tufts of growing grass. The centre pits were occupied by the two pieces and the outside ones were speedily converted into habitations for the men.

When the trenches were not being subjected to hostile shelling, the enemy devoted most of his time in endeavouring to destroy the numerous O.P.'s dotted about here and there. These were constructed for the most part of reinforced concrete, but the particular one used by us, called "Frascatis," had not yet been discovered, so we were free to carry out shoots to our heart's content.

A favourite diversion was sniping with one of our pieces, which was a particularly accurate one, and several points of observation and snipers' posts were carefully registered. Then we would lie in wait, observe some movement, and let fly one round only. This method exasperated and annoyed the enemy exceedingly.

One of the enemy's principal forms of amusement was to blow parts of our front parapet away and train a machine gun on the space left vacant, and snipe at any unsuspecting person who happened to pass along. On many occasions we were able to bring assistance to the harassed infantrymen, by spotting the offending snipers, and by, in turn, sniping at them with our "How." till we finally silenced them.

At dusk the enemy invariably harassed all roads of communication, and dropped innumerable shells of large calibre into the stricken city; and we made a habit of sitting at the entrance to the little shack, used as the officers' mess, smoking our evening pipes, interested spectators, while the shells screamed overhead, and alighted somewhere in the town, sending up columns of brick dust.

All the batteries in the line were now busy constructing new battery positions, while fresh O.P.'s were also erected, and it was thought that these preparations were preparatory to making an attack to enable us to improve our position by the capture of Pilkem Ridge, but, although the work was completed, nothing further developed.

Soon there were whispers of an impending gigantic attack away down in the south, and for several days before the opening of it our shelling was considerably increased, while the infantry made a series of raids. This was done throughout the whole length of the front, in order to keep the enemy from guessing the exact point of eruption, and we had a warm time in consequence. For a long time after the battle had commenced, we continued making demonstrations, which undoubtedly helped to prevent the removal of many reserves from the locality.

But we were not content to remain here. There was a great scrap taking place elsewhere, and were we going to be left completely out of it, to eat our heads off, in Flanders? It seemed very unlikely that the Division would not be called upon on such an occasion, and great was the joy when one day orders came through that we were soon to proceed to the scene of action. Within two days we pulled out to our old resting place, where preparations were completed for our transference to the battle area.

Our first acquaintance with the dreaded Salient was at an end, and, although the time spent there was always strenuous and difficult, we were not what could be called uncomfortable, and our casualties happily did not exceed expectations.

CHAPTER 5

On the Somme

At the beginning of August, the Division detrained in the neighbourhood of Doullens, and, proceeding in a south-easterly direction, the Brigade established itself near the small village of Couin. In a few days' time we went "in," and the Battery took up a position on the southern outskirts of Hebuterne, overlooking the enemy stronghold at Serre. This portion of the front was now in a normal state once more, as, on the opening day of the great battle, the British assault from Hamel, northward to Gommecourt, had met with no success, and the attack was not further pressed. The enemy was content to remain quiet, and most of the firing was carried out by us.

A considerable number of hostile "Minnies" made conditions somewhat unpleasant for the infantry in the trenches, and during the night the battery position was subjected to indirect machine-gun fire, which necessitated a certain amount of caution in moving about. The O.P.'s were well placed, and afforded us an excellent view, for we overlooked the enemy's lines, and could see some distance beyond them. We were now on the fringe of the battle, and away half right, on clear days, we could see the struggle progressing, as a considerable dent had already been made. The sight was a very grand one, especially after dark. The Verey Lights and various S.O.S. rockets, which were frequently sent up by our opponents, made a fine spectacular display, far finer than any firework exhibition we had ever witnessed in our own country in pre-war days.

Gradually the Division was side-slipped to the south, and our next position was close to the station of Mailly. We did not remain there long, however, as the time had now arrived for us to put in an appearance in the battle itself. We spent one night close to Amiens, and availed ourselves of the opportunity to hold a dinner there, which was attended by all the original officers in the Brigade—a last night of fun and merriment before the long, stiff fight ahead of us, for who knew how many would survive the ordeal. The next day brought us to Vaux, on the River Somme, and, in the first week in September, we found ourselves immersed in the battle. We took up our first position in the lately captured second line German system, facing Montauban and covering Guillemont, which had just been taken by an Irish Division.

Very stiff lighting was in progress on this sector, as we were now nearing the summit of the Ridge, the possession of which would be invaluable, as the enemy's territory would be laid bare to us, and he would lose his observation over us. It was not surprising, therefore, that he fought with the courage of despair and initiated counter-attack upon counter-attack, all of which we had to meet with great determination.

The weather was extremely hot, which added much to the discomfort: and, as progress had been very slow for some time, it was impossible to clear up the battlefield, and the stench was almost insupportable. At length the village of Guinchy was captured, and, with our men installed on the further side of the slope, the fighting for position came to an end. We were now entering on the third stage of the great battle, which had commenced more than two months previously. An attack, on a large scale, was planned, the object being to drive the enemy down the slope of the hill into the low-lying country beyond. Field batteries were moved up into forward positions, in order to assist the infantry, by placing a creeping barrage—a new and most successful invention, afterwards employed on all occasions—in front of the advancing waves of men: and the "heavies," of which, for the first time, we possessed a preponderance, pounded the enemy communications far behind his lines.

The assault was delivered over a wide area, early in the morning of the 15th of September, but in no way did it come up to expectations—in fact, it might almost be counted a reverse. Some divisions did well, and took their objectives, but others were completely held up, at certain strong points, which necessitated the withdrawal of the remainder, in order to keep the line uniform.

The Guards met with instant success, and took their final objectives, only to discover that the Division on each side of them had made little progress and could get no further. They were reluctantly forced to return, and it was while doing so that heavy casualties were inflicted on them, as they were raked with fire from the sides as well as in front. During the withdrawal, a party of machine-gunners occupied a trench, and attempted to screen the retirement of the main body of troops, by holding the enemy at bay. In order to use this machine-gun to the best advantage, the piece was placed on top of the parapet, exposed to the full view of the oncoming hordes, but our men never wavered in serving it, and, as soon as one gunner dropped at his post, another instantly took the vacant place, although it meant certain death within a few moments.

Next day they were pulled out to refit, and, as they marched back to rest, a very touching sight was witnessed. A certain battalion, a mere remnant, swung along, headed by its band. All the officers had become casualties, and the Battalion Sergeant-Major was in command, but as many of the dead officers as could be recovered were brought back on stretchers and placed each in his proper position. Headed by the body of their late Commander, the column proceeded on its way, the men marching at attention, and, although covered with mud and blood-stained, they might have been proceeding down the Mall. Such is the discipline of the Guards, and every tribute of respect was paid them by the troops through whom they passed.

The next battle was timed for the 25th inst., and our infantry came back to the line a couple of days before that date. There was much suppressed excitement and curiosity, for the mysterious Tanks were to participate on this occasion for the first time, and it was thought that the secret had been so well kept that they would come as a complete surprise to the enemy. This proved to be the case, and the attack was a great success. What was known as the Flers line was everywhere penetrated, and all gains were held. The Tanks did splendid work. They advanced well ahead of the infantry, and battered down barbed wire, overran trenches, smashed machine-gun emplacements, killing the gun crews, and even waddled as far as the village of Gueudecourt. There they effected much execution and caused great panic among the enemy reserves, which were concentrating for the inevitable counter attack.

Thus the battle continued, sometimes breaking out into fierce fights and at other times reduced to isolated scraps, but all the time the enemy was being gradually and relentlessly pushed down into the valley, and the villages of Morval, Les Boeufs, and Gueudecourt fell into our hands.

It was almost uncanny the way in which villages would completely disappear. For instance, at the time when these hamlets first came within our vision, on our reaching the crest of the hill, they appeared almost intact, but a few days rendered them unrecognisable—they had become merely so many heaps of rubble. There are many places on the Somme which have literally not one brick standing on top of another, and one would never imagine for a moment that a prosperous little village had ever existed there.

Many changes of battery positions were made, and, whenever possible, we burrowed down into the ground, as the enemy's heavy pieces were out after our blood. The great concentration of guns and the few suitable localities for placing them in action added to our difficulties, and we were thus rendered an easy target for the hostile counter batteries. Innumerable brigades were huddled close together, in what was known as the Death Valley, for the simple reason that there was no other suitable spot wherein to place them, and heavy casualties resulted. We had the good fortune, however, to be somewhat isolated from the others, and occupied a forward position, where the guns were hidden in an old German communication trench. The enemy never found it, but subjected us, now and again, to a general burst of harassing fire: his main volume of hate passed us by far overhead.

And, meanwhile, what of our friend the F.O.O.? In those days his lot was by no means an enviable one, and it was a task of no mean magnitude to keep communications going between the trenches and the guns. However, it had to be done, or at least attempted, and the following is a brief account of a typical day in the life of a gunner subaltern.

Orders would be given that a certain hostile trench was to be subjected to a severe, annihilating bombardment, and this necessitated the laying out of a wire to a part of our front line, from which the shoot could be registered, as the target could not be observed from any other locality than the trench immediately opposite it. The F.O.O. rises early in the morning, and sets out with his little squad of telephonists and linesmen. He requires to post a signalman and linesman at frequent intervals, called Relay Stations, in order to preserve communication, as the wire is being continually broken by hostile gunfire. Progress, in a case like this, is necessarily slow, and he has to pick his way among the shell-holes, seeking as much protection, for the line, as circumstances will permit.

The signallers follow in his footsteps, staggering along under the weight of a large reel of wire. All goes well until they reach the summit of a ridge, when, suddenly, a barrage from a "whizz bang" battery is placed right down on top of the party. There is nothing for it but to remain crouched in a friendly shell-hole, which affords a little protection, until the storm blows over or to risk the chances of being hit in the open. The journey is then resumed, and much relief is felt when at last the ground over a nasty dip is traversed without mishap, as this is known to be a favourite target for hostile gunners.

A muddy, unkempt communication-trench is now entered, and the party proceed, up a slope, towards the support system, and eventually arrive at their destination—a post in the front line overlooking its objective. Difficulty is experienced in preserving the wire from the unguarded feet of infantrymen, who look askance at the party as it passes, cursing the idiosyncrasies of each fire bay. The instrument is connected with the end of the wire, and all hold their breath in order to hear the answering buzz which tells them that they are through to the battery. Several futile buzzes may be made by the telephonist, and then, no response being forthcoming, a linesman is sent down the wire towards the first relay station. A break in the wire is discovered and speedily mended, the next attempt is successful, and the battery is called to action.

During registration the wire often breaks, and serious delays occur, but, at length, the last gun is duly pronounced O.K. by the officer. Just in the nick of time, too! for the enemy commences a sharp retaliation on the portion of the trench occupied by the little party. Refuge is sought in an old enemy shaft close by, and there it awaits the time for the "show" to commence. Several other batteries also take part in the shoot, and it is quite impossible to pick out the shells which belong to each one as they fall. Complete success crowns the effort, but on the particular day here described the F.O.O. and party failed to see the end of the bout, as they were subjected to very heavy fire, and were all blown down the mouth of the shaft by the explosion of a shell. Luckily, though badly shaken, all escaped without injury.

Meanwhile the wire has been broken in many places and is beyond repair, but it has already served its purpose, and, when fire has died down, the party starts on the return journey. On arriving at the first relay station, the telephonist on duty is found dead at his post, the receiver still clutched in his hand and held to his ear. A nasty gash in the forehead reveals the place where he has been hit and instantly killed. His companion is nowhere to be found, although bloodstains denote that he has at least been wounded, and, on investigation, it is ascertained that the linesman has been hit, picked up by passing comrades, and taken to an aid-post.

The journey is resumed, the party carrying the dead with them, and presently another hostile barrage is encountered. Again the men lie low until it ceases, and then pick up the remaining linesmen, and return to the battery utterly exhausted. Many questions are asked, and it frequently happens that the F.O.O. is cursed by his Battery Commander for not keeping the wire going, and even the Brigade joins in the chorus. The young officer pays little heed, and inwardly reflects that they should be extremely thankful that communication was established at all, and that those of the party who returned did so in safety. So, in spite of everything, he consumes a hearty dinner and retires to bed, sleeping the sleep of the just, and soon becomes oblivious of all his little worries and sombre surroundings.

Towards the middle of October the weather broke, and conditions became intolerable. The roads, which had been partially repaired, were still soft and broken, and developed into quagmires—mud and water to a depth of two and three feet made vehicular traffic almost out of the question. All ammunition had to be transported to the guns by means of horses carrying pack saddles, a slow and tedious method, which took a lot out of men and beasts alike. As yet no *deccaville* railways had been constructed as far as battery positions. Very heavy work thus fell on those at the wagon lines, who were kept busy most of the day and night. Although the distance to the gun position was under five miles there and back, the journey rarely took less than ten hours to accomplish.

If a horse fell down in this sticky mud, heavily laden as it was, attempts at rescue proved unavailing, except on rare occasions, even with the aid of drag-ropes, and the unfortunate animal had to be "dispatched." Was it a sense of humour that prompted those in authority to send the subalterns, in turn, to the wagon lines for a "rest"? Anyhow, it was considered anything but that by the poor unfortunates who went, and right glad they were when the time came round for their next period of duty with the guns!

As the weather rapidly became worse, operations came to a standstill, and all proceeded to dig themselves in for the coming winter. Every endeavour was made to make our quarters water-proof, as well as shell-proof, and some attempts at mining were commenced, but the condition of the ground was all against such an undertaking, and the work was abandoned. Then whispers spread abroad that we were to be relieved for a short rest, and, after ten weeks of incessant fighting, we were withdrawn from the line and marched to a little village named Hangest, a few miles west of Amiens. There we were glad to find ourselves installed in billets with a roof covering us once more. A week of leisure helped greatly to restore our spirits, and again we set out for the line.

Our destination this time was Combles, and we took over a battery position from the French, who politely made us acquainted with our new surroundings. Our allies, who had been fighting side-by-side with us on our right flank throughout the great battle, were then withdrawn, and the British front was extended to the south as far as the banks of the River Somme. Evidence was speedily forthcoming to convince us of the severe nature of the recent fight. The ground was strewn with wreckage and material of all descriptions, and many hostile guns were found abandoned or lying where they had been put out of action by the irresistible dash of the Poilus.

The country, in this part, was undulating, and better suited to the concealment of battery positions, and nowhere was the enemy able to overlook our territory. Our area included the defence of the joint villages of Sailly-Saillisel, situated on commanding ground, which the French had recently bravely stormed. Combles, too, which lay in a basin shaped hollow, was interesting as having been the centre of supplies for the southern portion of the German Army operating in the battle, and much booty was discovered in the huge catacombs which ran underneath the town.

Xmas passed in much the same way as in the previous year. A smart bombardment was carried out in the morning in order to advise the enemy that anything in the way of fraternising would not be countenanced by us. At mid-day the men partook of their 'Xmas fare, which had been fetched from Amiens, and a short service was conducted by the Padre in one of the gun-pits. A slight disturbance took place at dusk, when the S.O.S. went up from the front line and all batteries immediately opened out. It seemed a rather extraordinary occurrence, as the evening was unusually quiet, and, presently, it was discovered to have arisen through an error, due to the fact that the enemy had put up a coloured light in between two ordinary Verey lights which constituted our own S.O.S.

About this time the enemy caused considerable annoyance to a certain Battalion Headquarters, situated in a quarry close behind the lines, by occasionally dropping a shell right into it, the position having probably been discovered by his aircraft. Retaliation tactics were adopted, which consisted of subjecting the hostile trenches to a sharp half-hour's bombardment from eight batteries, firing a total of 2,000 rounds. The enemy was well known to be very thick-skinned, but these measures met with instant success, and it was only necessary to remind him once again that we were not to be trifled with in this way.

After the New Year, a severe spell of frost set in, with an occasional heavy fall of snow, and we were somewhat annoyed when orders came through to sideslip our position further south, as we had made our quarters fairly comfortable by this time, and expected to remain undisturbed throughout the winter. The new position was situated behind the ruined village of Rancourt, facing St. Pierre Vaast wood, and was one of the worst and most disagreeable localities it was ever our lot to occupy, as we were, more or less, water-logged the whole of our time there. Much difficulty was experienced by both friend and foe in entering their respective front line, so much so that, by common consent, sniping by rifle fire was discontinued until parapets were constructed and made fit for occupation. However, sniping was still indulged in by the artillery, and no parties of any size were permitted to go about freely near the front line under observation.

Affairs continued thus until the middle of February, when it became apparent that something unusual was taking place in enemy territory, and great explosions were heard, after which volumes of smoke were seen to rise in large columns. These, as was afterwards proved, were due to preparations being made by the enemy to evacuate the low-lying country, into which they had reluctantly been forced, as the result of the battle of the Somme, prior to falling back upon the great prepared defences known as the Hindenburg Line.

Instantly every one was on the alert for further signs of evacuation, and one morning a patrol reported that the enemy had vacated their front line. Further patrols were at once pushed out, through St. Pierre Vaast wood, in order to maintain contact with the retreating foe. Every precaution had to be taken, as it was soon discovered that many forms of booby-traps had been cunningly laid by him in his wake, and progress was necessarily slow. Added to this, there was great difficulty in manoeuvring the guns over the innumerable trenches which existed in the neighbourhood, and the pieces sank up to their axles in the clogging mud, and were only extricated after hours of labour.

The enemy retired slowly and most methodically, destroying everything of value and wantonly reducing the small villages and hamlets to mere shells, by means of incendiary bombs. The inhabitants also were removed beforehand, and, when the troops advanced, they might have been traversing a wilderness, so complete was the ruin and desolation on all sides.

The time had now arrived for the Brigade to have a much-needed rest and also to refit, so, at the end of March, we were withdrawn from the contest. Marching westward, we arrived at the village of Morlancourt in the first week of April, well content at the prospect of returning to civilization for a protracted period.

CHAPTER 6

Messines

It was not long before those in authority discovered that the neighbourhood of Morlancourt was peculiarly favourable for the carrying out of manoeuvres, with the result that a period of "intensive training" set in. Drill orders took place four days a week, and batteries were specially trained in the methods of open warfare, while many hours were devoted to tactical schemes.

At this time units were reorganised, all batteries were increased to six guns, and there was plenty of work to keep everyone busy. The narrator of these rambling notes, after a period of two years' service with the Brigade, here transferred his allegiance to the sister howitzer battery of the Division, known as "The Grey Battery," from the fact that all the horses were of that colour. Sentiment ran strong for his "old love" and those he was obliged to leave, but he was already well acquainted with both officers and men of his new unit, and soon settled down happily amongst them.

All guns were carefully calibrated on a range due west of Peronne, and the "hairies" picked up rapidly in condition, owing to the good care and attention that was bestowed upon them. The big battles of Vimy Ridge and Arras were now in full swing, and it seemed unlikely that we would be called upon to take any part in them so late in the day.

Many forms of amusement were created for the men, and football matches, both "rugger" and "soccer," were freely indulged in between batteries and brigades, while the full regimental band of one of the Guards' regiments was kindly lent to the Divisional Artillery. It gave many a fine entertainment in the evenings.

Time thus sped by at an amazing rate, and various visits of inspection paid us by officers from the C.R.A. up to the Army Commander made it very apparent that we were undoubtedly being "fattened up"—but for what? The question was more than we could answer, but speculations were rife as to our possible destination, for we knew that the Somme would see us no more—in the meantime, at all events.

Six weeks had come and gone, and yet we remained inactive in this peaceful village; then sudden orders were issued for us to be ready to entrain at short notice, and, in the second week of May, the Battery glided out of the station at Meulte prepared for anything. A long and circuitous route was taken *via* Amiens, Abbeville, Etaples, Boulogne, Calais, St. Omer, and at length we arrived at Arques, near which we remained, in billets, for some considerable time. It was while we were there that we learnt that it was the intention of the British Commander to gain possession of the great Messines Ridge, which towered over our lines, and was a stronghold of inestimable value to the enemy.

As long as he held this ridge, which was the keystone of his armies in Flanders, he was immune from any vulnerable attack on our part, and was free to launch any offensive operation from it by using it as a stepping-off place. Added to this, the northern end of the heights afforded him an uninterrupted view of the southern portion of the Ypres salient, which was a source of great annoyance to our forces on that part of the front. It was vital, therefore, for the future operations of the British Armies, that this important ridge should be captured and kept in our hands.

Preparations were accordingly set on foot, and artillery of all calibre was silently concentrated from all parts, and proceeded to dig itself in for the coming fray. For a long time this sector had been free from any serious operations, and was considered a kind of resting place for exhausted troops, but soon the peace and quiet of the neighbourhood was to receive a rude awakening, when the tide of battle broke out upon it once more.

Proceeding through Hazebrouck and Bailleul, the Brigade arrived at its wagon lines, a short distance west of Neuve Eglise, and immediately each battery sent work parties to the scene of action, in order to construct emplacements and make its position habitable. The spot allotted to our battery was in a little hollow close to the cut roads, near the small ruined village of Wulverghen. Our front line was placed on the top of an undulating rise, with the ridge itself beyond.

Our principal business was to avoid attracting the attention of the enemy to our preparations, and in this we were aided by the fact that there was a considerable amount of cover beside us, in the form of trees and undergrowth, the foliage of which was now in full leaf.

Row upon row of batteries were placed in position behind hedges, or artificially concealed, the barrels of the pieces peeping out from all imaginable lurking places. The Divisional Artillery was situated in the most advanced position, the 18 pr. batteries ranging from within 600 to 1,000 yards of the front line, with the howitzer batteries immediately behind them. On account of our proximity to the enemy, the two brigades had orders to remain silent until the day of the show, and we were only allowed to fire enough rounds to enable us to carefully register the pieces, and this was completed without giving away any of the positions.

All ammunition was conveyed to the guns by night, and was distributed in small quantities near to them. Before long the enemy became alive to the fact that we were contemplating some move, and consequently increased his devastating fire by night, with the result that many dumps in the vicinity were exploded by him. He was bound to hit something, the countryside was so packed with all manner of ammunition.

He had no idea, however, of the magnitude of our coming effort, and firmly believed his position to be impregnable, and that it was beyond our power to free ourselves from his grip.

He contented himself with drenching our little valley with chemical shell whenever conditions were favourable, but so accustomed were the men to their gas masks that no serious consequences resulted, although it was distinctly unpleasant to have to pass each night enveloped in these stuffy contrivances, especially as the weather remained hot and oppressive.

The Battery had more than their average share of good fortune throughout these operations, and it is worthy of putting on record that the unit did not sustain a single casualty to either man or horse. This was all the more remarkable as the engineers had constructed a wide plank road, which passed through the centre of our position, and could not be concealed from our foes, who lavishly besprinkled it with shrapnel after dark. Many casualties were caused to the transport, and the Officers' Mess virtually became an aid-post, where every assistance was rendered the wounded men.

Our sister howitzer battery was lined up alongside of us, and, when the two positions were first inspected, much chaff ensued as to which had the better place, and the men of our battery were certainly all of the opinion that, had the selection devolved upon them, we would unanimously have plumped for the other one. They had no landmarks likely to attract hostile fire, and thus occasion them the unpleasant sensation of living on top of a volcano, while we were slap-bang in the middle of a conspicuous cross road, with a constant stream of traffic coming and going through: yet, so strange and fickle are the fortunes of war that, while we escaped unharmed, our comrades next door suffered a heavy gruelling.

The preliminary bombardment commenced, and continued throughout five days, but, in order to deceive the enemy as to our weight of artillery, not more than fifty per cent. of the guns in the line were allowed to take part at one time. A row of O.P.'s had been constructed on Hill 65, which overlooked the valley and town of Messines. A fine sight was witnessed as that stronghold was gradually reduced to a mere shell by our heavies, which effected extraordinarily good work in smashing the elaborate structures of the enemy's defence.

The preparations were all that could be desired, and everything was carefully worked out to the minutest detail: not a stone was left unturned to render the operations a complete success. The labour and expense was well rewarded too, for surely no battle ever ran so smoothly from first to last, and it will always be looked back upon by the British soldier as a model of triumphant organisation. The battle only lasted a single day, but in that time the formidable network of trenches was neatly and clearly shorn off, and the enemy, who relied so much on the security of these positions, found himself suddenly pushed down the slope into unsuitable ground, where he could no longer be a menace to us.

The "feet" of our Division were not in the line, being held in reserve, and, as it turned out, they were not called upon at all at this juncture, so well did the course of the battle progress. We were covering the infantry of an English Division, and, on the evening previous to the attack, the troops passed us noiselessly and in perfect order on their way to their various points of assembly. All were in excellent spirits, which augured well for the next day, and a feeling of calm confidence appeared to prevail amongst them. A stream of gas and tear shells was maintained by the foe throughout the night, but it was mostly directed on the zone which contained the battery positions, consequently the infantry was caused little inconvenience.

Early the following morning, shortly before dawn, the attack was heralded by the explosion of the mines, which had been in course of preparation for months beforehand. This was the sign for the guns to open out, and the assault was launched from north of St. Eloi in the Salient to the neighbourhood of Ploegsterte in the south, the men following close in the wake of the now familiar and popular creeping barrage.

The force of the explosions was terrific, and the vibration was felt far and wide; even strong concrete "pill-boxes" were swung to and fro, and the occupants were tossed from side to side as if they were on board ship in a rough sea. Some indication of the colossal nature of these upheavals may be gauged from the fact that the craters were, in some cases, more than 200 ft. in diameter, and that the earth thrown up obliterated every hostile trench in the vicinity, completely burying the unfortunate garrisons who manned them.

At the same moment the sky was lit up by all manner of S.O.S. lights and the innumerable flashes from our guns, which were now showing their maximum strength for the first time. They belched forth concentrated death, the roar reached such a deafening crescendo that conversation was entirely out of the question—indeed it was impossible to hear one's own voice. However, the scene was truly impressive, and the grandeur was beyond anything hitherto seen.

As daylight crept in, the infantry were observed to be making rapid progress, although, here and there, stiff opposition was encountered. Soon the summit of the ridge was gained, and the men swept on and disappeared over the crest, leaving the mopping-up parties to complete their work. The Tanks bravely waddled up after them, in a vain effort to keep up, for the attacking infantry went so fast, in the first stages, that they easily outstripped those ponderous giants and left them far behind.

Meanwhile the field batteries which had been in position farthest in the rear, and so were already out of range, limbered up and dashed into action in front of our Brigade. As soon as the next row was also out of action, they too galloped past and took up their place again in "No Man's Land," while the Engineers worked at their highest pressure to pull down trenches and prepare the way for the gunners. Thus we were able to give the fullest possible support to the infantry, and the fire never ceased, while the men always found the creeping barrage laid down in front of them.

Early on in the fray prisoners came dribbling back in a more or less dazed condition, and, as they passed the array of guns, they paused and gazed in evident wonder at the huge concentration—probably realising how fortunate they were in escaping the fate of so many of their comrades.

Now, the enemy, although he knew an attack was imminent, had failed to anticipate the correct zero day, with the result that, on several portions of this front, various reliefs were in process of taking place at the actual time of the assault. The consequence was his defence was thrown into a state of confusion, while the extra numbers in the trench offered a double prey for the bayonets of our men, who were not slow in seizing the chances thus afforded them.

The whole of the first objectives were quickly in our possession, as well as the villages of Messines and Wytscheate, and there was a slight pause to give a breathing space to the infantry, and to allow time for the field guns to take up their allotted positions beyond the recently captured enemy trenches, before entering upon the second and final stage of the battle. When the creeping barrage, which had remained stationary during this period, went forward once more, the infantry encountered stronger opposition, but by this time the Tanks were well up in support, and were instrumental in breaking up the machine-gun nests and thus enabling the men to proceed up to schedule time.

The enemy lost a number of field artillery pieces, but had taken the precaution to withdraw most of the heavy ones several days before, when our bombardment commenced. His shooting, therefore, was rather wild and erratic, as he evidently had not had sufficient time to register his guns properly in the new positions. The result was that, fortunately for us, most of his energy was misplaced, and, for a battle of this magnitude, the casualties were not as heavy as might have been expected.

By early afternoon the final objectives were everywhere in our hands, and the work of consolidating the fruitful gains that the last few hours had yielded was immediately begun.

Several counter-attacks were attempted by the enemy, but were not pushed with much vigour, and no success was secured in that direction: our infantry remained firm and could not be dislodged.

Trenches were swiftly constructed, the work proceeding without intermission, and by evening the men were, more or less, securely "dug in," except in a few places where the line was slightly irregular, and which was afterwards rectified by means of a small operation.

By the time the battle had finished we found ourselves the farthest back Brigade in the line, the immense number of batteries which, at the beginning, had been in our rear were now well in front of us, and on this sector the Divisional Artillery were the only two Brigades who did not move forward during the course of the fight. Moreover, by this time we were firing almost at extreme range close to the enemy's new front line, which gives some idea of the distance our men covered.

The day had been an exhausting one for the gunners, and, in order to give some indication of the work and labour they had been called upon to do, our battery alone fired over 4000 rounds of ammunition. This was by no means a bad performance when one takes into consideration that each shell weighs 35 lbs., and necessitated a goodly amount of manhandling, but the men all had their "peckers well up," and displayed much determination throughout.

For a few days following the battle there were a number of small isolated scraps for positions, and one or two enemy counter-attacks, before the new front settled down into something like normal conditions again. *Deccaville* and light railways were pushed up smartly by the R.O.D., and the Engineers constructed new roads, while Labour Battalions were busily employed repairing the old ones and clearing up the litter of the battlefield.

Ever since we came into action it had been no secret that our stay in this area would be of short duration, and that we were only to be employed in the battle itself, and were only to remain as long as our services were really required. It was no surprise when, five days later, orders came through for us to withdraw from the line. We pulled out back to our wagon line, and from there proceeded through Bailleul to the little hamlet of Borre, a few miles east of Hazebrouck, where we remained pending removal to our next destination. We all had the feeling that our recent tour had been a great success, and were well satisfied with the part we had taken in the operations, for this was the first occasion on which we had witnessed a battle go smoothly, without a hitch from start to finish, and was a great contrast to any previous one in which we had participated.

A few days in rest sufficed to put the Brigade shipshape once more, and we were now ready for the next bout. No delay was made in transferring us to another neighbourhood, and we set out in a northerly direction, which boded little good, for we knew that unpleasant events were developing in that quarter.

CHAPTER 7

Ypres Again

In the middle of June the Division arrived in the neighbourhood of Ypres, and at once took over from the Belgians from just below Boesinghe northwards. We were thus back on familiar ground, as we had occupied the next sector to the south in the previous year. Although we were not actually in the Salient itself, we were situated at the northern re-entrant to it. The Yser Canal constituted "No Man's Land," the eastern bank of which was held by the enemy and the western by ourselves.

The battery positions on this occasion were placed a considerable distance behind, mainly around the village of Elverdinghe, as the enemy had close observation and overlooked us from Pilkem Ridge. We did not take long to discover that our opponents were well acquainted with the situation of our new homes, for the majority of the batteries were subjected at once to an avalanche of shells as soon as they opened fire in order to register the guns. It became imperative for us to build alternative positions or go elsewhere, while other sections moved forward and undertook most of the firing.

We had not been settled more than a few days when the enemy suddenly conceived a violent attraction for the house occupied by the officers' mess, and, after several direct hits had been made on it, we decided that the place was becoming too hot, and searched round for a more suitable abode. We packed up, made a hasty flight, and secured accommodation in a house which was strengthened by concrete, but even there we had to be wary, especially at night, for we were very close to a road fork, beloved by the enemy gunners.

The majority of the O.P.'s were also obvious to the keen eyes of the foe, who paid them much attention on every possible occasion, and it was just as well for the occupants that they had been strongly constructed with steel girders and concrete. On one occasion an officer, doing a night O.P. duty, along with his telephonist, was subjected to a full hour's bombardment by two hostile batteries, which fired salvoes regularly every minute. Next morning there was nothing left of the house except the skeleton, with the O.P. structure standing out defiant in bold relief in the midst of it.

These then were the conditions on this sector at the time of our taking it over, and it will be seen that the enemy did more or less what he chose, and was undoubtedly top dog as far as gunnery was concerned. However, this was not to remain long so, as almost immediately preparations were set on foot for the coming offensive, which had already been decided upon.

A host of new O.P.'s were erected, new roads and light railways constructed, while large working parties prepared fresh gun pits in advanced positions, and all were carefully camouflaged where they were exposed to enemy view. Every day new units arrived, and the country appeared to be overrun with troops. Most of the forward work had to be done during the night, and, as each position was completed, the guns were silently concentrated. While this was in progress, the Divisional Artillery only were maintained for the defence of the line, as it was not advisable that the enemy should know until the last possible moment that anything unusual was afoot. The scheme was a much more ambitious one than that in which we had recently taken a part, and, if everything went forward according to plan, it meant that we would be on the go for a considerable time, and there even appeared to be a chance of getting a taste of the long-talked-of open warfare.

About this time a most amusing episode was witnessed by

one of our Subalterns who was doing a liaison with the infantry at a battalion headquarters. This place was situated most unpleasantly, and was well known to the enemy, consequently accommodation had to be sought underground as much as possible. While the F.O.O. and his companion, the Intelligence Officer, were performing their ablutions early one morning outside the mouth of the cellar, a Brigadier with his Staff suddenly appeared on the scene to pay a visit to the Commander.

The two Staff Officers remained outside, and opened conversation with them. The Intelligence Officer, being something of a wag, brandished his shaving brush in one hand and with the other jocularly shoved the Staff Captain down the steps into their retreat, and asked him what he thought of the bedchamber. The other officer, although much amused, stood aghast, and, after the visitors had departed, he asked his companion to whom he had been speaking. He replied that he did not know, for, although the Captain's features appeared familiar, he could not "place" him, though he was a jolly sort of chap anyhow. On being told that it was none other than the Prince of Wales that he had been familiarly digging in the ribs for the past quarter of an hour, he was incredulous, and exclaimed, "And to think I nearly killed the youngster down these stairs!"

At length preparations were completed, and the two Brigades of the Divisional Artillery took up new advanced positions alongside the reinforcing batteries already in line, while the heavies were thickly aligned close in the rear. The preliminary bombardment broke out about the middle of July, and at first it was keenly resented by the enemy, who perceived that we were gradually wrestling the initiative from him, but when, day after day, our fire continued unabated, he apparently resigned himself to his fate. Hurricane shoots by field batteries soon began to make a difference in the appearance of his trenches, and the heavies, by means of aerial registration, demolished his strongholds far back over the crest, and destroyed many of his battery positions.

Several thick woods were facing us across the canal, and these grew thinner, and yet more thin, disclosing cunningly concealed pill-boxes, which were then dealt with by the heavies, until at last only a few stumps remained to indicate that a wood had ever existed there. The enemy's alarm grew daily, and soon our aeroplanes reported that the hostile batteries were being withdrawn further out of danger, and that work was proceeding feverishly upon new defences far behind his lines.

By this time we had complete control of the air, and the heavens were alive with our aircraft, though the enemy tried his best to equalise matters by bringing along his famous "travelling circus" to the scene of action, and many thrilling fights were witnessed. The batteries were subjected to much chemical shelling during the night, and the enemy were known to bring forward special guns under cover of darkness for this purpose, and to withdraw them out of range again before daybreak.

It was during this period that he introduced the new mustard gas for the first time, and it must be admitted that he surprised and inflicted considerable casualties on us at first by this latest specimen in his assortment of poison.

Our initial attack had to be postponed for several days, as the French, who came in immediately on our left, were delayed in putting in their appearance, consequently they had many hours' bombardment to make up, but, when it did commence, it was no uncertain one, and the noise was terrific. In the meantime our bombardment was continued also, though in a lesser degree, and the destruction of the enemy's lines was, as far as we were able to judge, thorough and complete.

This delay proved a blessing in disguise to the Guards, who were to deliver the assault on our sector. The problem of effecting a crossing of the canal was a most serious and difficult one, and it had been arranged to send the men over on floating mats, as a good deal of water still remained in parts of the bed. In others so much mud and slime were encountered, while carrying out a series of raids, that it was almost impossible to cross without some such assistance, and it will be readily understood that it was imperative to waste no time in this manoeuvre, especially as the foe was awaiting them on the further bank.

Whether it was that the enemy could not maintain communications between his front line and the rear, on account of our intense bombardment, or whether, as has been suggested, he suspected a repetition of Messines, and that we had mined underneath the canal bed, at all events three days before the attack he evacuated the canal bank and retired just over the crest of the hill some 800 yards beyond. This movement, however, had not been carried out unperceived by our valiant airmen, who, flying at a low altitude, returned and reported the situation. Immediately strong patrols crossed the canal and pushed up the slope on the other side, in order to remain in contact with the enemy and gauge his whereabouts. A series of posts were thus established 500 to 600 yards east of the canal, and orders were given to hold them at all costs, so that on the day of the battle our infantry could start off from there without having any serious obstacle in their way. Many men crossed the canal by means of hastily constructed foot bridges or floating rafts made of biscuit and petrol tins ingeniously lashed together.

On this occasion we will follow the fortunes of the F.O.O.'s detailed to accompany the infantry on their journey over the top on the first day of the battle. The party consisted of two officers and fourteen signallers and linesmen from the Brigade, who, during the past fortnight, had received full instructions as to their duties. Every detail had been carefully worked out beforehand: the men had been divided into several groups, each armed with telephones, reels of wire, flags, and Lucas lamps, all these things being necessary for the provision of each relay station. One of the officers was to accompany the attacking waves of infantry with his staff, consisting of a telephonist, linesman, and signaller, while the duty of the other was to work in conjunction with him and to maintain, as far as possible, uninterrupted communication with the Brigade after laying down the wire.

The morning before the battle, the wire was laid out over the canal as far as the series of outposts, in order to save time on the following day. The same evening, at sunset, the party set out, after receiving wishes for the best of good luck from those who had been fortunate enough to escape being detailed for this arduous task. Officers and men proceeded to their appointed places in the front line, or rather in what had once been an enemy support trench, though now it was scarcely recognisable as such, owing to the effects of our bombardment, there to remain for the night and await coming events.

Now, in consequence of the enemy's premature retirement over the crest, he lost most of his observation on us, but he was aware we had effected a crossing and held posts on his side of the canal. He therefore lavishly besprinkled this area with all manner of high explosive shells—one here, one there: never two in the same place—and the members of the party began to wonder whether they would survive to witness the fortunes of the battle.

It always appears to be a matter of conjecture as to what are the real feelings of an F.O.O. about to take the plunge, so perhaps it might be of interest in this case to acquaint ourselves with them. As he lies out there with his men, where are his thoughts? Are they of his home, his parents, wife, or children? Will he ever see their dear faces again? No—! all that agony has been fought out over and over again long ago, during the previous fortnight or so, since he has been detailed for this particular job. Then, what does he think about? If the truth be told, he is rapidly running over in his mind all the little things which may perhaps, at the last moment, have been omitted or forgotten. He questions Gunner "So-and-so" to make certain that that extra piece of wire has been brought along, and asks what the h—l Gunner "Somebody else" is doing standing there without a "tin-hat" on, and enquires of the Bombardier if he has adjusted the Lucas lamp properly, which has been giving some trouble previously.

These and a hundred-and-one other such questions flash through his brain as he lies on the ground with his little party, all vigorously puffing pipes or cigarettes. The hours go by very slowly, and conversation on any old topic is attempted from time to time, sleep being entirely out of the question, as everyone is much too excited for anything of that nature. Meanwhile the bombardment continues without intermission, and the night becomes intensely cold and eerie. Will the darkness never pass and let us get started on the job?

Soon after midnight the infantry, who are to make the assault, arrive at their places of assembly, full of quips and jests, a sure sign that they are cheery and in good form for the coming fray. Rum is served out, and the men lie down in little bunches, either to snatch a few minutes' sleep or else to resume their constant arguments and bickerings on every subject under the sun except anything connected with the war. Zero hour at last draws near, and everyone grows more restless, for this period is much the most trying time to endure, and all topics of conversation have long since been exhausted.

Then a short, sharp order passes down the line, and the answering shouts announce that all are present and ready— the "quarter to zero" has arrived. Another crisp order comes along, and there are a series of ominous clicks as each man adjusts his bayonet to the rifle, then the men line up in perfect extended order, ready for the word to go. A faint grey appears in the sky to the east, but only the next man is visible to his neighbour, as the darkness is still upon us.

The F.O.O.'s and party are also up and ready, final instructions being rapidly given to the signallers, who nod assent that everything is prepared and understood. Then suddenly the guns bark out afresh, and a creeping barrage drops down like a curtain in front of the men, who follow after it at an easy walk. Fortune attends the little party, as the wire has only been cut in three places, and these are speedily repaired; and, as soon as the second wave of men is clear of the trench, the line is laid out as rapidly as possible behind them.

The ground is difficult to traverse, being full of deep craters, so the party progresses more slowly than the infantry, and presently the third wave gains on and passes it by. At first the enemy puts down a nasty barrage, just beyond our stepping-off place, but most of his heavy stuff falls on the canal bank, and, as the majority of the troops have already crossed, the damage is not severe. By this time the party has gained the top of the crest, and, after establishing a relay station in a pill-box lately occupied by their opponents, the remainder proceed on their way. Many are the temptations to dawdle, instead of getting on with the work, so much of interest is taking place around them, including the amusing, and at that time not too frequent, sight of scores of the enemy, with uplifted hands, emerging from pill boxes, where they must have been packed like sardines.

An auxiliary wire tapped into the main F.O.O. line is led to another pill-box, now to be used as a new infantry headquarters for the time being, and the party comes under the fire of a hostile machine gun emplacement, which necessitates their lying in a shell-hole for a while. On arrival there, the "mopping up" party is found still at work, but it soon completes its grim task. The officer who has proceeded with the infantry now sends his first message through to the effect that the first objectives are taken, the wire fortunately holding out well at the moment, every sound being clear and distinct. The Lucas lamp is then fixed on top of the relay station, and communications established in case the wire goes, but the morning dawns in mist, and signalling by this method is unsatisfactory.

After a short pause, the infantry proceed on the second stage of their adventure, the F.O.O. and party following up and laying out wire close behind them. More messages are sent through to Brigade, and the wire breaks on several occasions, but is speedily dealt with by the linesmen, who are kept busy patrolling up and down the line. Meanwhile, items of extreme interest are taking place around the pill-pox of the Central Relay Station. Numerous batches of prisoners are drifting back, for the most part unattended, composed entirely of youths of nineteen and twenty years of age, the Guards having refused to kill these babies, only "despatching" the older men, for the Division up against them was very mixed, and may best be described as a "dud" lot, and it did not put up much of a fight.

The lads all look weary and mud-stained, although there is an expression of relief on their faces, as they steadily munch the bread that has been good-naturedly handed to them by their captors, for they have been starving for the past three days or so, no food having reached them on account of the terrific bombardment. An aid-post is hastily placed in a huge shell-hole close by, and the wounded straggle back; those who are but slightly hit and can walk help each other along, while the others are carried on stretchers. Here, a man, ghastly wounded, minus one leg and with the other almost severed, lies on a stretcher, calmly puffing at a cigarette given him by the bearers, and attempts to raise himself on his elbow that he may gaze at the curious scenes taking place around him. Others just stagger along, their pinched faces showing signs of suppressed pain, yet all have a quip or a jest on their lips as they smoke the inevitable cigarette.

The sight is truly a wonderful one! The courage and calm that these wounded display in the midst of their sufferings is beyond words, but they are "Greatheart's all." Reinforcements are passing all this time on their way up to the battle line, ready to throw themselves into the conflict when their time arrives.

Again the infantry move forward to the third and final objective, under cover of the friendly barrage, and, by the time they arrive at their allotted destination, an advance of some three miles from the canal bank has been effected since morning. The wire is linked up, and the F.O.O. selects a good point of vantage, and makes himself and his staff as comfortable as possible, and then proceeds to gather as much information as he can obtain to send back over the line. The infantry are now busy digging themselves in, and are being subjected to heavy shell-fire, but they stubbornly resist all efforts to dislodge them. By this time the batteries have all limbered up and advanced to new positions, mostly out in the open, and an order comes over the telephone from the B.C.'s for the F.O.O. to register the guns afresh: so he at once picks up some dependable landmark, and with much difficulty observes the rounds as they fall, and thus gives the necessary corrections.

Then the wires break on account of the shelling, and some time is lost before communications are again established. The enemy has now recovered somewhat from the initial shock of the attack, and displays much determination to recover lost ground—counter attacks are launched without success. The F.O.O. now has an important message to convey, but, when the telephonist endeavours to send it through, there is no answering buzz. Thereupon the linesman is despatched as a runner, and, on reaching the first relay station, he transfers the written message to another linesman, who immediately sets out for the next relief, and so on, until the message duly arrives at headquarters.

Thus the day wears on: sometimes direct communication is possible, and at others the wire is "dished," but, on the whole, a good deal of information is passed through. The relay posts are constantly shelled, and the bombardier in charge is wounded, while one runner was killed in his gallant endeavour to pass through a heavy barrage with an important communication. In the evening the party, much exhausted with the strenuous and never ending work of the day, is relieved by a fresh group of officers and signallers, who take over from them, and the little party wind their way homewards profoundly thankful to find themselves back with their unit safe and sound.

The situation, at the end of the opening day of the battle, was roughly this:—In the north all had gone well, and most of the objectives aimed at were successfully taken, but, such stiff resistance was met with further south, that the assaulting troops were held up after they had gained only about half of those allotted to them, and, although they fought stubbornly and determinedly, they were unable to make further ground. Thus the left wing was forced to mark time while the troops on the right made a series of attacks in order to straighten out the line, otherwise the army to the north would have found itself enclosed in a nasty salient.

The artillery, over the whole battle front, also encountered great difficulty in advancing the guns, the ground was so ploughed up by the effects of the long preliminary bombardment. Even the horse gunners, who were detailed to move up in immediate support of the infantry, were unable to proceed further than a few hundred yards on the other side of the canal. Huge craters, placed lip to lip, met them in all directions, and an advance was found to be out of the question till new tracks were prepared and the road cleared of debris. This naturally took some time to accomplish, and, meanwhile, all the field batteries were advanced as close to the canal bank as possible, but even then they were much too far behind, and were firing at almost extreme range.

No serious attack could be delivered, therefore, for some ten days, until sufficient time had elapsed to enable the gunners to occupy new positions some way across the canal, and, on this occasion, Langemarke fell into our hands, as well as the line of the Broombeke. Progress remained slow further south, consequently our front became stationary.

Now, it so happened that most of our batteries were in extremely awkward positions, as we had expected to be moved forward at any time. They were right out in the open, devoid of any cover, and, for the most part, placed in shell holes which had been hastily converted into pits. Here we were subjected to the most "gruelling" time that was ever our lot to endure, and the battle developed into a gigantic duel between batteries, in which our position was no worse than the others. We lived in shell holes, scantily covered with corrugated iron and a layer or two of sand-bags, scarcely splinter proof, nor had we any means of making ourselves more secure. The enemy's heavy counter batteries swept and searched over the slope where the majority of our batteries were congregated, and never before or after were they seen to reach such a pitch of efficiency.

Never a day passed without casualties, and often a number of gunners were buried as the result of an explosion, and had to be hastily dug out, and early on we lost one of our subaltern officers, who was borne away to the dressing station with no less than a dozen wounds on him. It was with great difficulty that the battery was kept in action sometimes, and, though we soon shifted our position to a flank, this did not relieve the situation. A 60 pdr. battery not far behind us developed the fatal habit of becoming particularly active during "flash time," and, as its flash was notoriously conspicuous, it was not surprising that its location was promptly pin-pointed by the enemy, who proceeded to knock it out: and this they succeeded in doing without much delay. During this particular contest we always got the short rounds, and, as they were not peas that were coming over, but 8" and 11" shells, the atmosphere was unpleasant, to say the least of it!

We considered ourselves lucky if we could keep 50 per cent. of the guns in action at the same time, while every nerve was strained to dig out the remainder, and it was a very heartless job, as a gun had no sooner been recovered and set up in position than it was knocked out again almost immediately. One morning, after a wild night of shelling by the enemy, on going to ascertain the damage, we found one gun with its barrel buried deep in the ground, the trail standing perpendicular pointing towards the sky; another completely turned over on its back pointing in the opposite direction, while a third had been blown right out of the shell hole in which it had been placed, and hurled a considerable distance away.

Casualties to our establishment mounted at a most alarming rate, and one night our B.C. was mortally wounded by a high explosive shell, and, although such assistance as it was possible to give was rendered, he did not survive long after reaching the casualty clearing station. His loss was much felt, not only by reason of his own cheerful personality, but also on account of the way in which he inspired all those under him to do their utmost, especially in times of stress and danger, when he always proved himself a true leader.

The Captain now succeeded to the command of the battery, and the Senior Subaltern became second-in-command. It soon became evident that we could not carry on much longer under these conditions, and in the last week of September we were pulled out to refit, and remained near the village of Herszeele for a few days before again entering the fray.

Meanwhile a subaltern with a working party was busily occupied preparing new emplacements for our reception, and on the day of their completion he was wounded while riding his bicycle back to his billet: thus we lost yet another officer. But, try as we would, it was impossible to escape the vigilant eye of the enemy, who engaged battery positions one after another, and the number of guns knocked out was prodigious. Through a lucky chance it had been decided to take the guns "in" at dawn, instead of during the night, and by reason of this we escaped a most violent hostile bombardment which was directed against the position, and which damaged at least two of the pits and completely destroyed several dug-outs which the work party had recently striven so hard to build. We set to work and repaired most of the damage, and, whether or not it was the enemy thought he had disposed of us thereby, at all events he did not repeat the performance beyond subjecting us to the ordinary night harassing fire.

Another attack was impending, which again necessitated the forward movement of all batteries, and this time we were more fortunate in the selection of a site, and had several German pill-boxes in which to live and take refuge. Owing to the congestion on the one and only good road in the neighbourhood and the hostile shelling thereof, it was a matter of luck to find ourselves safely installed behind Abri Wood, and we immediately set out preparing for the new fight.

Unfortunately, the weather again came to the assistance of our foe, and a spell of rain and wind made conditions extremely difficult for both infantry and gunners. However, the battle was proceeded with, and the result was an advance over the mud and slime of the river Broombeke as far as the outskirts of Houthoulst Forest, a distance of about two miles; our French allies, on the left, keeping in step with us throughout this operation.

Then the inevitable forward move of the batteries was resumed, and this time we occupied positions down the further slope of the hill immediately across the rivulet of the Steenbeke. In consequence of torrents of rain, which continued daily, the low-lying ground became flooded, and it was all we could do to prevent the guns sinking in the sodden earth, and they frequently disappeared in the mud up to their axles. Dry accommodation was nowhere to be found except in a great pill-box, which we added to and strengthened, and it was popularly called the "Rabbit Hutch," for the obvious reason that it held the majority of the four batteries of the Brigade.

Now, our last attack had advanced us considerably further than the men on the right, who throughout the past month had encountered very stiff opposition, so we had perforce to remain stationary and mark time, while the battle continued to the south. On several occasions we rendered assistance by putting up what is commonly known as a "Chinese barrage," i.e., the artillery carries out the ordinary programme preceding an attack, but no action follows on the part of the infantry. Conditions were equally disagreeable at the wagon lines, which speedily developed into quagmires, and it was almost impossible to walk about the lines unless attired in waders, and, even then, there was always the possibility of completely disappearing in the mud. Over and above that, the wagon lines were subjected every now and then to the attentions of a high velocity gun, as well as frequent visits from hostile night bombing machines, which were following the example set by our airmen and were endeavouring to pay us back in our own coin.

Much damage was done in and around the neighbourhood, but our lines escaped exceedingly lightly. The question of ammunition supply became acute, and the use of pack saddles was again necessitated, and, because of the great distance between wagon lines and gun position, the round journey sometimes took eighteen hours to accomplish, and naturally the strain eventually told greatly upon both men and horses.

The battery positions were not long in being located by the enemy, who expended great quantities of ammunition in his attempts to destroy them: and he made much use of chemical and mustard shell, which in time saturated the low-lying ground on which the guns were placed. In this way he effectively gassed the B.C., a subaltern, and several of the men, who were all despatched to the wagon line, and the Captain assumed command for the time being and brought up reliefs with him. By this time the Battery was again in a very bad way, and a rest was promised on several occasions, only to be held up time and again with the exhortation to hold out yet a little while longer. Winter was rapidly approaching, and it was necessary to adjust our line before fighting came to a standstill: and a considerable distance had yet to be traversed before the goal—Passchendaele and the ridge on which it was situated—could be reached.

The battery, meanwhile, waited on in patience. All the remaining officers were affected by the mustard gas, as well as the majority of the gunners, and a sorry sight we presented when, in the first week in November, an incoming battery took over from us. We then proceeded to the new wagon lines, near Proven, in an utterly exhausted condition.

CHAPTER 8

Cambrai

Everyone thought that our long-expected rest was now forthcoming, so it was a great surprise when we were ordered to hold ourselves in readiness for a long march.

What did it all mean? Were we marching into our new area and having our rest there or were we to be pitch-forked into another scrap?

No indication of our destination was given, and everything seemed most mysterious: and, when the Brigade arrived in the neighbourhood of Merville, there did not appear to be any sign of a definite halt. At all events the journey was being performed in easy stages, as if we were filling in time, and we were always making further south, till, passing behind Bethune, the vicinity of Arras was reached. Here news of the surprise attack at Cambrai first reached our ears, the secret of which had been kept so well, and, heading in the direction of Bapaume, we were acquainted with the fact that we were again "for it."

Now, the initial attack, which came as a complete surprise to the enemy, had met with instant success, and, with the aid of a considerable number of Tanks, the great Hindenburg line had been breeched over a distance of from 6 to 8 miles, with the result that the fall of Cambrai a centre of great importance to the Germans appeared imminent.

However, after the first couple of days, the attack was not pressed home as it might have been, for some reason or other, and the fight came to an abrupt standstill, leaving our troops in a particularly baggy salient. These were the conditions that prevailed when the Division gradually moved nearer the scene of action.

In the beginning of the fourth week of November, we entered the battle, taking over from a famous Scottish Division which had fought with great distinction on the opening days.

The battery was placed in action to the north of Flesquieres, well inside the salient facing Bourlon Wood, in a position only recently completed by the enemy and which had not even been occupied by him. There was plenty of accommodation for everyone in the deep mined dug-outs prepared by him some thirty to forty feet below the ground, and the officers' quarters were spacious and lavishly constructed.

From this point the domes and the spires of the city of Cambrai could be clearly distinguished; indeed, they appeared such a short distance away, it looked as if a saunter would carry us into the heart of the town.

It was most interesting and instructive studying the elaborate system of the Hindenburg defences. First, there were three separate belts of closely-entwined barbed wire, each being some thirty yards wide, and behind them came a deep, narrow fore-field trench that was only intended to be lightly manned. Communication trenches led back to the main Hindenburg trench some distance behind, in most cases being out of immediate view from our lately occupied positions.

This trench was both deep and wide, being some twelve feet across and duck-boarded throughout, raised on wooden stakes to prevent the water reaching the level of the pathway. At short intervals shafts led down to the spacious dug-outs beneath, which were all connected and linked up with one another. In fact, practically speaking, one could walk from one end of the line to the other below the surface of the ground.

Skilfully concealed, at frequent intervals, were emplacements for both trench-mortars and machine-guns, all heavily concreted and covered on top with turf.

The enemy must have thought himself very secure in this vast stronghold, but in a way this very fact contributed, in a great measure, to his undoing; for, it is common knowledge that the more one frequents deep dug-outs the less inclination there is to emerge from them when a scrap is taking place.

Finally, some 500 yards in the rear, a support line ran along, which, though not constructed with the same strength, was formidable enough in itself.

To judge by the indescribable mess, and by the mass of material left littered about, the enemy must indeed have beat a hasty retreat. The dug-outs were filthy to the last degree, and there was no sign of any system of sanitation having been used by these people, who considered their *"Kultur"* to be superlative, and who desired to impose it on the rest of mankind. All through the campaign, whenever one had the opportunity of inspecting hostile trenches and billets, one always found the same thing, filth and lack of sanitation.

Now, for some little time our hold on Bourlon Wood had been precarious, so a further attack was initiated, and the Guards went in to straighten the line. They swept through the Wood, taking the villages of Bourlon and Fontaine, but a gigantic counter attack pressed them back again owing to reinforcements being late in arriving to render assistance. They were so badly mauled and cut up that it was necessary to withdraw them from the line to refit, and infantry from an "Old Contemptible" Division took their place. Bourlon Wood became so saturated with gas that, after a great tussle, neither side was able to tenant it any longer, and so withdrew, leaving a screen of outposts to prevent any surprise attack.

This was the situation when dawn broke on the 30th of November, a day which proved to be one of ups and downs for us, and caused many misgivings to arise in the old country. The object of the enemy was to pinch either side of the jaws, and, if his attack on the north had met with equal success with that on the south, there would have been little hope for the troops in the salient, who undoubtedly would have been surrounded and cut off. However, as events turned out, our men held out and remained firm. Moreover, it was afterwards discovered from captured documents that the enemy's scheme was a large and ambitious one. Not only was it his intention to retake the whole of our recent gains, but to press on further through Havrincourt Wood, and establish himself on a line beyond it.

The Germans employed the same tactics as we used on the opening day of the battle—there was no preliminary bombardment, and their troops advanced under cover of a heavy mist and preceded by a creeping barrage. They put an overwhelming number of troops into the fight, the odds against our men being something like three to one, but our infantry in the north fought valiantly, although they were forced to give ground step by step in the initial stages. As the day wore on and the mist rose, we were able to see the hostile infantry advancing in masses, but they were paying a heavy toll at the hands of our machine gunners, who cut many a line in their ranks.

The situation became tense when the enemy succeeded in driving our men across the Bapaume-Cambrai road, and were seen to be approaching Anneux and Graincourt. The 18 prs. batteries which were lying alongside of us dragged their guns out of their pits on to the crest in front, and proceeded to rake the enemy, firing as rapidly as they were able, through open sights, the gunners stripped to the waist, toiling and sweating in their endeavour to stop the oncoming tide. The fight swayed backward and forward throughout the whole day, but finally the enemy was held in check without gaining further ground, and he incurred very heavy casualties.

In the south the situation was very obscure, and somehow or other the enemy broke a gap in the defences between La Vacquerie and Gouzeaucourt, capturing the latter place as well as the village of Gonnelieu, and commenced streaming through. He had advanced a considerable distance before the importance of his move was fully realised, consequently most extraordinary incidents occurred, stories of which are now familiar to everyone. Battery positions were rapidly overrun, and even wagon lines were captured, while Labour companies, working on the roads far behind the front, on looking up, discovered the foe almost on top of them.

There were no reserves in immediate support, and affairs were taking on a most serious complexion. Something had to be done and that right speedily! Therefore the Guards, who had only two days previously been withdrawn from the fight, were again called upon. They were lying in rest around Bertincourt, Ytres and Ruyaulcourt, and were hurriedly conveyed in 'buses and motor lorries to Metz, where they formed up and set out on their big counter-attack, supported by our sister Brigade and another gunner unit which chanced to have been pulled out on the previous night. Now, the enemy troops appeared to be as much surprised at their success as we were, and continued advancing in a bewildered kind of fashion, astonished at the little or entire lack of opposition with which they met. Suddenly, however, they came face to face with the full strength of the best disciplined troops in the world, whereupon they paused, staggered, and at length commenced to fall back, in confusion and disorder, with the result that the day was saved just in the nick of time, and most of the ground was recovered, in addition to some 50 guns.

Meanwhile the wagon lines were situated in the village of Ribecourt, right inside the salient, and, although it was known that a scrap was taking place, no one had any idea as to its stupendous nature. The fact that the village lay in a valley, surrounded by hills, prevented much noise of the conflict reaching those in it. However, shortly after breakfast, it became apparent that something was amiss, and the place became subjected to a heavy bombardment. The horses and vehicles were evacuated as quickly as possible, without suffering undue casualties, and collected on the hillside a short distance away, facing Bourlon Wood, where they "stood to" awaiting further orders.

Hostile aeroplanes put in an appearance, flying daringly low hither and thither across the salient, endeavouring to pick up as much information as possible, and sometimes dropping bombs. Many a tussle took place between them and our airmen, who did not allow them undisputed sway for long.

At noon instructions came through to be prepared to withdraw the guns at any moment, but in the end this was found unnecessary. Even at this time we were unaware that the enemy had penetrated our line to the south, and the first indication we had that something unusual was taking place, was the arrival of some reinforcements, who hurried along the top of the hillside behind us, and took up positions facing in the opposite direction! A short time elapsed, and then we were astonished and horrified to see a creeping barrage roll along, top the crest, and gradually draw nearer us from the rear. Fortunately, it stopped before actually reaching us, for by this time the enemy had attained his furthest point of penetration, and the counter attack had already been launched. Throughout the rest of the day the wagon line "stood to" ready for any emergency, and at dusk the limbers were sent up to the position, and the guns were withdrawn the same night and placed in action in the railway cutting immediately behind the ridge to the south of Flesquieres.

It became evident, after the experiences of the previous day, that, as long as we remained in this awkward salient, we would undoubtedly be exposed to further attacks at the hands of the enemy. The Germans meanwhile had concentrated huge forces in the vicinity, so a continuation of our advance was now out of the question, and a modification of our front was decided upon. The infantry constructed a new line running north of Flesquieres Ridge, and, as soon as it was completed, our troops fell back on it under cover of darkness, unperceived and therefore unmolested by the enemy, who only made the discovery on the following day, and then cautiously followed up until they came in contact with us once more. The salient presented a curious aspect at night to those inside it, and we seemed to be almost surrounded by Verey lights, as indeed we were, except where the narrow neck led out towards Metz.

The enemy did not, as was expected, attempt any further operations on a large scale, but contented himself with making things very uncomfortable for us. In spite of our withdrawal, the line was still saggy to a large extent, and he could bring his guns to bear on any part of the salient and enfilade it. He also paid much attention to bombing, and his planes came over at dawn and dusk and caused a good deal of damage. The wagon lines came in for their share of unpleasantness, and in the course of a fortnight we were forced to quit no less than three positions in turn. The battery was specially handicapped by the colour of its horses, and was evidently easily spotted by hostile aircraft, for we had more than our share of ill fortune at this period. To take the worst case that befell us, one night the wagon line lost 35 horses. A covey of enemy planes had been over at daybreak, and apparently made a mental note of our location, as they returned the same evening and dropped several bombs, though, strange to say, no damage was effected. However, towards midnight, a 4.2 battery suddenly opened fire with instantaneous fuse action, and many casualties were inflicted before the horses could be removed, owing to difficulties in the pitch darkness.

The most wonderful fact in the whole proceedings was that, although there was little or no cover for the men, who were ensconced in bivouacs, except a few who were in an old disused trench close by, only a couple of them were hit. The officers were rudely awakened by large splinters entering their tent, and only just missing their heads as they lay on their valises, while the sergeants had a most miraculous escape. They had formed a Mess in a bay of the trench, the sides supported and heightened by some of the Q.M.S.'s stores, and covered on top by a large tarpaulin.

A shell dropped practically on top of them, fortunately detonating instantly against several boxes of iron rations, which undoubtedly contributed to saving their lives. An officer arrived on the scene immediately afterwards, and found them all lying unconscious as the result of the explosion, but they soon revived and took a stout part in rescuing the horses. The construction was completely wrecked, and the clothes they wore were stripped into ribbons, but only one of them had a scratch on him.

No delay was made in attending to the wounded horses, and in conveying the remainder to a place of safety. The drivers were all splendidly cool and collected under the trying circumstances, but many of the poor beasts were beyond human aid, and had to be destroyed.

The scene next morning was a gruesome one, and it was a most pathetic sight to watch the drivers, with tears running down their cheeks, bidding a last farewell to their lost charges before burial, for the men become exceedingly attached to their four-legged comrades, especially when they have had charge of them for a considerable time. No time was lost in selecting a new locality, as it was considered wise to get out of the salient altogether, and thus avoid the risk of incurring further unnecessary casualties; so the wagon lines were removed to the vicinity of Ruyaulcourt.

A spell of hard frost set in, with an occasional fall of snow, which added to our difficulties as well as to our discomforts, for it must be remembered that both battery position and wagon line were occupied at a moment's notice, and no time could be spent in making any preparations beforehand for our reception. Affairs were now settling down for the winter, and nothing unusual was taking place beyond a good deal of artillery activity on both sides, consequently we were only awaiting orders to withdraw from the line. These came through in a few days' time, and the Brigade pulled out in the middle of December to the ruined village of Beaulencourt, situated south east of Bapaume. On the following day a long march was undertaken, and we proceeded by way of Achiet-le-Grand, Ayette, and Beaumetz to the village of Montennescourt, due west of Arras, a distance of 25 miles.

It says much for the battery that it accomplished this long trail with no less than 43 horses below establishment, and without any outside assistance, in spite of the heaviness of the roads. The guns were pulled by six-horse teams, and the vehicles and other baggage wagons by four-horse teams, made up by requisitioning all the available outriders, yet none of the horses suffered to any great extent from the extra strain imposed on them.

It was with feelings of great gratification that we learnt that at last we were going to have our long-delayed rest, and that it would fall to our lot to spend the coming Christmas-tide and New Year season in more congenial surroundings than had been the case in the two previous years. All were prepared to enjoy themselves on this occasion, as it was felt, on reviewing the past six months, during which time we had been fighting incessantly in *"pukka"* battles, in which we had acquitted ourselves not badly, that we had thoroughly earned a week or two of complete rest and quiet.

CHAPTER 9
At Arras

The next fortnight was spent under most happy conditions, and all ranks had an enjoyable time. As Christmas approached, active preparations were made to excel anything we had ever had before in the way of festivities, and this was possible now that we were out of action. Quarter-Master-Sergeants, puffed out with importance, were to be seen strutting hither and thither, returning with mysterious sacks and parcels, presumably filled with good cheer.

Plucked geese and turkeys appeared in large numbers, suspended from the ceilings of billets, and several large barrels arrived on the scene, and were duly placed under lock and key in the canteen, awaiting the auspicious day. Much competition took place between batteries for the possession of the only two live pigs in the village, which eventually went to the highest bidders, while the remainder procured their joints in the form of pork from Doullens. One of the batteries meanwhile grew so attached to its prospective Christmas fare that it was almost decided to spare his life and adopt him as a mascot. His fate was sealed, however, when one day it was discovered that he had disposed of several parcels of food which had, inadvertently, been placed within his reach by some of the men.

Concerts were arranged, and the village school-room was kindly lent and artistically decorated for these occasions. The weather was all that could be desired now that we were safely lodged in billets, and it was a typical old-fashioned Yuletide, with a plentiful fall of snow followed by hard frost. The little village was in a sheltered hollow, and a small rivulet passed through it on its way down the valley, while the scenery might have been that surrounding any hamlet in the south of England.

An open air service was conducted by the Padre, for the Brigade, on 'Xmas morning, and the rest of the day was given over to sports and concerts, and the climax of enjoyment was reached at night when the men partook of their dinner. Gramophones were well to the fore, but all kinds of musical instruments took part in the gaiety which followed.

A certain amount of latitude was given the men for a few days after, in order that they might recover from the orgy, for indeed they had never had such a gorge since their arrival in France. All were in excellent spirits, and these were by no means diminished when it became known that our next area was in front of Arras. It was recognised to be an enviable part of the line to be situated in, especially during the winter months. It was also a locality with which we had not as yet made acquaintance, and it was always interesting to visit a new portion of the front, as we disliked being too long in the same surroundings without a change of scene.

The day following New Year, the Division entered on its period of duty in the sector north of Monchy to the vicinity of Gavrelle, with the heights of Vimy, which had fallen into our hands in the previous spring on its left.

The battery position was reached by following the Arras-Plouvain road along the valley of the river Scarpe, and we took over from a Scottish Division. The enemy lines were everywhere overlooked, consequently he wisely refrained from showing much activity.

A magnificent view was obtained from the rear O.P. on the heights facing Vitry, and, on a clear day, Douai was plainly visible and even the country far beyond it.

Our front line ran along at the bottom of the slope, having the ruined piles of Roeux, which was the scene of such furious fighting in the latter stages of Arras battle, immediately in its rear. Half right, to the south of the river Scarpe, what remained of the village of Monchy stood out like a sentinel on the top of the hill. This point afforded a splendid view in all directions and was the veritable keystone of the whole position. Four of our pieces were placed in a quarry, a few yards off the road leading through Fampoux, on its western extremity, while the other two guns were moved forward, east of the same village, behind a bank, and carefully camouflaged.

As this sector was extraordinarily quiet and there was not sufficient work to keep everyone occupied, the Battery Commander decided to commence construction and endeavour to make our position a model one. Two pits, which were already in existence, were pulled down and rebuilt, and two others were constructed alongside, and all of them were placed just as near the front bank of the quarry as would permit of the guns clearing the crest. The whole position was completely camouflaged, as, it will be readily understood, a quarry made a conspicuous target for the enemy at any time, and if he suspected the presence of a battery therein, there would have been little peace or quiet for us. However, as things turned out, we had evidently made a good job of our work, and to our surprise, not a single shell dropped in the quarry during our period of occupation.

Walls were white-washed and ammunition and charge shelves elaborately painted, the platforms were neatly tiled or bricked with material taken from the surrounding ruins, and all manner of "eye wash" was employed in making the pits look well. A communication trench was dug from one extremity to the other, riveted and duck-boarded throughout, and led to the men's quarters. These when completed were palatial, and put in the shade any headquarter unit in the line.

The near side of the quarry, which consisted of chalk, was easily and rapidly mined, and, in the course of three weeks, the men had comfortable quarters. Beds made of wire netting stretched on wooden frames, a spacious dining hall, telephone pit, cook house, and they even possessed a moderate sized bath room, which was highly valued and put to great use. The officers' quarters were no less sumptuously fitted out. Each had sleeping accommodation, in cellars of the ruined houses, running along the main street close to the quarry, nicely lined with wood and canvas to keep the damp out, while the Mess itself was a work of art.

The latter was built entirely by the officers and their batmen, under the personal supervision of our energetic B.C.

The floors, walls and roof of the cellar were lined with three inch timber, and one day a subaltern, who had been out exploring, came back triumphant, bearing in his arms a huge roll of wall paper found buried under some rubbish, at a spot which probably denoted the one time existence of a decorator's shop. The Mess was therefore duly papered, with frieze complete, and with the addition of easy chairs, book shelves, a stove and gramophone, there was nothing left to wish for, and the place was most cosy and snug. The entrance, too, was the admiration of everybody, nicely tiled and decorated with fancy carvings from the utterly destroyed church. Iron girders, beams, and countless bricks to the height of several feet rested on top of our home. It is not to be wondered at, then, that this model position was frequently visited by high personages, brought hither by our Brigade-Commander or C.R.A., who appeared almost as proud of the place as we were ourselves. Moreover, as we were in such close proximity to the road leading up to the front line, it was only natural that officers should drop in to this half way house and rest and regale themselves before resuming their journey, so before long our Mess was known as "The Pub" throughout the Division.

The forward position was treated in the same fashion, and never before had both officers and men had such comfortable quarters. Thus we settled down to a life of ease, such as we had not known since the Laventie days of two winters ago, and proceeded to thoroughly enjoy ourselves.

Frequent trips were made into Arras, either on horseback or by river, for there was a steamboat service, running daily on the Scarpe, which landed one close to the Officers' Club, a large wooden erection similar to a Y.M.C.A. hut, run by the Expeditionary Force Canteen.

The town had not been irreparably destroyed, and in most parts the inhabitants had returned, and were carrying on their usual routine, while many shops were re-opened and doing good business. The Cathedral was badly damaged, as well as other prominent buildings, but, on the whole, the town had escaped wonderfully considering how close the enemy had been to it for so long. Now, of course, the enemy was over six miles away, and the city could not be reached by any other than his high velocity guns, and they seldom troubled to shell the place, and when they did so, from time to time, the fire was chiefly directed on the railway station and sidings in the vicinity.

An equally peaceful time fell to the lot of those who were at the wagon lines. They were situated just off the main Arras-Souchez road, within easy reach of the former place. Accommodation for Officers and men was provided by Nissen huts, containing stoves, while the horses had good covered-in standings, with mud walls surrounding them for protection against bombing raids.

The transport of ammunition to the guns was easily conducted, as excellent roads ran the whole way, and every care was taken to keep the horses up to condition. The frost did not continue and in the early months of the year the weather was wonderfully bright and mild, and many a good gallop could be had in the neighbourhood, as there was a fine stretch of open ground close to the wagon line.

The horses undoubtedly had a better time than it is usually possible to give them during the winter months. The war horse is an extraordinarily intelligent animal and appreciates anything done for him in the way of comfort. He also becomes very cute and cunning, and always knows the routine of the day, and can tell his time of feeding almost to the minute, and, if allowed, would go by himself automatically to the water troughs and return to his own particular standing in the stable.

One horse familiarly known by the name of "Shrapnel," owing to several wounds of that kind which refused to close up, and completely heal, knew at once when he was "warned" for the line. Now, he disliked going out at nights, and consequently was in the habit of "scrimp-shanking," and proceeded forthwith to go lame. At first he managed to fool everybody, but on close investigation it was discovered that nothing at all was the matter with him.

Another fine beast, which at one time must have been ill-treated, when he came to us had a bad rope gall on his near hind, and was extremely nervous at being touched. After hours of coaxing he allowed his section officer and driver to handle him, and, at length, showed great affection to them both, but woe betide any other member of the battery, who attempted to go near him, back went his ears and out went his feet at once!

About the middle of February, a feeling of uneasiness evidently entered the minds of those in authority. It was known that the enemy was transferring large numbers of troops, which had been released by the collapse of Russia, to the Western front. Consequently every unit got busy at once, the Infantry dug new trench systems in rear of their existing ones, constructed strong points, and mile upon mile of barbed wire was laid down.

The gunners prepared new battle and reinforcing positions, in case a retiral should be necessary, and filled them with ammunition against all eventualities.

In a little more than a month everything was completed, and during the third week of March, the troops were warned of an impending great enemy offensive, and became fully on the alert.

Chapter 10

March the 21st

The morning of the 20th broke calm and the enemy did nothing to indicate that anything out of the ordinary was about to take place, but this did not deceive us, as it was known to our Command that the blow was going to fall on the following morning. Silence reigned supreme, except for the ordinary harassing artillery fire, up till midnight, but shortly afterwards the German guns opened out their annihilating fire, and drenched our forward system and battery positions with a severe gas bombardment.

In this area the majority of batteries had, at the last moment, taken the precaution to change their positions, as these were known to the enemy, and thus avoided being entirely demolished by the heavy concentration which poured all manner of shell into those they had lately vacated.

At dawn, which, unfortunately for us, broke in a thick mist, after a sustained bombardment of some four to five hours' duration, the enemy launched his gigantic attack over an area of fifty miles, from Guenappe, immediately below Monchy in the North, to the neighbourhood of La Fere in the south. Under cover of the mist, he congregated large numbers of field guns, which were able to accompany and closely support the attacking waves, while at some places he employed his new Tanks. These, however, though rendering some assistance to him, by no means came up to expectations, and were ponderous and clumsy, in spite of the fact that he had previously captured several of ours from which to copy, but they proved to be far behind ours, both in construction and usefulness.

A "Chinese barrage" was put down by the enemy on our sector, but no attack developed. The same evening the Division was hurriedly withdrawn from the line, and heading in a southern direction arrived in the neighbourhood of Tilloy and prepared for instant action.

In spite of the favourable conditions, our foes made little or no ground, throughout the day, on the whole of the Army front, and were held in our fore-field. Further south, much the same thing happened, although they penetrated further in some places, but nowhere had they broken through, so the news on the whole was good and reassuring.

The German attack was renewed on the following day, and still the Northern Army remained firm, but they succeeded in effecting a serious breech in the Army to the south, where the British had lately taken over from our French allies. So swift was the enemy's progress at this point that our troops on either side of this bulge soon became endangered, and a general retirement was immediately necessary in order to keep the line straight.

This applied to the Northern Army also, but not to anything like the same extent. The Division again moved south, and took up positions behind the Henin Ridge, between the village of that name and St. Leger, for the purpose of covering the retirement.

The whole line thus became mobile, and, for several days, a stiff rear-guard action was fought, which resulted in very heavy casualties being inflicted on the enemy. He was by this time flushed with his success further south, and attempted to advance as if he were already the conqueror, which led to his own undoing, as virtually he was only permitted to gain ground at our time and will. It cannot be denied, however, that the days were anxious ones and the infantry were kept very heavily engaged and became much exhausted. However, they made the most of their opportunities, and had hitherto rarely found such ready targets, and their machine guns effected great execution on the enemy ranks as the men came along laden with full packs. A story is told, and is believed to be true, of one machine gunner that, in the course of his morning's work, he slaughtered over 200 German's single handed with his weapon, after which he became a raving lunatic and had to be forcibly removed.

The infantry, too, admitted that they were getting tired of killing Boches, and the casualties inflicted on our men were a mere nothing as compared with those suffered by our foes. The gunners were equally busy dropping into action here and there and falling back as the circumstances required, until at the end of a week, the line became more or less stationary. The front line now ran through Mercatel, Boisleux and Moyenneville and thence, in a south westerly direction, towards Serre. Thus the Germans were again almost back on the line they had held, prior to the big retreat on the Hindenburg line in the spring of 1917.

It seemed a great pity to vacate the Henin Ridge, for the opposing sides found themselves facing each other in a hollow, with rising ground on either side, which made battery positions difficult to conceal. So many disused trenches, which had previously formed part of the old German line system, helped to shelter us, to a great extent, for we were at this point nearly two miles east of the permanent line of a year ago.

Everyone feverishly sat about digging and constructing new trenches, and an enormous amount of work was accomplished in a comparatively short space of time, for it was felt that the enemy had by no means expended all his strength, and would endeavour, in the near future, to resume active operations. There could be no doubt that he would be dissatisfied to remain where he was, especially as, so far, he had little to show on this particular part of the front for his gigantic effort and huge loss of men.

It was no surprise therefore when, at the beginning of the

second week in April, after a short sharp bombardment, the enemy made a strong attack from Monchy, north to the Vimy Ridge, with the object of seizing Arras and the heights before mentioned. The result was a costly failure, as he was everywhere held up in our fore-field system, and the British Divisions opposed to him had the time of their lives. We were very interested to hear about this battle, as, of course, it was fought over the sector in which we had lately spent a number of happy months and where we had done such an amount of work. It was distinctly gratifying, too, when a wire was received from the Division who took over from us thanking our Division for the wonderful defensive construction made by us. It was due to that work that they were enabled to bring the enemy so quickly to an abrupt standstill.

They had seemingly experienced a veritable field day and thoroughly enjoyed themselves on that occasion.

After this unsuccessful effort, the enemy evidently gave up the attempt to gain possession of Arras and Vimy by a frontal attack and turned his thoughts elsewhere.

Unfortunately, however, in the course of these operations, Monchy had to be evacuated by the British, which enabled the Boche to gain observation on the city which, thereafter, came in for a good amount of shelling, and again the inhabitants were forced much against their will to leave the stricken place.

All manner of heavy shell fell in the town, and the damage caused was considerable, and it was no longer the haven of rest for the troops which it had been a few months previously. Our wagon lines, meanwhile, had not escaped undamaged, and were forced to change positions on several occasions until, at last, comfortable quarters were obtained in the little village of Bretencourt, where the houses still had roofs covering them, as the hamlet was just outside the devastated area. When affairs settled down once more, the battery positions were gradually advanced, and we dug a new position east of Ficheux, where the guns were meanwhile situated.

A forward section was established ahead in the railway cutting of the Arras-Albert line, and we subjected the enemy to as much unpleasantness as it lay in our power to devise.

We were not, however, any length of time in this sector, and were removed to the adjoining one immediately to the south.

The line required rectifying in several places, and in a brilliant minor operation, the village of Ayette was carried and remained firmly in our hands.

Our new position was situated on the high ground to the north of Adinfer Wood, immediately behind the village of the same name, but the neighbourhood was much more peaceful than that which we had recently quitted, as everywhere we had observation over the enemy, and naturally he never created trouble under such circumstances.

The wagon lines were again moved, this time much further behind, to the small village of Gaudiempre, where one might have imagined one was completely out of the war area, it appeared so quiet.

The place was intact and all were ensconced in snug little billets, while the horses were well off also, as opportunities for grazing were afforded round about the neighbourhood.

Then the enemy's second great offensive opened on the Lys, and all eyes were turned in that direction, but everyone held the opinion that, sooner or later, he would be brought to a standstill, which proved to be the case.

In fact, throughout the whole of this trying period, the confidence among all ranks was extraordinary. No one had the feeling that we were going down and under, and it would have done the pessimists at home a world of good to have caught a glimpse of conditions out in France and of the cheery optimism that prevailed there. There was even disappointment, in some quarters, that the enemy had not attempted to attack us on this front, but he evidently thought discretion was the better part of valour, for the defences were, by this time, very strong, and it would have been strange if he had managed to penetrate to any depth.

About the middle of May, it was the will of those in authority to rest the Division a while, and although we were not in any urgent need of a rest, we were not disinclined for it, as the season of the year was favourable, and we pictured all manner of good times in store.

The Brigade, therefore, withdrew to the wagon lines, marched the following day to Humbercourt, the village appointed for our resting place.

CHAPTER 11

The Turn of the Tide

It invariably happened, when the Brigade came out for a period of rest, that expectations of a real holiday were never fully realized, and although the time passed pleasantly enough and we were favoured with fine weather, all ranks were kept pretty busy. Many tactical schemes were practised, and we had always to hold ourselves in readiness to render assistance, at short notice, to the troops who were in the line, for our Command was taking no risks and had not entirely given up the possibility of a hostile attack on this area.

It must be admitted, however, that in the end everybody enjoyed rehearsing these schemes, and we would have been well acquainted with our duties had the emergency arisen. Our resentment, also, at being called upon to partake of violent exercise so early in the morning, completely disappeared after a while, the country looked so beautiful at dawn, and we usually returned in time for breakfast, with well-whetted appetites, after some three or four hours in the saddle.

Unfortunately, at this time, the scourge known as "Flanders Grippe," which had been prevalent throughout the Army, developed in our Brigade. For a considerable time this epidemic paralysed us, more or less, as about half our number was down with the disease at the same time. Although it passes after taking its three days' course, one is left very weak and groggy for some time, and several of the men were very seriously ill.

Inevitable inspections by Corps Commanders and minor officials passed off without incident, but, of course, much labour and "eye-wash" was expended as is always the case on these occasions. The Divisional Horse Show, held towards the end of our rest, was undoubtedly the principal diversion of our time out, as each unit naturally did its utmost to out-shine all others. The battery entered a gun team complete, consisting of six dapple-grey horses, and we succeeded in securing the second prize in the gunner's Derby. Curiously enough, the winners, our sister howitzer battery, won with five, out of six horses which had been shown, over two years previously at Zeggers Capelle, in Flanders, and who then carried off second prize in the competition with a team of blacks. H.R.H. The Duke of Connaught afterwards inspect-ed the prize-winners, and evinced much interest on being told that ours was a complete battery of grey horses.

Paris leave opened for both officers and men as a conso-lation for home furlough being stopped, and many availed themselves of the opportunity of having a few days' enjoy-ment in the "Gay City."

In the first days of June the Division returned to the line and occupied the sector we had already been in prior to mov-ing to Adinfer. The area had become very quiet with one or two exceptions, and the enemy did not subject our infantry to much shelling, and contented himself with occasionally annoying them with trench mortars. But if, at any time, he discovered the location of a battery position, that unit had a most unhappy time. Four of our guns were placed in the rail-way cutting, where we had previously had a forward section, and the remainder were again detached some distance away. Mine shafts, which were already in existence, were enlarged and the men had plenty cover on top of them.

Some little time afterwards certain indications pointed to the fact that the enemy contemplated business once more on this front, and as our guns were situated awkwardly where it would be impossible to withdraw them quickly, we were directed to construct a new position further behind. The work proceeded briskly, and, when completed, four of the pieces were withdrawn and placed there, the other two remaining in the railway embankment. The main position was a long way back, and the guns could only just reach the enemy support trenches, consequently they were only to be fired in case of a general S.O.S., and all the shoots were accomplished by the forward section.

Much time was spent in making our new quarters shipshape, and the ground was well suited for mining, as it consisted principally of chalk, and eventually all ranks were comfortably installed in spacious underground quarters, although, at the moment, they were quite unnecessary, and many lay out in the open during the warm summer nights. The principal thing to do now was to make sure that the officers and men did not stagnate for lack of occupation and to find means to keep them hard and fit. Physical exercises were indulged in during the morning, and sports of all kinds were organised, both at the battery positions and at the wagon lines—the latter having taken up their quarters at the village of Baillemont.

A modified kind of base-ball, introduced by an energetic and enthusiastic Canadian subaltern, became very popular with the men, while the corps ran a polo-club of sorts for the officers. A fairly level patch of ground was selected which possessed a certain amount of grass, and the numerous shell holes were filled in and levelled off by fatigue parties, with the result that it became moderately good. The polo ponies, however, left something to be desired, and it was no uncommon sight to see a young officer appear mounted on a stalwart wheeler, the best he could do for himself from among the horses in his section. Possibly the explanation was that he had found a horse which he could suitably "rein in".

Meanwhile the enemy's third big offensive had come and gone and the British Commander-in-Chief's famous "back to the wall" order of the day to his armies. Still we waited, but nothing unusual happened; then in the middle of July the French were heavily attacked, and once more the clouds appeared on the horizon. There was great enthusiasm when it became known that our Allies had counter-attacked, and were driving the enemy out of the Marne pocket, and when the daily bulletins arrived there was always a scramble among the men to read them.

Then the British stroke fell south of the river Somme at Villers Brettonneux, and excellent news, as to our progress, came through, which raised everyone's hopes to a high degree. Our artillery fire was increased daily, and affairs became more lively, while flying was in full swing and continued night and day. Both sides paid much attention to bombing, and our Airmen freely besprinkled enemy territory with their bombs by day, whereas the foe rarely attempted raids over our lines during daylight. However, after dusk, the air was filled with the planes, as the weather was particularly favourable, and the hum of the machines coming and going was incessant throughout the whole night.

At times one could scarcely get any sleep for the continual drone they made, like the hum of gigantic bees around their hives. One thing certain was that we had almost complete control of the air and both out-numbered and out-witted the enemy to a marked extent. It was most unpleasant to hear the noise of the hostile planes drawing nearer, for one could not mistake the beat made by the German machines. The amount of bombing experienced by us was quite bad enough in all truth, but we used to smile when contemplating what our foes must be suffering at the hands of our Airmen, as truly it was ten times worse.

During this period the two counter offensives were progressing favourably in the south, and we suspected that something would be doing on our front before long, as the din of battle was creeping further north. It came as no surprise, therefore, when serious fighting commenced north of the Somme, and the enemy retreated from Serre and later withdrew in error from Ablainzevelle. As soon as he discovered his mistake he attempted to retake it, but, by that time, our men were firmly lodged there and could not be shifted from the village.

In the middle of August, to everyone's satisfaction, it became known that we were to be up and doing at no distant date, and preparations were immediately and silently set on foot. Throughout each night a continual stream of teams and wagons conveyed thousands of rounds of ammunition up the line to battery positions, and fresh dumps were placed in forward localities. New battle positions were constructed in advanced positions and stocked with shells, and we only awaited the order to occupy them.

Instructions were issued to wagon lines that all surplus kit and stores were to be left behind, as a strenuous time was in store for us, and all ranks responded with a will to the hard work these preparations necessitated. Drivers were elated at the prospect of a change from their humdrum existence, and their enthusiasm knew no bounds. New reinforcing batteries appeared like mushrooms during the night, and lay safely ensconced in their appointed places in readiness for the coming fray, while the neighbourhood behind the lines bristled with activity and also with new arrivals. We believed that probably these preparations were being made in order to take the Henin Ridge in front, and no one imagined that the coming operations would consist of more than a local attack with a limited objective, as little or no information had been given to anyone. It is true that rumours were abroad, that our opponents were preparing to withdraw during the coming winter to their defences in the Hindenburg Line, which meant that we would be left most uncomfortably situated in the wilderness throughout that season.

Little did we dream, however, that this was the commencement of a long series of hammer blows, lasting over several months, and employing millions of men, and destined to be the last and greatest battle the world has ever seen, ending with the complete demoralisation of the enemy's forces. The turn of the tide was at hand at last!

CHAPTER 12

Through the Hindenburg Line

Before the serious work ahead of us could be undertaken, it was necessary to shear off an awkward little bulge in the enemy's line, which included the ruined hamlet of Moyenneville. The corps on our right were to take part in an assault two days previous to the commencement of our own advance, so it was considered expedient to accomplish the above task at the same time. Consequently, during the big attack, delivered in the south on the 21st of August, which brought our troops level with the Arras-Albert railway line, our small side-show passed off successfully almost unnoticed.

Desperate fighting had also taken place in the neighbourhood of Morlancourt, just north of the river Somme, in which the enemy troops had been driven back after stubborn resistance. They thereupon evacuated the town of Albert, as the place was getting too hot for them, and retired on positions to the east of it. Our guns were now moved into their battle positions, and on the eve of the attack everything was ready and in order. For once in a way the weather was favourable, and this augured well for the speedy advancement of the guns, which was essential for the success of the operations.

At dawn, therefore, on the 23rd inst., without any preliminary bombardment, but, preceded by a dense creeping barrage and supported by innumerable tanks, the infantry set out on their long journey. The men swept on, capturing the villages of Boyelles and Hamelincourt at an early hour, without meeting much opposition or suffering undue casualties. The day went well throughout and all objectives were taken, and by nightfall, the vast machinery in the rear commenced to move slowly forward. Batteries were advanced and supplied with ammunition, by their echelons, ready for the next bout, and wagon lines occupied the positions only just vacated by the guns.

The attack was continued on the following morning, which necessitated the moving up of the guns once more, and the same thing continued day after day. The enemy was slowly and relentlessly pressed back without a pause or breathing space, and once this gigantic force was set in motion it was exceedingly difficult to stop it, as our opponents were soon to find out to their cost.

As the fight proceeded, our comrades on the left joined in, and gradually the battle spread further north, assuming huge dimensions, until it reached the river Scarpe. The enemy was caught napping before Monchy, and the Dominion forces in one bound everywhere overwhelmed their opponents, not only capturing the village but gaining ground to the extent of two miles beyond it. By this time, Croisilles and St. Leger had fallen into our hands, but the enemy made a most determined stand in front of Ecoust, and a very stiff tussle took place for several days before we eventually gained possession of it.

Some extraordinary incidents took place during the course of these operations. The long-hoped for open warfare was upon us at last, and the gunners' dream of galloping into action and firing with open sights at close range was an accomplished fact almost before we were aware of it. On one occasion, the whole Brigade, immediately at the close of executing a creeping barrage, limbered up, and topping the crest in front came face to face with the enemy, and dropped into action alongside our advancing infantry.

The enemy machine gunners were lined up on a ridge some four hundred yards away, but on seeing us they decamped with all speed, probably believing us to be a regiment of cavalry. At any rate, if they had stood their ground and manned their guns, they would have assuredly wiped us off the face of the map almost before we could have opened fire on them. At the end of another day's work, our battery position was scarcely two hundred yards behind our front line, where the infantry had installed themselves.

The wagon lines were now well over late enemy territory, on the ground where his batteries had been situated, and the mess was almost beyond description. In some cases his positions were entirely obliterated, which spoke volumes for the accuracy of the fire of our heavies, directed by our gallant airmen, and if it had not been for the quantities of ammunition and dead horses littered around, it would have been impossible to have known that positions ever existed there. Mine shafts had been entirely closed up by the explosion of the great shells, and a conglomeration of huge craters marked their locality.

There was no rest for anyone these days, and no men were called upon to perform more strenuous work than our little drivers, whose untiring and never failing energy was worthy of the highest praise and admiration: not only had they to care for their pair of horses, but were incessantly on the go twixt gun positions, dumps, and wagon lines under the most trying and difficult circumstances, and, at the same time, the latter were changing positions frequently. However, they never faltered or grumbled, and had always a cheery smile on their faces, even when they returned in the middle of the night dead beat. For days on end it was impossible to get out of one's clothes, and sleep was almost an unknown quantity: however, what did it matter as long as we continued to advance, and in spite of everything—this was a long way better than the monotonous routine of trench warfare. Everybody looked upon it in this light, and the excitement and never ending novelty of the experiences under which we were living, carried us on through thick and thin.

The corps on our left, meanwhile, had by a superhuman effort penetrated the great Drocourt-Queant switch of the

Hindenburg line, and firmly maintained their grip on the ground to the east of it, and all counter attacks made by the enemy, to dislodge them, proved unavailing. The troops to the south had also effected good progress, and the ill-fated town of Bapaume had again changed hands and passed for the last time into the keeping of the Allies. Thus it came about that the enemy troops, in spite of their very determined resistance in the neighbourhood of Ecoust and Mory, found themselves in a most perilous position, as the Dominion forces were now well in their rear, and were carrying out a turning movement from a northerly direction. Therefore, they were forced to do something, without further delay, which resulted in a swift retirement on to the Hindenburg line some six miles to the rear.

It was a most interesting and instructive chase, and the enemy retreated so fast that it was with the greatest difficulty that we could keep up and maintain contact with him. The battery had reluctantly to abandon a captured German field gun which had been doing valiant work as the seventh gun for several days against its late owners, for we had neither time or the means to convey surplus equipment along with us. It was the kind of day that one reads about in "Field Artillery Training" or even endeavours to imitate while manoeuvring out in rest, but for the first time we were doing it in reality. The battery dropped into action on innumerable occasions during the course of the day, and had only time to fire a few rounds before the enemy had decamped out of range. Then we would limber up with all speed, the teams waiting the orthodox two hundred yards in rear and to the flank, and gallop forward and take up a new position right out in the open, and help the enemy on his way with a few reminders that we were up and after him, and that he would do well to hurry.

By evening our foes had snugly entrenched themselves behind the great Hindenburg barrier, and we again came face to fare with this formidable obstacle. The line had, meanwhile, been kept in an excellent state of preservation, and it was quite out of the question to make a frontal attack on it without first cutting the belts of broad wire and treating the emplacements to a prolonged bombardment. Another formidable hindrance in our way and placed between us, moreover, was the famous Canal Du Nord, which was entirely dry in most places. It was a considerable breadth across, and could obviously not be bridged as long as the enemy kept watch over it from the opposite side, and it varied from forty to seventy feet in depth.

Thus, for the time being, the line settled down stationary until this task could be accomplished, for it was not the intention of our Command that we should sit down for the winter before this great fortress, as our enemies wished and expected us to do.

Our opponents were too busily engaged removing their heavy pieces of Artillery back to a place of safety to subject us to a great amount of annoyance, and, as the weather remained good, the work of bringing our heavies up was accomplished quickly and effectively. The battery took up a position in our former front line facing Bourlon Wood, with the ruined village of Mouevres immediately ahead, while the forward section was placed in part of the Hindenburg line itself, southeast of Pronville. Wire cutting was undertaken and carried out by all field batteries, and the heavies pounded enemy emplacements and communication trenches in the rear.

Bombing by aircraft became intensive on both sides, and the enemy adopted new tactics by coming over after dark, and, waiting for the gun flashes, proceeded to drop bombs on the batteries. A fine spectacle was witnessed two nights in succession in the form of a super-Gotha bombing machine brought down in flames. Our small fighting planes were in the habit of flying at a high altitude, keeping watch over our lines and lying in wait for these monsters. As soon as one of them was picked out in the rays of a searchlight, others would concentrate at once on it, whereupon the archies immediately opened fire.

Then far above a light would twinkle out several times, which was a sign for the anti-aircraft batteries to cease fire.

Everything remained still for a while, the searchlights always focused on their prey, which endeavoured to dodge out of the brilliant light, but in vain, owing to its unwieldiness. Then suddenly from out of the darkness a little object shot alongside the giant plane and spat tracer bullets into it, whereupon it instantly caught fire, and slowly heeling over commenced its downward journey to destruction.

Fierce fighting continued to the south, and by a series of brilliant operations our troops had everywhere come in contact with the Hindenburg Line, and commenced pounding its defences for the further advance. At the beginning of the fourth week in September preparations were almost complete for the coming assault, which would require all the energy and fortitude we could display. The Division was side-slipped down to the neighbourhood of Havrincourt, as it was familiar ground to us, after our experiences in November and December of the previous year. The policy at this juncture was, as far as it could be carried out, to place Divisions in localities with which they had already become acquainted.

Our battle position was situated on the outskirts of the small hamlet of Demicourt, and we were to cross the canal a few hours after zero by means of a ramp already prepared and carefully camouflaged at a point where it passed through our lines. If all went according to expectations we were to follow a line due east, and, passing to the north of Havrincourt, take up a position, already known to us, on the railway cutting south of Flesquieres, although as yet it was in enemy possession.

The great battle opened on the morning of the 27th inst., under excellent conditions, and it is now known to everyone how the crossing of the canal was effected by means of scaling ladders, and, in some instances, by the use of life-belts.

From first to last the day went smoothly and well, and by nightfall the great Hindenburg Line, upon which the enemy depended so much and in which he had such faith, was everywhere behind us, and we were through, at last, to open country beyond!

It only remained for the Allies' great Commander-in-Chief to deliver the final knock-out blow at his own time and discretion.

At this time the writer was reluctantly forced to leave the Battery on account of ill health, and was sent home, and it is a source of keen regret to him that on that account he missed the closing weeks of the great campaign.

It is now a matter of history how our Armies, after hot and incessant fighting, swept the enemy divisions out of France.

On Armistice Day, the Division was in possession of Maubeuge, and thus the Guards found themselves on territory which they had occupied in the early days of the War, prior to the retreat from Mons.

After three and a half years of strenuous warfare, the Battery is now lying at rest in Cologne, where it keeps its silent "Watch on the Rhine."

With the British
Guns in Italy

To The High Cause Of Anglo-Italian Friendship And Understanding

Nella primavera si combatte e si muore, o soldato.
M. Puccini, *Dal Carso al Piave*

So they gave their bodies to the commonwealth and received, each for his own memory, praise that will never die,
and with it the grandest of all sepulchres; not that in which
their mortal bones are laid, but a home in the minds of men,
where their glory remains fresh to stir to speech or action as
the occasion comes by. For the whole earth is the sepulchre
of famous men; and their story is not graven only on stone
over their native earth, but lives on far away, without visible
symbol, woven into the stuff of other men's lives.
Funeral Speech of Pericles

Dying here is not death; it is flying into the dawn.
Meredith, *Vittoria*

Preface

So far as I know, no British soldier who served on the Italian Front has yet published a book about his experiences. Ten British Batteries went to Italy in the spring of 1917 and passed through memorable days. But their story has not yet been told. Nor, except in the language of official dispatches, has that of the British Divisions which went to Italy six months later, some of which remained and took part in the final and decisive phases of the war against Austria. Something more should soon be written concerning the doings of the British troops in Italy, for they deserve to stand out clearly in the history of the war.

This little book of mine is only an account, more or less in the form of a Diary, of what one British soldier saw and felt, who served for eighteen months on the Italian Front as a Subaltern officer in a Siege Battery. But it was my luck to see a good deal during that time. Mine had been the first British Battery to come into action and open fire on the Italian Front. And, as my story will show, it was either the first or among the first on most other important occasions, except in the Caporetto retreat, and then it was the last.

I have camouflaged the names of all persons mentioned throughout the book, except those of Cabinet Ministers, Generals and a few other notabilities.

For permission to reproduce photographs, I wish to thank the representatives in London of the Italian State Railways (12 Waterloo Place, S.W.), and my friend and brother officer, Mr Stuart Osborn.

H. D. London, February, 1919

CHAPTER 1

The Anglo-Italian Tradition in the War

Anglo-Italian friendship has been one of the few unchanging facts in modern international relations. Since the French Revolution, in the bellicose whirligig of history and of the old diplomacy's reckless dance with death, British troops have fought in turn against Frenchmen and Germans, against Russians and Austrians, against Bulgarians, Turks and Chinamen, against Boers, and even against Americans, but never, except for a handful of Napoleonic conscripts, against Italians. British and Italian troops, on the other hand, fought side by side in the Crimea, and, in the war which has just ended, have renewed and extended their comradeship in arms in Austria and Italy, in France and in the Balkans.

During the nineteenth century Italy in her Wars of Liberation gained, in a degree which this generation can hardly realise, the enthusiastic sympathy and the moral, and sometimes material, support of all the best elements in the British nation. There were poets—Byron and Shelley, the Brownings, Swinburne and Meredith—who were filled with a passionate devotion to the Italian cause.[1] There were statesmen—Palmerston, Lord John Russell and Gladstone—who did good work for Italian freedom, and Italians still remember that in 1861 the British Government was the first to recognise the new Kingdom of United Italy, while the Governments of other Powers were intriguing to harass and destroy it. There were individual, adventurous Englishmen, such as Forbes, the comrade of Garibaldi, who put their lives and their wealth at the disposal of Italian patriots. But, beyond all these, it was the great mass of the British people which stood steadily behind the Italian people in its long struggle for unity and freedom.

Mazzini, Garibaldi and Cavour, "the soul, the sword and the brain," which together created Modern Italy, all had close personal relations with this country. Mazzini, driven from his own land by foreign oppressors, lived a great part of his life in exile among us, and here dreamed those dreams, which still inspire generous youth throughout the world. When Garibaldi visited us in 1864, he was enthusiastically acclaimed by all sections of the nation, by the Prince of Wales, the Peerage and the Poet Laureate, no less than by the working classes. It is recorded that, used as he was, as a soldier, to the roar of battle and, as a sailor, to the roar of the storm, Garibaldi almost quailed before the tumultuous roar of welcome which greeted him as he came out of the railway station at Nine Elms. Cavour was a deep student and a great admirer of British institutions, both political and economic, and in a large measure founded Italian institutions upon them. And the first public speech he ever made was made in London in the English tongue. These great men passed in time from the stage of Italian public life, and others took their places, but amid all the shifting complexities of recent international politics, no shadow has ever fallen across the path of Anglo-Italian friendship. And indeed during the Boer War Italy was the only friend we had left in Europe.

Italy's membership of the Triple Alliance was always subject to two conditions, first, that the Alliance was to be purely defensive, and second, that Italy would never support either of her partners in war against England. Thus, under the first condition, when Austria proposed in 1913 that the Triple Alliance should combine to crush Serbia, victorious but exhausted af-

---

1: Even Tennyson, who was not very susceptible to foreign influences, invited Garibaldi to plant a tree in his garden.

ter the Balkan Wars, Italy at once rejected the proposal. And, under the second condition, as German naval expansion became more and more provocative and threatening to Britain, we were able to transfer nearly all our Mediterranean Fleet to the North Sea, secure in the knowledge that, whatever might befall, we should never find Italy among our enemies.

****

The part which Italy has played during the war just ended, the great value of her contribution to the Allied cause, and the great sacrifices which that contribution has involved for her, have been often and admirably stated. But I doubt whether, even yet, these things are fully realised outside Italy, and I will, therefore, very shortly state them again.

When war broke out in August 1914, Italy declared her neutrality, on the ground that the war was aggressive on the part of the Central Powers, and that, therefore, the Triple Alliance no longer bound her. By her declaration of neutrality, she liberated the whole French Army to fight in Belgium and North-Eastern France, and rendered our sea communications with the East substantially secure. Bismarck used to say that, under the Triple Alliance, an Italian bugler and drummer boy posted on the Franco-Italian frontier would immobilise four French Army Corps. The Alliance disappointed the expectations of Bismarck's successors.

But if Italy had come in at this time on the German side, she might well have tilted swiftly and irremediably against us that awful equipoise of forces which, once established, lasted for more than four years. There would have been small hope that France, supported only by our small Expeditionary Force and faced with an Italian invasion in the South-East, in addition to a German invasion in the North-East, could have prevented the fall of Paris and the Channel Ports, while Austria, freed from all fear on the Italian frontier, perhaps even reinforced by part of the Italian Army, could have turned all her forces against Russia. Or alternatively, part of the Italian

Army might have attacked Serbia through Austrian territory, with the probable result that Rumania and Greece, as well as Bulgaria and Turkey, would have been brought in against us in the first month of the war.

At sea our naval supremacy would have been strained to breaking point by the many heavy tasks imposed upon it simultaneously in widely-separated seas. Our communications through the Mediterranean would, indeed, have been almost impossible to maintain.

Many bribes were offered to Italy at this time by the Central Powers in the hope of inducing her to join them—Corsica, Savoy and Nice, Tunis, Malta, and probably even larger rewards. But Italy remained neutral.

In May 1915 she entered the war on our side, in the first place to free those men of Italian race who still lived outside her frontiers, under grievous oppression, and whom Austria refused to give up to their Mother Country, and, in the second place, because already many Italians realised, as Americans also realised later, that the defeat of the Central Powers was a necessary first step towards the liberation of oppressed peoples everywhere and the building of a better world. Italy entered the war at a time when things were going badly for us in Russia, and looked very menacing in France, and when she herself was still ill-prepared for a long, expensive and exhausting struggle. The first effect of her entry was to pin down along the Alps and the Isonzo large Austrian forces, which would otherwise have been available for use elsewhere.

She entered the war nine months after the British Empire, but her losses, when the war ended, had been proportionately heavier than ours. According to the latest published information the total of Italian dead was 460,000 out of a population of 35 millions. The total of British dead for the whole British Empire, including Dominion, Colonial and Indian troops, was 670,000, and for the United Kingdom alone 500,000. The white population of the

British Empire is 62 millions and of the United Kingdom 46 millions. Thus the Italian dead amount to more than 13 for every thousand of the population, and the British, whether calculated for the United Kingdom alone or for the whole white population of the Empire, to less than 11 for every thousand of the population. The long series of Battles of the Isonzo,—the journalists counted up to twelve of them in the first twenty-seven months in which Italy was at war,—the succession of offensives "from Tolmino to the sea," which were only dimly realised in England and France, cost Italy the flower of her youth. The Italian Army was continually on the offensive during those months against the strongest natural defences to be found in any of the theatres of war. On countless occasions Italian heroes went forth on forlorn hopes to scale and capture impossible precipices, and sometimes they succeeded. Through that bloody series of offensives the Italians slowly but steadily gained ground, and drew ever nearer to Trento and Trieste. Only those who went out to the Italian Front before Caporetto, and saw with their own eyes what the Italian Army had accomplished on the Carso and among the Julian Alps, can fully realise the greatness of the Italian effort.

It must never be forgotten that Italy is both the youngest and the poorest of the Great Powers of Europe. Barely half a century has passed since United Italy was born, and the political and economic difficulties of her national childhood were enormous. For many years, as one of her own historians says, she was "not a state, but only the outward appearance of a state." Her natural resources are poor and limited. She possesses neither coal nor iron, and is still partially dependent on imported food and foreign shipping. She is still very poor in accumulated capital, and the burden of her taxation is very heavy.

From the moment of her entry into the war her economic problems became very difficult, especially that of the provision of guns and munitions in sufficient quantities, and the extent to which she solved this last problem is deserving of the greatest admiration. Her position grew even more difficult in 1917. After the military collapse of Russia she had to face practically the whole Austrian Army, instead of only a part of it, and a greatly increased weight of guns. The Austrians had 53 millions of population to draw from, the Italians only 35. Moreover, just before Caporetto, a number of German Divisions, with a powerful mass of artillery and aircraft, were thrown into the Austrian scale, while from the Italian was withdrawn the majority of that tiny handful of French and British Batteries, which were all the armed support which, up to that time, her Allies had ever lent her. Only five British Batteries and a few French were left on the Italian Front. By the defeat of Caporetto she lost a great quantity of guns and stores and practically the whole of her Second Army, while half of Venetia fell into the hands of the enemy, and remained in his possession for a year. The inferiority of the Italian Army to its enemies, both in numbers and in material, was thus sharply increased.

But the Italians held grimly on; they turned at bay on the Piave and in the mountains, and checked the onrush of Austrians and Germans. Then, supported by French and British reinforcements, but still inferior in numbers, they continued for a year longer to hold up almost the whole strength of Austria. That winter the poor were very near starvation in the cities of Italy, and the peasants had to cut down their olive groves for fuel. The following spring part of the French and British reinforcements were withdrawn to France, together with an Italian contingent which numerically balanced the French and British who remained in Italy.

The Austrians also lost their German support and sent some of their own troops to France, but they retained their numerical superiority on the Italian Front. In June they launched a great attack on a seventy-mile front, which was to have made an end of Italy; but the Italians beat them back. Then four months later, after an intense effort of preparation, Italy, still inferior in numbers and material, struck for the last time and utterly destroyed the Austrian Army in the great battle which will be known to history as Vittorio Veneto. The Austrians lost twice as many prisoners and four times as many guns at Vittorio Veneto as they had taken at Caporetto.

The war on the Italian Front was over, the Austrian Army was broken beyond recovery, the Austrian State was dissolving into its national elements, which only tradition, corruption and brute force had for so long held together. Italy, heroic and constant, had endured to the end, and with her last great gesture had both completed her own freedom, and given their freedom to those who had been the instruments of her enemies.

CHAPTER 2

From Folkestone to Venice

On the 6th July, 1917, I arrived at Folkestone armed with a War Office letter ordering my "passage to France for reinforcements for Siege Artillery Batteries in Italy." I had a millpond crossing in the afternoon, and that evening left Boulogne for Modane.

Next morning at 2 a.m. I was awakened from frowsy sleep by a French soldier, laden with baggage, who stumbled headlong into the railway carriage which I was sharing with three other British officers. We were at Amiens. I was last here ten months before, when my Division was coming back from rest to fight a second time upon the Somme. I did not sleep again, but watched the sunrise behind an avenue of poplars, as we passed through Creil, and the woods of Chantilly shining wonderfully in the early morning light. I spent that day in Paris and left again in the evening.

Next morning, the 8th, I awoke at Bourg in High Savoy. Here too the poplar dominates in the valleys. We ran along the shores of Lake Bourget and up the beautiful valley of the Arc in misty rain. We arrived at Modane at 10 a.m., and I was booked through to Palmanova, a new name to me at that time. The train left an hour later and, as we lunched, we passed through the Mont Cenis tunnel and slid rapidly downwards through Alpine valleys, charming enough but less beautiful than those on the French side of the frontier. Very soon it became perceptibly warmer, electric fans were set in motion and ice was served with the wine.

I found that I had six hours to wait at Turin before the train left for Milan. My fleeting impression of Turin was of a very well-planned city, its Corsi spacious and well shaded with trees, its trams multitudinous, its many distant vistas of wooded hills and of the Superga Palace beyond the Po a delight to the eye. But I found less animation there than I had expected, except in a church, where a priest was ferociously declaiming and gesticulating at a perspiring crowd, mostly women, who were patiently fanning themselves in the stifling, unventilated heat. I was an object of interest in the streets, where the British uniform was not yet well known. Some took me for a Russian and some little boys ran after me and asked for a rouble. A group of women agreed that I was Spanish.

The train for Milan goes right through to Venice, so, being momentarily independent of the British military authorities, I decided to spend a few hours there on my way to the Front.

The carriage was full of Italian officers, chiefly Cavalry, Flying Corps and Infantry. It is their custom on meeting an unknown officer of their own or of an Allied Army to stand stiffly upright, to shake hands and introduce themselves by name. This little ceremony breaks the ice. I saw many of them also on the platforms and in the corridor of the train. The majority, especially of their mounted officers, are very elegant and many very handsome, and they have those charming easy manners which are everywhere characteristic of the Latin peoples.

Nearly all Italian officers speak French. In their Regular Army French and either English or German are compulsory studies, and a good standard of fluent conversation is required. In these early days my Italian was rather broken, so we talked mostly French. At Milan all my companions except one got out, and a new lot got in. But I was growing sleepy, and after the formal introductions I began to drowse.

****

125

I woke several times in the night and early morning, and, half asleep, looked out through the carriage window upon wonderful sights. A railway platform like a terrace in a typical Italian garden, ornate with a row of carved stone vases of perfect form, and vines in festoons from vase to vase, and dark trees behind, and then a downward slope and little white houses asleep in the distance. This I think was close to Brescia. Then Desenzano, and what I took to be the distant glimmer of Lake Garda under the stars. Verona I passed in my sleep, having now crossed the boundary of Lombardy into Venetia, and Vicenza and Padua are nothing from the train. At Mestre, the junction for the Front, all the Italian officers got out, and I went on to Venice.

Except for three British Naval officers I was, I think, the only foreigner there, and a priest, whom I met, took me for an American. Everything of value in Venice, that could be, was sandbagged now for fear of bombs, and much that was movable had been taken away. I spent three hours in a gondola on the Grand Canal and up and down the Rii, filled with a dreamy amazement at the superb harmonies of form and colour of things both far away and close at hand. And even as seen in war-time, with all the accustomed life of Venice broken and spoiled, the spaciousness of the Piazza S. Marco, and the beauty of the buildings that stand around it, and at night the summer lightnings, and a rainstorm, and a café under the colonnade, where music was being played, will linger always in my memory. All the big hotels were closed now, or taken over by the Government as offices or hospitals, and the gondolas lay moored in solitary lines along the Grand Canal, and even the motor boats were few and, as a waiter said to me, "no one has been here for three years, but the people are very quiet and no one complains."

CHAPTER 3

From Venice to the Isonzo Front

I left Venice next morning by the 5.55 train, and reached Palmanova at half-past ten. As one goes eastward by this railway, there is a grand panorama of hills, circling the whole horizon; to the north and north-east the Carnic Alps and Cadore, their highest summits crowned with snow even in the full heat of summer; eastward the Julian Alps, beyond the Isonzo, stretching from a point north of Tolmino, down behind the Carso, almost to Fiume in the south-east; and yet further round the circle to the southward the mountains of Istria, running behind Trieste and its wide blue gulf, whose waters are invisible from this railway across the plain.

Of Palmanova I will write again. This was the Railhead and the Ammunition Dump for the British Batteries. I stayed there that day scarcely an hour, and then went on by motor lorry to Gradisca, the Headquarters of "British Heavy Artillery, Italy." Here I lunched and was well received by the Staff, who were expecting no reinforcements and were astonished at my coming. It was decided, after some discussion, to attach me temporarily to a Battery which had one officer in hospital, slightly wounded by shrapnel. I continued my journey in another motor lorry after lunch. Gradisca lies on the western bank of the Isonzo, which is crossed close by at Peteano by a magnificent broad wooden bridge, the work of Italian engineers. Gradisca had not been badly damaged, the Austrians having made no great resistance here against the Italian advance in May 1915, but Peteano had been laid absolutely flat by Austrian twelve-inch guns. It had been utterly destroyed in half an hour's intense bombardment some months before, and many Italian hutments in the neighbourhood had been destroyed at the same time.

Within sight of this bridge, at a distance of a quarter of a mile, is the confluence of the Vippacco with the Isonzo. From this point the road follows the Vippacco to Rubbia, the Headquarters of Colonel Raven, who commanded the Northern Group of British Batteries. which I was now joining. The five Batteries of this Group, known as "B2," were all in positions on or near the Vippacco, firing on the northern edge of the Carso, and eastward along the river valley. The southern Group, "B1," were on the Carso itself and operating chiefly against the famous Hermada, a position of tremendous natural strength, directly covering Trieste. B2 had the more comfortable and better-shaded positions, but B1, though their guns were among the rocks and in the full heat of the sun, were in easy reach of the sea, and had a Rest Camp at Grado among the lagoons.

Raven's Group, B2, formed part of an Italian Raggruppamento, or collection of Groups, under the command of a certain Sicilian Colonel named Canale, a dapper little man who generally wore white gloves, even in the front line. He was a fearless and capable officer and did all in his power for the comfort of our Batteries.

From Rubbia I drove in a car to the Battery. As I left the Group Headquarters, a number of wooden huts at the foot of the wooded slopes of Monte San Michele, which rise upwards from the road, I went under the railway which in peace-time connects Gorizia with Trieste. It is useless now, being within easy range of the Austrian guns, which have, moreover, broken down the high stone bridge on which the line crosses the Vippacco. A young Sicilian Sergeant accompanied me as a guide and pointed out Gorizia, some six miles away to the north, a widely-scattered town, very white in the sunlight, lying at the foot of high hills famous in the history of the war on this Front, Monte Sabotino, Monte Santo, Monte San Gabriele, of which there will be more for me to say hereafter.

The gun positions of my new Battery were situated just outside the little village of Pec, inhabited mostly by Slovene peasantry before the war, now all vanished. The village had been much shelled, first by Italian and then by Austrian guns, and there was not a house remaining undamaged, though several had been patched up as billets and cookhouses by British troops. Another of our Batteries had their guns actually in the ruins of the village, but ours were alongside a sunken road, leading down to the Vippacco. The guns themselves were concealed in thick bowers of acacias, the branches of which had been clipped here and there within our arc of fire. I doubt if anywhere, on any Front, a British Battery occupied a position of greater natural beauty. The officers' Mess and sleeping huts were a few hundred yards from the guns, right on the bank of the Vippacco, likewise hidden from view and shaded from the sun by a great mass of acacias, a luxuriant soft roof of fresh green leaves. Our Mess, indeed, had no other roof than this, for there was seldom any rain, and, as we sat at meals, we faced a broad waterfall, a curving wall of white foam, stretching right across the stream, which was at this point about seventy or eighty yards wide. Innumerable blue dragon-flies flitted backwards and forwards in the sunlight. Though the weather was warm, it was less hot than usual at this time of year, and the surroundings of our Mess reminded me vividly of Kerry. In the first days that followed I could often imagine myself back in beautiful and familiar places in the south-west corner of Ireland. Only Italian gunners coming and going, for several of their Battery positions were close to ours, and the Castello di Rubbia across the water, slightly but not greatly damaged, broke this occasional illusion.

These Italians took us quite for granted now, and that evening I began to learn about their Front. Things were pretty quiet at present on both sides, but greater activity was expected soon. I made the acquaintance of Venosta, an Italian Artillery officer attached to the Battery. He was from Milan, a member of a well-known Lombard family, and had a soft and quiet way with him and a certain supple charm. At ordinary times he preferred to take things easily, and was imperturbable by anything which he thought unimportant. But in crises, as I learned later on, he could show much calm resource and energy.

****

I woke next morning to the sound of the Vippacco waterfall, and the following day I got my first real impression of this part of the Italian Front. The Battery was doing a registration shoot and I went up in the afternoon with our Second-in-Command to an O.P. on the top of the Nad Logem to observe and correct our fire. It was a great climb, up a stony watercourse, now dry, and then through old Austrian trenches, elaborately blasted in the Carso rock and captured a year ago. The Nad Logem is part of the northern edge of the Carso, and from our O.P. a great panorama spread out north, east and west, with the sinuous Vippacco in the foreground, fringed with trees. From here I had pointed out to me the various features of the country. The play of light and shade in the distance was very wonderful. Our target that afternoon was a point in the Austrian front line on a long, low, brown hill lying right below us, known officially as Hill 126. The Austrians some days before had sent us an ironical wireless message, "We have evacuated Hill 94 and Hill 126 for a week so that the British Batteries may register on them." They evidently knew something of our whereabouts and our plans!

Coming back we stopped at the foot of a hill on which stands the shell-wrecked monastery of San Grado di Merna, a white ruin gaunt against the darker background of the Nad Logem. Here a new Battery position was being prepared for us, only three hundred yards behind the Austrian front line, but admirably protected by the configuration of the ground from enemy fire. An Italian drilling machine was at work here, operated by compressed air, drilling holes in the rock for the insertion of dynamite charges, and, by means of gradual blasting, gun pits and cartridge recesses and dug-outs were being created in the stubborn rock. Here a heavy thunderstorm broke and we sheltered in the Headquarters of an Italian Field Artillery Brigade, likewise blasted out of the mountain side. I returned with Venosta. I asked him to show me the famous Bersagliere trot, and by way of illustration we doubled along the road for about half a mile. On the British Front the spectacle of two officers thus disporting themselves for no apparent reason would have caused much remark and amusement. But the Italians, whom we passed, seemed to see nothing remarkable in our behaviour. They are, perhaps, more tolerant of eccentricity than we are.

It may be of interest at this point to say a few words about some of the special characteristics of the Italian Army. Every modern Army has adopted a distinctive colour for its wartime uniform, chosen with a view to minimising visibility. Thus we wear khaki, the French horizon-blue, the Germans field-grey. The Italians have adopted an olive colour, commonly spoken of as *grigio-verde*, or grey-green.

The various Italian Corps, Regiments and Brigades wear distinctively coloured collars on their tunics which, except in the case of the Arditi, fit closely round the neck. For example, the Granatieri, or Grenadiers, who both in their high physical standards and military prestige resemble our own Guards Battalions, wear a collar of crimson and white. The colour of the Artillery is black with a yellow border, that of the Engineers black with a red border. Of the Infantry, the Alpini collars are green and the Bersaglieri crimson, the bands of colour being shaped in each case like sharp-pointed flames turning outwards. For this reason the Alpini are often called the *fiamme verdi*, or green flames, and the Bersaglieri *fiamme rosse*, or red flames. The Infantry Brigades of the line, who bear local names,—the Avellino Brigade, the Como Brigade, the Lecce Brigade and so forth,—have each their distinctively coloured collars.

These local names mean very little, for, as a matter of policy, men from all parts of Italy are mixed indiscriminately together in each Brigade. The Parma Brigade, for example, will contain only a few men from Parma, and them by chance. One of the objects of this policy is to help to break down those regional barriers, which still linger owing to historical causes, between different districts of Italy. It is often remarked that men from many parts of Italy know more of foreign countries than of other parts of their own country, and most of the numerous local dialects are hardly intelligible to men who live far from the districts where they are spoken. Ordinary Italian, which is in fact the local dialect of Rome, is, as it were, the *lingua franca* of the whole country, but the great majority of Italians speak not only Italian but one, or sometimes several, local dialects, and the latter are used by all classes in their own homes. Some of these dialects differ widely from Italian. In many remote districts some of the peasants cannot speak Italian at all.

The Alpini and the two Sardinian Brigades, Cagliari and Sassari, are exceptions to the rule mentioned above. The Alpini are in peace-time recruited entirely from the men who dwell in the Alps, though I believe that during the present war a certain number of men from the Apennines have also been included in Alpini Battalions. The Alpini are specially used for warfare in the mountains. They wear in their hats a single long feather. Closely attached to the Alpini are the Mountain Artillery, armed with light guns of about the same calibre as our own twelve-pounders. They too are recruited from the mountaineers and wear the Alpino hat and single feather. The Alpini have a magnificent regimental spirit and, in my judgment, are the equals of any troops in the world.

The Cagliari and Sassari Brigades, two of the best in the Italian Army, are composed entirely of Sardinians. When in the front line they use the Sardinian dialect on the telephone. Even if the Austrians succeed, by means of "listening sets," in overhearing them, it hardly matters, for it is not likely that anyone in the Austrian front line will understand!

The Bersaglieri, another famous Italian Regiment, are recruited from all parts of Italy, but only from men of high physical fitness. They correspond roughly to the Light Infantry of other Armies, and always drill and march to a very quick step, even when carrying machine guns on their shoulders. Their hats decked with a mass of green cocks' feathers are familiar in illustrations. The Bersagliere Cyclist Companies, used for scouting purposes, form part of the Regiment. The Bersagliere undress cap is a red fez with a blue tassel.

The Arditi, or Assault Detachments, correspond to the German Sturmtruppen. They were instituted in the Italian Army in 1917. They also consist of picked men, and undergo a special training to accustom them to bomb-throwing at close quarters and to other incidents of the assault. In the course of this training casualties often occur. Only young unmarried men of exceptionally good physique can become Arditi. They are only used in actual attacks and never for the purpose of merely holding trenches. They therefore spend a large part of their time behind the lines and receive, I believe, extra pay and rations. They are armed with rifles and *pugnali*, or small daggers, and wear a low-cut tunic, with a black *knottie* and a black *fez*. On each lapel of their tunic they wear two black flames, similar to the crimson flames on the collars of the Bersaglieri. They are, therefore, known as *fiamme nere*, or black flames.

A large proportion of Arditi are Sicilians, and their fighting quality is very high. Certain detachments of Bersaglieri are also classified as Assault Detachments and wear low-cut tunics like the Arditi.

The Italian Mountain and Field Artillery are excellent; their Heavy Artillery is handicapped, in comparison with ours, by its smaller ammunition supply and fewer opportunities for prolonged practice, but its methods are scientific and its personnel very keen and capable. The Italian Engineers have done much wonderful work, to which I shall refer later.

CHAPTER 4

The War on the Isonzo Front

From Monte Nero to the Adriatic the distance is, in a straight line, some 35 miles. Allowing for the curves of the actual line, the length of Front is between 40 and 50 miles. This portion of the Italian and Austrian lines is commonly spoken of as the Isonzo Front. It is not like the Front in the higher Alps, where, as on the Adamello, trenches are cut in the solid ice, where the firing of a single gun may precipitate an avalanche, where more Italians are killed by avalanches than by Austrians, where guns have to be dragged up precipices and perched on ledges fit only, one might think, for an eagle's nest, where food, ammunition, reinforcements, wounded and sick have all to travel in small cages attached to wire ropes, slung from peak to peak above sheer drops of many thousand feet, where sentries have to stand rigidly stationary, so as to remain invisible, and have to be changed every ten minutes owing to the intense cold, where Battalions of Alpini charge down snow slopes on skis at the rate of thirty miles an hour, where refraction and the deceiving glare of the snow make accurate rifle fire impossible even for crack shots,—the Isonzo Front is not so astounding and impossible a Front as this, but it is yet a very different Front from any on which British troops are elsewhere fighting in this war.

It is a country with a strange beauty of its own; it is, in its own measure, rough and mountainous, and it is within sight of other and loftier mountains to the north-west. At my first view of it I remembered a speech of Carlo, the hero of Meredith's *Vittoria*, concerning Lombard cities away on the other side of the Trentino:

> Brescia under the big Eastern hill which throws a cloak on it at sunrise! Brescia is always the eagle's nest that looks over Lombardy! And Bergamo! You know the terraces of Bergamo. Aren't they like a morning sky? Dying there is not death; it's flying into the dawn. You Romans envy us. You have no Alps, no crimson hills, nothing but old walls to look on while you fight. Farewell, Merthyr Powys....

To me those words were always recurring on the Italian Front. "Dying here is not death; it's flying into the dawn." I would have liked to have them engraved on my tombstone, if Fate had set one up for me in this land, whose beauty casts a spell on all one's senses.

****

The Isonzo Front is divided into two parts by the Vippacco river, which flows roughly from east to west and joins the Isonzo at Peteano. Of these two parts the northern is three times as long as the southern. The northern part was held by the Italian Second Army, under General Capello, the southern by the Italian Third Army, under the Duke of Aosta. In the north the Isonzo runs through a deep ravine, with Monte Nero rising on its eastern side. Monte Nero is some 6800 feet high. The Alpini took it by a marvellous feat of mountain warfare in the first year of the war. South of Monte Nero, also on the east bank of the river, lies the town of Tolmino, the object of many fierce Italian assaults, but not yet taken. Here the Isonzo bends south-westward and continues to flow through a deep ravine past Canale and Plava, with the Bainsizza Plateau rising on its eastern bank. This Plateau is of a general height of about 2400 feet, and is continued south-eastward by the Ternova Plateau, rising to a general height of about 2200 feet.

Bending again towards the south-east, the Isonzo flows out into the Plain of Gorizia. Here stand Monte Sabotino and Monte Santo, the western and eastern pillars of this gateway leading into the lower lands. East of Monte Santo, along the southern edge of the Plateau, stand Monte San Gabriele and Monte San Daniele. Here the Plateau falls precipitously down to the Vippacco valley, only the long brown foothill of San Marco breaking the drop.

Gorizia has scattered suburbs: Salcano to the north, in the very mouth of the gorge, the fashionable suburb in days before the war; Podgora to the west, on the other side of the Isonzo, industrial. The Isonzo Front was the only possible field for an Italian offensive on a great scale, and the possession of the Carso, of the Bainsizza and Ternova Plateaus and of Monte Nero are as essential to the future security of the Venetian Plain as the possession of the Trentino itself. The frontiers of northern and north-eastern Italy were drawn according to the methods of the old diplomacy after the war of 1866, when Bismarck, seeking to keep Austria neutral in the next war on his schedule, that with France, willingly sacrificed the interests of his Italian Allies. For half a century Lombardy and Venetia have lived under the continual threat of an Austrian descent from the mountains, both from the Trentino, thrust like a wedge into the heart of Northern Italy, and across the Isonzo from the east. Nor has this threat been remote. When Italy was plunged in grief at the time of the Messina earthquake, the Austrian General Staff almost persuaded their Government that the moment had come to strike her down into the dust, and recover Lombardy and Venetia for Francis Joseph and Rome for the Pope. And so to-day an Italian Army fighting on the Isonzo Front fights in continual danger of having its line of communications cut by an Austrian offensive from the Trentino.

The population of the Trentino is indisputably Italian. East of the Isonzo the people are mainly Italian in the towns and mainly Slovene in the country districts. It has been the deliberate policy of the Austrian Government to plant new Slovene colonies here from time to time and to render life intolerable for Italians. But, even so, the population is still sparse, and all the country is infertile, except for the Vippacco Valley, which, though wretchedly cultivated hitherto, would richly repay the application of capital and modern methods. Here, I think, is a clear case where strategic considerations, which are definite, must prevail over racial considerations, which are dubious. These lands must be Italian after the war, if, with even the dimmest possibility of war remaining, Italians are to have peace of mind. Nor does a strong defensive frontier for Italy here imply a weak defensive frontier for her eastern neighbours. For the tangle of mountains continues for many miles further east.

****

Venosta told me that, when they took San Michele in July 1916, the Italians lost 7000 in killed alone, seasoned soldiers of their old Army, whom it has been hard to replace. But when San Michele fell, they swept on and took Gorizia and all the surrounding plain at one bound, and, in the same offensive, Monte Sabotino. This victory has a special significance in modern Italian history, for it was the first time that an Army composed of men from all parts of United Italy fought a pitched battle against a great Army of Austria, Italy's secular enemy and oppressor. Monte Cucco and Monte Vodice were taken in the offensive of May 1917, and here, as at Monte Nero, the Alpini performed feats of arms which, to soldiers accustomed to fighting on the flat, must seem all but incredible. In one case twenty Alpini climbed up a sheer rock face at night by means of ropes, and leaping upon the Austrian sentries killed and threw them over the cliff without a sound, so that, when the main body of Alpini, climbing by hardly less difficult paths, reached the summit, they took the Austrian garrison in the rear and by surprise, and the heights were theirs.

Monte Santo was still Austrian when I came, though the Italians held trenches half-way up. On the summit the white ruins of a famous convent were clearly visible. Here some of the bloodiest Infantry fighting of the whole war took place in May 1917. The Italians were on the top once in the full flood of that offensive, but could not hold it. Four gallant Battalions charged up those steep slopes only to find that the Artillery preparation had been insufficient and that the convent wall had not been destroyed. Austrians poured out from deep caverns in the rock, where they had taken refuge during the bombardment, and threw down bombs from the top of the wall upon the Italians below. For these there was no way round and no question of retreat, so they all died where they stood, struggling to climb a wall thirty feet high, clambering upon one another's shoulders.

South of the Vippacco we held the Volconiac and Dosso Faiti, but not Hill 464, though this had been taken and lost again, nor yet the hills further east, nor any of the northern foothills of the Carso, except Hill 123. To the south again the Hermada had proved a great and bloody obstacle.

****

Three striking characteristics of the warfare on this Front impressed themselves upon my mind—first, the shortage of ammunition; second, the enormous natural strength of all the Austrian positions; third, the work of the Italian Engineers.

Judged by the standards of warfare in France and Flanders, both Italians and Austrians were very short of ammunition. For Italy, a young and poor country, possessing neither coal nor iron and thrown largely on her own resources for manufacturing munitions of war, this was no matter of surprise. It was astonishing that the Italian Artillery was so well supplied as it was. But, to bring out the contrast, one may note that, whereas in Italy *fuoco normale* for Siege Artillery was six rounds per gun per hour, in France at this time a British Siege Battery's "ordinary" was thirty rounds per gun per hour. And one may note further that the number of Siege Batteries on a given length of Front in France was, even at this time, more than four times as great as the corresponding number on the Italian Front. The Austrians to some extent made up for their small quantity of guns and shells by a high proportion of guns of large calibre. Their twelve-inch howitzers were disagreeably numerous. It resulted, however, that neither Italians nor Austrians could afford to indulge in continuous heavy bombardments, such as were the rule in France. There was here on neither side a surplus of shell to fire away at targets of secondary importance, and therefore there was less destruction than in France of towns and villages near the lines. Ammunition had to be accumulated for important occasions and important targets. Thus battles were still separate and distinct in Italy, with perceptible intervals of lull, less apt than in France to become one blurred series of gigantic actions. So too counter-battery work on a great scale was not practised on either side out here, partly for reasons of ammunition supply, and partly for technical reasons connected with the nature of the ground. For in a good *caverna* one was perfectly safe, though outside high explosive produced not only its own natural effect, but also a shower of pieces of rock, thus combining the unpleasant characteristics of high explosive and shrapnel. One of our gunners had his ribs broken by a blow from a large piece of rock, though standing three hundred yards away from where the shell burst. But often after a heavy bombardment it was found that the enemy had been sitting quietly in *caverne*, ready to emerge with his machine guns when the attacking Infantry advanced. Aeroplanes also were less numerous than in France. And, when I arrived, gas was not much employed on either side.

In the second place, I was deeply impressed with the natural strength of the Austrians' positions. Almost everywhere they held high ground. On no other Front in this war have stronger positions been carried by assault than San Michele,

Sabotino, Cucco, Vodice, Monte Nero, and, in the end, Monte Santo. No one who has not seen with his own eyes the heights which Italian Infantry have conquered, backed by no great Artillery support, can realise the astounding things which the Italians have performed. The Italian Infantry have died in masses, with high hearts and in the exaltation of delirium, crumpled, rent and agonised, achieving the impossible.

And in the third place I would say something of the work of their Engineers. Italian Engineers are famous all the world over, but they have done nothing more magnificent than their swift building of innumerable roads, broad and well-laid and with marvellously easy gradients, both in these inhospitable and undeveloped border lands beside the Isonzo, and along the whole mountain Front. They have made possible troop movements and a regular system of supply under the most difficult conditions. It is a work worthy of the descendants of the old Romans, who by their road building laid the foundations of civilisation throughout Western Europe. And only second to their road making, I would place the work of the Italian Engineers in blasting *caverne* and gun positions and trenches in the rock, an invaluable and unending labour.

We British Gunners spent our first Italian summer in khaki drill tunics and shorts[1] and Australian "smasher hats." When these hats were first issued, one Battery Commander declared them to be "unsoldierly" in appearance and asked for permission to return them to the Ordnance. But this was not allowed. The men stood the heat well, though at the beginning, before they had got accustomed to the change of climate, there was some dysentery. I myself, a few days after my arrival and before I had a smasher hat, had a touch of the sun and lay about all day cursing the flies. But next day I was all right again.

Our rations at this time were a special Anglo-Italian blend; less meat, bacon, cheese and tea than in the British ration, but macaroni, rice, coffee, wine and lemons from the Italian. It

---

1: Next summer the introduction of mustard gas made it unsafe to leave our knees uncovered.

was a good ration and no one suffered from eating a little less meat than at home. In order to check the spread of dysentery, it was ordered by the medical authorities that no meat was to be eaten at midday.

We were not doing a great deal of firing when I came, though we had always to be prepared to come suddenly and quickly into action, especially at night. Most of our prearranged daylight shoots were observed from an O.P. in a ruined house at S. Andrea, on the plain just outside Gorizia, where one had a fine view southwards of the Tamburo and of the whole boundary ridge of the Carso from Dosso Faiti to the Stoll. Observation was beautifully easy on these high hills and in this clear air. What worlds away is this country with its wonderful cloudless sunshine from the dismal flat lands of the Western Front! Said one enthusiast of ours, "This is a gunner's heaven!" The Austrians fancied, I think, that we had our O.P. in Vertoiba, which is north of S. Andrea, for they shelled this frequently, but S. Andrea seldom. They shelled Vertoiba heavily, I remember, all one afternoon, while I was on duty at S. Andrea and while the Italian Staff were present in large numbers for two hours to watch our shooting. I remember thinking what a fine bag they would have got if they had lifted about four hundred yards! The Italian Staff were always most complimentary and enthusiastic over the work of our Batteries.

We had taken part in the Italian May offensive, the results of which had been claimed by the *Daily Mail*, with characteristic good taste and sense of proportion, as a "great Anglo-Italian victory." Our part had been more justly described by General Cadorna, who in a special Order of the Day had said that "amid the roar of battle was clearly heard the voice of British guns," and in his summary of the results of this offensive, which lasted from May 12th to May 30th, after remarking that the number of Austrians taken prisoners was 23,681 men and 604 officers, and that, in addition, at least 100,000 Austrians had been put out of action, continued as follows, "Our brave Infantry fought indefatigably for eighteen days, without pause and without proper food supplies, on difficult ground, in almost mid-summer heat, impetuous in attack and tenacious in defence. Most effective at all times was the fraternal co-operation of the Artillery, Siege, Field or Mountain, one Field Battery not hesitating to push right up to the firing line. Excellent help, too, was lent by ten Batteries of medium calibre of the British Army and by the guns of the Italian Navy."

Cadorna had inspected our Batteries soon after their arrival in Italy, and we had been visited and officially welcomed on behalf of the Italian Government by the Minister Bissolati, perhaps the most vivid and vital personality in Italian politics, and a wise counsellor, whose advice has more than once been disastrously ignored.[1]

Addressing at Pec detachments from a number of British Batteries on the 29th of May, Bissolati had said: "Officers and men of the British Force, I bring you the greetings of the Italian Government and the thanks of the Italian people. I greet you not only as an Italian Minister, but as a comrade in arms, for I consider it the greatest privilege of my life to have been in this war a soldier like yourselves. Our hearts beat with joy to see you here, because there is no Italian, however humble his station, who does not know how great is the debt of Italy to Britain for the brotherly help afforded her during the tragic vicissitudes of the glorious story of her Resurrection. We all remember how your fathers helped to create the Italian nation.... To-day we find ourselves fighting side by side in the same campaign, we to redeem this territory from the Austrian yoke, you to maintain the liberty of your national existence from the German menace, both of us,

---

1: From the outbreak of war in August 1914, Bissolati strongly advocated Italian intervention on the side of the Allies. When Italy declared war, he enlisted in the ranks of the Alpini, although over military age, was decorated for valour and seriously wounded. He then became Minister for Military Supplies, and acted as a connecting link between the Cabinet at Rome and the High Command.

moreover, to set the whole world free from the peril of falling under the dominion of that race, hard in temper as a granite rock, which finds in the Austro-Hungarian Empire a willing ally in its rapes and aggressions. I am here, then, to thank you, not only as an Italian, but as a man, and I am filled with joy at the thought that the British, even as the Italians, are showing themselves to be, now as always, the champions of justice, and the defenders of liberty and right. The sacrifices which we are making together, the mingling of our blood upon the battlefield, will render even stronger the age long, traditional friendship between our two nations.

"Viva l'Inghilterra! Viva l'Italia!"

CHAPTER 5
Palmanova

During my first month in Italy I lived a nomadic life. I was only "attached" to a Battery, and really nobody's child. July 17th to 22nd I spent at Palmanova in charge of an Artillery fatigue party which was helping the Ordnance to load and unload ammunition, and from August 2nd to 10th I was in charge of another working party of gunners at Versa, a fly-bitten, dusty little village, which our medical authorities had stupidly selected as a site for a Hospital, though there were many suitable villas in more accessible and agreeable places not far away. But in this first month I was lucky in being able to multiply and vary my impressions of the Eastern Veneto.

****

I rode down to Palmanova from Gradisca on a motor lorry. What a country! The white houses, the white roads, the masses of fresh green foliage, chiefly acacias, the tall dark cypresses, the cool blue water of the Isonzo, the blue-grey mountains in the distance, and on their summits the sunshine on the snow, which is hardly distinguishable from the low-lying cloud banks in an otherwise cloudless sky.

Italian troops, dusty columns marching along the road, throw up at me an occasional greeting as the lorry goes by. Long lines of transport pass continually. *"Sempre Avanti Savoia!" "Sempre Avanti Italia!"* I find my eyes wet with tears, for the beauty and the glory and the insidious danger of that intoxicating war-cry;

145

for the blindness and the wickedness and the selfish greed that lurk behind it, exploiting the generous emotions of the young and brave; for the irony and bitter fatuity of *any* war-cry in a world that should be purged of war.

****

And so I came to Palmanova to supervise the loading of shell, in the company of Captain Shield and another Ordnance officer. Shield had travelled much and mixed with Italians on the borders of Abyssinia. He told me that with no other European race were our relations in remote frontier lands more harmonious. They and we have, he said, a perfect code of written and unwritten rules to prevent all friction. He told me, too, of a young Englishman out there, quite an unimportant person, who had a bad attack of sunstroke and whose life was in great danger. The only hope was to get him through quickly to the coast, and the shortest road lay through Italian territory. So application was made to the Italian authorities for a right of passage, which they not only granted, but mapped out his route for him, for it was difficult country and unfamiliar to our people, and sent a guide, and had a mule with a load of ice waiting for him at every halting-place along the road, and so saved his life, treating him with as much consideration and tenderness as they could have been expected to show to a member of their own Royal Family.

****

Palmanova lies just within the old Italian frontier, a little white town surrounded by a moat, which in summer is quite dry, and by grassy ramparts shaped like a star. It was first fortified by the Venetian Republic four hundred years ago, and again by Napoleon. It can be entered only through one of three gates, approached by bridges across the moat, from the north, south-east and south,—the Udine Gate, the Gradisca Gate and the Maritime Gate. Each gate is double, so that you pass through a small square court, almost like a well, and at each gate you can see the remains of an old portcullis and drawbridge. Each is topped by two slender towers, and is wide enough to allow only one vehicle to pass at a time, and at each there is a guard of Carabinieri in their grey lantern-hats, to stop and examine all questionable traffic.

From the ramparts you can see the Carnic and the Julian Alps, sweeping round the Venetian plain in a great half circle. To the north the mountains seem to rise sheer out of green orchards and maize fields, but to the east there is a gradual slope of less fertile uplands, where the Austrians in the first days of war on this Front would not face the onrush of the Italians in the open, but fell back hurriedly to the more difficult country behind. At night all the inhabitants sit out on the ramparts, talking of the hot weather and the war, and watching the searchlights winking on the hills.

In the centre of the town is a large Piazza, planted round with myrtles which smell strong and sweet in the sun, and at midday an old woman sets up a stall here and sells the newspapers of Rome and Milan, Bologna and Venetia. In one corner of this Piazza is a restaurant, where one can play billiards and dine well and cheaply. A youth serves here who has been rejected for the Army because of defective eyesight. He speaks a little French and a little German and a very little English, and in moments of excitement words from all these languages come tumbling out together, mixed up with Italian. He has, I am sure, an Italian-English phrase book, which he consults hurriedly in the kitchen, for, whenever he sets a new course before one, he shoots out some carefully prepared and usually quite irrelevant sentence, and watches eagerly to see if one understands. In another corner of the Piazza stands a campanile with a peal of those absurd little jangling bells, which are among the most characteristic charms of Italy. Down a side street is the Albergo Rosa d'Oro, where for a week I was billeted. The *padrone*, a little round man, is always smiling. He thinks the war will last three years more and seems pleased at the prospect, for the town and the district round are full of soldiers, and he must be making great profits. But his wife, when one speaks of the war, says "it *must* end soon; we must go on hoping that it will end soon."

The station, where my fatigue party worked, lies outside the town. When the Austrians provoked war in 1914, they had special trains waiting here to carry away the Italian troops who, they hoped, would go and fight for them against the Russians,—a poor fool's dream! In normal times it must be a quiet place with little traffic. But now there is continual movement, Infantry going up to the front line and often waiting for hours at the station, and other Infantry coming back to rest, goods trains of enormous length passing through, motor lorries loading and discharging, driven very skilfully though sometimes very recklessly, horse and mule transport in great variety, both military and civilian, some of the horses wearing straw hats with two holes for the ears, and carts drawn by stolid, slow-moving oxen. With all this coming and going, and with a temperature of over a hundred degrees in the shade, the Albergo della Stazione does a great trade in iced drinks!

I made the acquaintance of two families in this town. At Signor Lazzari's any British officer was always welcome after dinner for music and talk and light refreshments. An Italian General was billeted there and two or three Italian officers of junior rank. A Corporal with a magnificent voice, an operatic singer before the war, came in to sing one night, and a Private from his Battalion played his accompaniment. In Italy, as in France, the art of conversation and a keen joy in it, are still alive, perhaps because Bridge is still almost unknown. Signor Lazzari's handsome and charming daughter was an admirable hostess.

At Signor Burini's I was also most hospitably received and drank some very excellent champagne. I used to talk to his three little girls in the evenings on the ramparts. Signor Burini's mother remembered Garibaldi's visit to Palmanova in 1867, the year after Venetia was liberated from the Austrian yoke and added to United Italy. She was speaking of this one evening to Shield and he said, "It rained very heavily that day, didn't it?" Whereat the old lady, much astonished and evidently suspecting him of some uncanny gift of second sight, replied that indeed it did. But the truth was that he had been reading an account of this historic occasion in a local guide book, which related that, just as Garibaldi came out on a balcony to address the crowd, a heavy thunderstorm broke and the Hero of the Two Worlds only said, "You had all better go home out of the rain."

****

It can still rain at Palmanova.

One day while I was there the temperature rose to 105 degrees in the shade, but in the evening a cool breeze stirred the dust and I sat outside the Albergo Rosa d'Oro, talking with various passers-by. About nine o'clock bright lightning began to fill the sky, but, as yet, no rain. And then about eleven, just after I had gone to bed, came a tremendous drenching thunderstorm and a great whirlwind. And then, very suddenly, all became quiet again, save for the rain-water pouring off the roofs into the street below.

CHAPTER 6

Aquileia and Grado

On July 22nd, the day before I returned from Palmanova to my Battery, Shield and I and two lorryloads of
men made an expedition in the afternoon to Aquileia and
Grado. Aquileia, at the height of the old Roman power,
was a great and important city, on the main road eastwards
from the North Italian plain. It was destroyed and sacked
by Attila and his Huns in the year 452, and again in 568 by
Alboin and his Lombards. It was the fugitives from Aquileia and the neighbouring towns, who, taking refuge in the
lagoons along the coast, founded upon certain mudbanks
in the fifth century the city which was destined to be Venice. And it was at Grado in the year 466 that the foundations of Venetian constitutional history were laid by the
election of tribunes to govern the affairs of the community
inhabiting the lagoons.

The two chief features of Aquileia to-day are a museum
of Roman antiquities, which I had not time to visit, and a
large church, with a bare interior, but with a magnificent
eleventh century mosaic floor, one of the best examples of
its kind in Italy. The interior of the church was decorated
with flowers in shell cases, to signify its re-conquest by the
Italians, who intend to make here a great national memorial
when the war is over. Beside the church, at its eastern end,
stood a glorious group of very tall cypresses, one of the best
groups I have ever seen, and opposite the western entrance

was a charming little avenue of young cypresses, planted since the re-conquest. We stayed for half an hour at Aquileia and then went on to Grado.

****

On the way Shield told me the story of how the British Batteries came to Italy. Our own War Office, as the habit of the tribe is, had wrapped the whole thing up in mystery, and the Batteries were christened "the British Mission" to a destination secret and unnamed. Passing through the South of France and up the Arc Valley to the frontier, with the gunners sitting on their guns in open trucks in the sunshine, the trains were loudly cheered by the French who, in that part of the country, had seen few of the sights of war. Once in Italy the official attempts at mystification mystified nobody. The engine-drivers at Modane hoisted Union Jacks on their engines and kept them flying all the way. Everyone knew who we were and where we were going, and at every station where the trains stopped there were official welcomes and immense crowds cheering like mad. At Turin our guns were wreathed in flowers and at Verona the station staff presented a bouquet to the General, on whose behalf Shield made a suitable reply in Italian.

****

Grado lies on several islands, in its own lagoons. The Austrians were developing it, in a haphazard way, as a watering-place before the war, and there are several large hotels and the beginnings of a Sea Front. The canals are filled with fishing boats with brown sails, which seldom put to sea now for fear of mines.

One approaches Grado by a steamer which starts from a little cluster of houses on the mainland known as Belvedere, and takes one down a long channel through a maze of 'wooded islands, one of which is now the Headquarters of an Italian Seaplane Squadron. The islands are thickly clothed with tamarisks and pollarded acacias and stone pines, and are reputed to be somewhat malarial. There is a long beach at Grado, where all the world bathes, and the water is deliciously warm, with a bottom of hard sand. Lying in the water, I could see right round the Gulf of Trieste as far as Capodistria, and straight opposite to me lay Trieste, the Unredeemed City of Italy's Desire, very clear against a background of hills. Through glasses I could even distinguish the trams running in her streets. I could easily fancy her scarcely a mile away across that sheet of blue sunlit sea. Thus must she often have appeared to Italians fighting and dying by sea and land to reach her, who remained ever just out of reach.

CHAPTER 7

A Gramophone and a
Chaplain on the Carso

The Battery moved up to its new position on the edge of
the Carso on the night of July 25th. The guns were drawn by
Italian tractors. It was a long business getting the guns out of
their gun pits, as we had not much room for turning, and a
still longer one getting them into the new pits, after unhook-
ing the tractors, down a steep slope and round two right-angle
turns. Owing to our nearness to the front line no lights could
be used and the night was darker than usual. For hours the gun
detachments were at work with drag ropes, lowering, guiding
and hauling, and the monotonous cry, that every Siege Gunner
knows so well, "On the ropes—together—heave!" went echoing round those rocks till 2 a.m. next morning.

****

This new position of ours was only three hundred yards
from the Austrians, though we had between us and them the
river Vippacco and a high hill, a spur of that on which the
ruined monastery of S. Grado di Merna stood. The trenches here ran on either side of the Vippacco. An Italian Trench
Mortar Battery had been here before us and, it was said, had
been shelled out. But our gun pits, blasted out of the hillside,
were almost completely protected against hostile fire, except
perhaps from guns on S. Marco, which might, with a com-
bination of good luck and good shooting, have got us in enfilade. Only howitzers capable of employing high-angle fire

153

could usefully occupy such a position, and, as it was, our shells could not clear the crest except at pretty large elevations. It resulted that we could not hit any targets within a considerable distance of the Austrian front line, but this, we were told, did not matter. We were here, we were informed, "for a special purpose" and for action against distant targets only. There was an orchard on the flat just behind our guns, a little oasis of fertility in that barren land, and wooden crosses marking the graves of some of the Italian Trench Mortar Gunners, who had preceded us.

Italian Field Artillery were in position all around us, and were firing a good deal by night. For the first few nights, with their guns popping off all round, and with blasting operations in full swing, an almost continuous echo travelled round and round the stony hillsides and made me dream that I was sleeping beside a stormy sea breaking in endless waves on a rocky coast. Blasting was going on all day and all night in this neighbourhood. One of our officers was walking one morning on the back of the Carso, out of view of the enemy and anticipating no danger, save the stray shell which is always and everywhere a possibility in the war zone, when suddenly the face of an Italian bobbed up from behind a rock with the warning, in English, "Now shoots the mine!" and disappeared again. The Englishman ran for his life and took shelter behind the same rock, and a few seconds later there was a heavy explosion, filling the air with flying fragments, unpleasantly jagged.

Our officers' Mess and sleeping huts were about two hundred yards from the guns and a little higher up the hill, just above one of the magnificent newly-made Italian war roads, along which supplies went up to Hills 123 and 126 and the Volconiac and Dosso Faiti. Just outside our huts and opening on to the road was a broad, natural terrace, with a fine view backwards over the plain. Several times, during our first week in this position, the Austrians shelled a British Battery at Rupa about a mile in rear of us and an Italian Battery alongside it. It was very hot and dry and they had been given away by the huge clouds of dust raised by the blast of their guns firing. The Austrians shelled them with twelve-inch and nine-four-fives, getting magnificent shell bursts, which some of us photographed, great columns of brown-black smoke, rising mountains high, in the shape of Prince of Wales' feathers, and hanging for about ten minutes in the still air. But very little damage was done, and after a short interval both Batteries opened fire again.

From this terrace of ours we had fine views of fighting in the air. On August 2nd we saw an Austrian plane brought down by two Italians, who dived down upon him from above, firing at him with machine guns as they swept past him. The Austrian, who was flying high, gradually seemed to lose his head and hesitate in what direction to fly, then he began to turn over and over, recovered for a moment, but finally lost all control and came down nose first into his own trenches, just across the river. Another evening, about ten o'clock, a whole squadron of Austrian planes came over, flying in regular formation and signalling to one another with Morse lamps. They were going, it appeared, to bomb Gradisca. They were heavily shelled by the "archies" as they came over us, and several fragments of shell fell on our terrace. The night sky was full of starry shell-bursts, and a dozen of our searchlights fussily got busy. Then suddenly all our artillery, as it seemed, began to go off, and for about five minutes there was a deafening burst of fire from guns of all calibres. And then all grew suddenly quiet again. Perhaps it was a raid, perhaps only the fear of one.

One day an Italian plane dropped some booklets into the Austrian trenches, and some were blown back into our own lines. They contained photographs of Austrian prisoners of war in Italian camps, very contented apparently, and explanations in German, Magyar and various Slav tongues, showing "men who yesterday were living from hour to hour in peril of death, now waiting happily and calmly in perfect safety for the war to end, when they shall return to their homes to embrace once more their wives and little children. Here you will be able to recognise many of your friends." A good propaganda to induce desertions and surrenders! The Italians generally had the mastery over the Austrians in the air. Their machines, and especially their Capronis, could always be distinguished from the Austrians' by the deeper hum of their engines.

Venosta had a gramophone, which played most evenings after dinner on the terrace, chiefly marches and martial music and Italian opera. Italy's Libyan war, whatever else may be said of it, has produced one magnificent marching song, "A Tripoli," which deserves to live for ever. Fine, too, even on the gramophone, are the "March of the Alpini," the "March of the Bersaglieri" and the famous "Garibaldi's Hymn." I met an English doctor once, who had heard this last played in Rome on some great occasion with some of the old Garibaldian veterans in their red shirts marching in front of the band. He had felt a lump in his throat that day, he said. When Venosta's gramophone played, the Italians encamped near by clustered round the edge of the terrace in obvious enjoyment, and sometimes one or two would dash indignantly down the road to stop limbers and carts, which were making a rattle on the stones.

****

Our Mess was a great centre for visitors, both English and Italian, we being at this time the British Battery in the most advanced and interesting position. Among our visitors, especially on Sundays, was a Chaplain, whom I will call Littleton, who used to conduct our Church Parades. In the British Army, and I believe in most others, the principle of compulsory religious observance is still intermittently enforced, when it does not interfere with the still more important business of fighting. I liked Littleton very much in many ways, but sometimes he infuriated me. He was lunching with us one day and describing how for some months in France, during some murderous fighting, he was attached to an Infantry Battalion.

"I have never in my life enjoyed myself more," he said, "than during those months."

I could not help asking, "What did you enjoy, seeing the poor devils getting hit?"

I told him afterwards that I knew he did not really delight in spectacles of agony and bloodshed, but that "enjoy" seemed to me an unfortunate word to use.

On another occasion I attended, in the capacity of Orderly Officer for the day, one of Littleton's Church Parades and heard him preach. It was clear that he was troubled by a suspicion that the war and the details of its development had discredited in some minds some of the ideas of which he was the professional exponent. He made a brave struggle, however, against this tide of unreason. "God does not make things too easy for us," he explained, "He gives us the opportunities, and if we choose not to use them, that is our fault. A loving father sets up a tremendously high standard for his son, and judges him severely, not in spite of, but because of, his love for him. In God's sight, three or four years of war may be tremendously worth while."

Then we sang a hymn. I felt inclined to sing instead a song, written by a soldier who was wounded in France:

> The Bishop tells us, 'when the boys come back
> They will not be the same; for they'll have fought
> In a just cause: they led the last attack
> On Anti-Christ; their comrades' blood has bought
> New right to breed an honourable race.
> They have challenged Death and dared him face to face.'
> 'We're none of us the same!' the boys reply.
> For George lost both his legs; and Bill's stone blind;
> Poor Jim's shot through the lungs and like to die;
> And Bert's gone syphilitic; you'll not find
> A chap who served there hasn't found some change.
> And the Bishop said 'The ways of God are strange!

It was hard for such a limited intelligence as mine, especially in this unending Italian sunshine, to imagine that it

157

could seriously be worth while to burn down a whole real world, in order to roast a probably imaginary pig. I found it very hard to believe, with the Chaplains, that the war was purifying everyone's character, and I was particularly sceptical as regards some of the elderly non-combatants who were unable to realise at first hand "the Glory of the Great Adventure."

CHAPTER 8

A Front Line Reconnaissance

Every day, in our Group, some officer carried out a Front Line Reconnaissance. This officer was chosen in rotation from the Group Headquarters and the various Batteries. Colonel Raven, our Group Commander, often carried out these reconnaissances himself. Of all British officers at this time serving in Italy, he had, I think, the greatest understanding of the Italians. He had travelled in Italy in peace-time and had studied Italian history. He fully appreciated the difficulties against which the Italian Army had to contend, and its military achievements in spite of them. He enjoyed social intercourse with Italians, and his invariable and slightly elaborate courtesy was, in an Englishman, remarkable. For, as Mazzini once said, an Englishman's friendship, when once secured, holds very firm, but it is manifested more by deeds than by words. But Colonel Raven had the gift of sympathetic imagination, and he had also in full measure the Allied spirit.

The purpose of these reconnaissances was twofold: first, to report on matters of military importance, any notable activity by the enemy, the direction and nature of hostile fire upon our trenches, the effects of our own fire, when not otherwise ascertainable, the precise position on the map, especially after any action, of our own and of the enemy's lines, including saps, advanced posts and the like; second, to maintain a real contact and spirit of comradeship with the Italian Infantry and to seek to give them confidence in the efficiency and promptitude of British Artillery support. Under the first head, valuable information was frequently brought back, and under the second I believe that, so far at least as our Group was concerned, the personal relations between the Artillery and the Infantry were exceptionally good. Hardly ever did we receive complaints that our guns were firing short, though such complaints are often made, and often quite groundlessly, when the Infantry lack confidence in the Artillery behind them.

At one time thin-skinned persons among us used to complain that Italians who passed them on the roads used to call out *imboscato! Imboscato* is a term very frankly used in the Italian army, generally though not necessarily as a term of reproach. It corresponds with the French *embusqué*, one who shelters in a wood, for which we in English have no precise equivalent. It is used by an Italian to indicate one who runs, or is thought to run, less risk of death than the speaker. It is chiefly used of men in the non-combatant services or in posts well behind the fighting front, including the Higher Staff and especially the junior ranks attendant on them. It is used also in jest by Italian patrols going out at night into No Man's Land, of their comrades, whom they leave behind in the front line trenches. Personally I was never called an *imboscato*, nor were any of my brother gunners, except once or twice when riding in side-cars or motors miles in rear of our guns. And to Infantry marching along dusty roads under an Italian sun there is something very irritating in a motor car dashing past, with its occupants reclining in easy positions, its siren hideously shrieking, and blinding dust-clouds rising in its wake.

German propaganda was insidiously active in Italy throughout the war, and spread many lying stories with the object of discrediting the British. Among these was one, the details of which do not matter now, concerning the fact that only British Artillery, and no British Infantry, had at that time been sent to Italy. Our reconnaissances, involving our visible and daily presence among the gallant succession of Italian Brigades, who held the blood-stained line on the Carso and across the valley of the Vippacco, were the most fitting reply which we could make to German propaganda.

****

I made my first Front Line Reconnaissance on July 27th, two days after we had moved forward to our new Battery position. That day I visited the trenches on the Volconiac, starting in the early afternoon and getting back at nightfall. I took with me as a guide a young Italian gunner, a Neapolitan by birth, who had been a waiter in an Italian restaurant in New York before the war. He had been in the Austrian offensive of 1916 in the Trentino, where all the guns of his Battery had been lost and nearly all his comrades killed or captured.

From the Battery position we followed the road behind Hill 123, up a glorious valley, whose sides were thickly wooded with pines, gradually thinning under the destruction wrought by Austrian shell fire and the Italian military need for timber. The only other vegetation here was a little coarse grass. On the lee side of Hill 123, sheltered from Austrian fire, was a whole village of wooden huts, admirably constructed, capable of housing several Battalions. At the head of the valley, the road, a good example of the war work of the Italian Engineers, turned sharply up the hillside, securing tolerable gradients by means of constant zigzags—tolerable that is to say for men on foot and for pack mules, for wheeled transport could not proceed beyond this point. It was a steep climb and I perspired most visibly right through my thin tunic. Three-quarters of the way up we stopped and got a drink of water from the Infantrymen in charge of the water barrels. There are no springs or streams on the Volconiac or on Dosso Faiti. All water has to be pumped up from below through pipes, and at the point where we rested, water barrels were being continually filled from the pipes and then hauled on by hand, on sleighs, for the remainder of the ascent. Water was also carried up from this point by individual soldiers in the *fiaschi*, or glass bottles encased in plaited straw, in which Italian wine is sold.

Just below the crest we entered the trenches, which were held at this time by the Florence Brigade. The construction of these trenches was very interesting. They were all blasted in the rock, and many drilling machines were at work as I passed along them, increasing the number of *caverne*, or dug-outs, and deepening those already in existence. Here and there, where the trenches were rather shallow, they were built up with loose rocks and sandbags filled with stones.

One of my objects was to get a view of the Austrian trenches and barbed wire on the Tamburo, in order to observe from closer quarters than was possible from any of our O.P.'s the effects of our recent bombardments, and to verify or disprove a report that certain new defensive works were being constructed by the enemy at night. Our own trenches here were on a higher level than the enemy's, and the bottom of the valley between the Tamburo and this part of the Volconiac was in No Man's Land, as was a relatively short slope on the Tamburo and a relatively long slope on the Volconiac. The latter slope was very steep, but thickly clothed with pines, most of which were now shattered by shell fire into mere dead stumps. Even these stumps, however, made it difficult to get an uninterrupted view of the Tamburo, and I had to go some miles along the trenches, gazing through numerous peepholes, before I reached a point from which I could satisfy myself that our bombardments had been effective and that the reported new works were indeed real. Having got this information, I smoked a pipe and talked with an Italian company commander in a rocky dug-out, and then started to return.

Things were quiet on this sector of the Front that afternoon, though Italian Field Guns were bursting shrapnel from time to time over the Tamburo. As I went along the trenches I was several times greeted by Italians who had been in America, "Hullo, John! How are you? How d'you like this damn country?" This type brings back with it across the Atlantic the frank, almost brutal, familiarity of a new and democratic civilisation. It contrasts oddly with the quieter ways of those Italians who have lived all their lives in Italy, amid one of the oldest and most mature civilisations of the world.

On our way down the hill we passed a seemingly endless string of pack mules coming up, laden with food and ammunition. Always at evening this wonderful system of supply was visibly working, triumphing over tremendous natural difficulties. We passed, too, a party of about fifty men hauling up on long ropes a heavy drilling engine, the sort of labour of which British fatigue parties have, luckily for themselves, no experience. Mists came down from the mountains as we descended, and rainstorms threatened, but did not break.

CHAPTER 9

An Evening at Gorizia

On the first day in August I had been doing some observation at S. Andrea in the afternoon, and, this duty over, I got permission to walk into Gorizia and visit the section of the British Red Cross stationed there, several of whose members I knew. It is a longer walk than one would think, for S. Andrea is practically a southern suburb of Gorizia, which, however, straggles over a large area of country. The railway bridge across the Isonzo is broken down by shell fire and so are two other bridges—all three of stone—but these could be soon repaired, if we made a big advance. It would be wasted labour to repair them now, for the Austrians would only break them down again. The Italians have run up a low, broad wooden bridge, sheltered from Austrian view behind one of the broken stone bridges. From time to time the Austrians hit this bridge, and then the Italians quickly make it good again. To be able to cross the Isonzo at this point is a convenience, but not a military necessity, for all movement of troops and supplies into Gorizia can be carried out on the left bank of the river and across bridges some miles further down-stream.

The suburbs of the town were badly knocked about, but the centre was not at this time much damaged. Gorizia lies in a salient of the hills, with the Austrians looking down upon it from the tops of most of them. But, still hoping to win it back, they do not shell it heavily or often. There are special reasons, too, for their forbearance. For Gorizia is a sort of Austrian

Cheltenham, whither Austrian officers retire in large numbers to pass their last years in villas which they take over from one another's widows. So the Austrian officer class has a sort of vested interest in the preservation of the place. So also have certain Hebrew Banks in Vienna, which hold mortgages on a great part of the land in and around the city, which just before the war was being rapidly developed as a fashionable Spa. It is a well laid out town, with large public gardens and good buildings, architecturally very like the larger Italian towns on the other side of the old frontier, Udine for example, but with a certain element of a heavier and more *rococo* style, the Viennese. There is still a fairly large civilian population in the town, and one restaurant still keeps open.

I found the British Red Cross in the Via Ponte Isonzo, in what had once been a big boarding-house, with a large untidy garden behind. Most of those stationed there were motor ambulance drivers, about twenty in number, some too old to fight, some rejected for health, some Quakers, unwilling to kill, but willing to risk their own lives on behalf of the wounded, others again boys under military age, who go, as soon as they can, to the Navy or the Flying Corps. It is brave and nervous work they do, driving ambulances in the dark, without lights and under fire.

After dinner I sat out in the garden in the twilight and talked with an old acquaintance of mine, who has had a large share in the organisation and daily work of the British Red Cross in Italy. The Italians, he said, are really beginning to feel their feet, as a united nation, in this war. Men of all classes from all parts of Italy are meeting and mixing with one another as they have never done before, and the old *regionalismo* is being rapidly undermined. He himself has almost ceased to think critically of the past or speculatively of the future, but just lives and works in the present. As to the state of the world after the war, he is very confident, provided we go on fighting long enough. Nothing that happens at home is of great importance, all the pressure is on the Fronts. Everything is looking now in the direction of democracy. Even Russia, in the long run unconquerable, has got her good out of the war already, whatever miseries and transitory anarchy she may have yet to undergo. In England and elsewhere many of the present political leaders are vile, but we shall all know what we want the world to look like, and to *be* like, after the war, and new leaders will arise and lead us. When the survivors of our smitten generation have grown old, there must be a peace of hearts, as well as a peace of arms, between the young of all lands. But our generation can never make personal friendships again with Germans, seeing that they have killed nearly all those who mattered most to us, and that we have to spend the rest of our lives without them.

****

He motored me back to the Vippacco bridge at Rubbia. When next I heard of him it was a month later at the height of the Italian offensive. He had been severely wounded on the Bainsizza Plateau.

The British Red Cross did splendid work in Italy and made a big contribution to Anglo-Italian friendship and understanding. They began their operations in Italy in September 1915, and were thus the first Englishmen to "show the flag" on the Italian Front. Thousands of Italians will gratefully and affectionately remember them till the end of their lives. More even than the British fighting troops who came after them, the British Red Cross will remain a historic legend in Italy in the days to come.

CHAPTER 10

A Cemetery At Versa

I was at Versa, as I have already said, from the 2nd to the 10th of August, to supervise a party working on the hospital. I walked one evening down the village street, where in the light of the sunset an Italian military band was playing to a mixed crowd of soldiers and civilians. Just outside the village I came to the gates of a cemetery, where six tall cypresses stand like sentinels on guard over the graves of many hundreds of Italian dead. This was at first a civilian graveyard, but all the dead have Italian names, except one Kirschner, and even he was called Giuseppe and has an Italian inscription on his tombstone. For this is Italia Redenta, in this one little corner of which a great company of Italian youth have already laid down their lives. And now the graves, in long straight rows, have filled one newly added field, and begun to flow across a second, and soon from the Field Hospitals in the village more dead will come.

Here, as in our war graveyards in France, no religious dogma or supernatural hope intrudes upon the little wooden crosses. On these, for the most part, you can read only the bare conventional attributes of each little handful of dust, which has passed through its quivering agony into the still sleep of decay,—its name and regiment, its civilian home, the place and date of its death. A few have more than this. Here lie the two brothers Bellina in one grave, with a cross at their head and another, rougher and larger, at their feet, announcing simply, *I due fratelli*, "the two brothers." And here is a tombstone engraved with an anchor, for one who, very early in the war, was hit while fording the Isonzo in face of the enemy's fire. *Al Pontiere Guazzaro Giuseppe che valorosamente sfidando le infide acque dell' Isonzo cadeva colpito dal piombo nemico. 25 Giugno 1915.*[1] And here is another inscription, typical of that Latin sense of comradeship, which is more articulate, though not necessarily more profound, than ours. *"Sottotenente Arcangeli Antonio, con commossa memoria,"* the officers of his Battery, *"il loro orgoglio infinite quì eternano."* "In deeply moved remembrance they here place upon eternal record their infinite pride in him." It is poor stuff in English, but a vivid and quite natural tribute in Italian.

Where the sun went down, the sky was a sea of rose red and golden green, studded with little long islands of dark cloud, and on the edge of this sea the evening star twinkled like a tiny illumined boat, dancing, a blaze of light, upon the waves. To left and right the cloudbanks were a deep purple blue, fast fading into the dim warm grey of an Italian night. East and north the mountains that bound the plain, silent witnesses of Italy's great struggle, were hidden in the dusk, and the cypress sentinels stood up sharp and black against the darkening sky. The band had ceased to play and one heard only the chirp of grasshoppers, and across an orchard the soft sound of Italian speech, and the distant song of two soldiers in the village street. But the warm air, which just now was throbbing with a military march, seemed to be throbbing still with an aching longing that happier days may come swiftly to this land of beauty and pain, so that the sacrifice of all these dead shall not be wholly waste.

****

Not many miles away, as the sun was setting, an Austrian shell burst in a British Battery, and three hours later through the dark under faint stars an ambulance lorry brought to us the bodies of four British gunners, whose dust will mingle with Italian dust, under Italian skies, for ever.

1: To the Sapper Giuseppe Guazzaro, who fell, while bravely defying the treacherous waters of the Isonzo, struck down by an enemy bullet, 25th June, 1915.

CHAPTER 11
Udine

I first saw Udine on the 5th of August. I was still on duty at Versa, but the conversation in the R.A.M.C. Mess bored me, particularly at meals; it was all sputum and latrines, gas gangrene and the relative seniority of the doctors one to another. There was nothing to keep me at Versa, for my gunner fatigue party did not in truth need any supervision. So I determined to go to Udine. I started, walking, about 10 a.m. It was not too hot. I walked about three miles and then picked up a lorry. One can generally get a ride on an Italian lorry if there is any room, by waving one's stick at the driver, shouting out one's destination, and looking agreeable. This one took me to Mogaredo and then stopped. I then walked another three miles to a point near Trevignano. Here I was within ten miles of Udine and picked up another lorry which took me the rest of the way. It was driven by a Triestino who, seeing what was coming, had left the Unredeemed City just before Italy declared war. His face was very sad, and he made a gesture of weeping, drawing his fingers downwards from his eyes across his cheeks, though his eyes were dry. "How long?" he asked. "How long before Trieste will be free?"

We approached Udine through a long avenue of plane trees, planted under Napoleon. It is a gay little town, with arcaded streets, clustering round a hill on the top of which stands a Castello, with a memorial tower to the martyrs of 1848, and on the hill slopes public gardens full of cypresses. Udine was at

169

this time a nest of British newspaper correspondents. I began to make their acquaintance in the afternoon. First an Anglo-Italian lady from Rome, whom I met sitting out behind the Hotel Grande d'Italia under the shade of trees. She was evidently something of a figure here and received several callers, all ladies of Udine, as we sat drinking coffee. One of these, on learning that I was a gunner, took out a locket and handed it to me. It contained a picture of a marvellously handsome boy. It was her eldest son, killed three months before in Cadore, a Lieutenant in a Mountain Battery. He was only nineteen. His mother began to weep as she handed me the locket, and it was the lady from Rome who told me these things. Then the mother cried, between her sobs, *"E troppo crudele, la guerra!"* And as I handed the locket back, I thought of the unmarried childless parson in khaki who considered that "three or four years of war may be tremendously worth while."

****

Later I met and dined with two of the male correspondents of the London Press. Conversation, in the sense of a mere flow of talk, is never difficult with newspaper men. They are among the most articulate of the British, although much that they articulate is only patter. These two had plenty of miscellaneous information, much of which I received in a sceptical spirit, but I learned some interesting facts, which I verified from other sources later on. Chief of these was the effect produced upon Young Italy by the personal gallantry of the poet D'Annunzio, who, when he is not flying at the head of the Italian bombing planes against Pola, is making fiery orations to the Infantry in the front line and distributing among them little *tricolor* flags bearing his own autograph.

Having talked till midnight, I found a bedroom at the Croce Malta, where I slept for four hours. Then I got up and dressed and walked to the railway station, where I drank coffee and ate biscuits. A train was due to leave for Palmanova, the nearest station to Versa, at 5.30 a.m. As I waited for it on the platform, I looked out at the station lights, a dull orange under their dark shades, and at the red signals beyond, four in a vertical line, and beyond again at the dim outlines of houses and dark trees against a sky, at first a very deep dark blue, but slowly lighting up with the beginning of the dawn. The train did not start till nearly seven. By this time it was quite light, and the sun had turned the distant Cadore into a ridge of pink grey marble, very sharply outlined against the morning sky, and in the middle distance, just across the maize fields which run beside the railway track, rose the *campanile* of some little village of Friuli, like a stick of shining alabaster.

Chapter 12

The British and the Italian Soldier

The sending of ten British Batteries to Italy had something more than a military significance. Otherwise the thing was hardly worth doing. It was evident that here was an international gesture. An effort was being made to promote a real Anglo-Italian understanding, to substitute for those misty and unreal personifications—"England" to an Italian, "Italy" to an Englishman—real personal knowledge and a sense of individual comradeship in a great cause. Our task, in short, was not only to fight, but also to fraternise. But would we fraternise successfully? For it has been said, not without some truth, that "England is an island and every Englishman is an island," and in the early days I was doubtful what sort of personal effect we should produce, and what sort of personal impressions our men would bring away.

When I got back to the Battery from Versa I began to take stock of my own impressions so far, and to notice, in the letters which I had to censor, the drift of general opinion. It was surprisingly satisfactory.

Some of these Italians, writes one gunner, *are the finest fellows you could wish to meet. Our men get on very well with them. The Italians*, writes another, *are very good soldiers and nice chaps. We get on well together. The other night*, writes a third, *I was out laying telephone wires in a graveyard. We saw some Italian soldiers carrying a tombstone for their Lieutenant who had recently been killed. The Italians look after their graves very well. A Sergeant, who had spent* most of his life in England, asked us in and gave us some coffee and cognac which was jolly acceptable. He asked if we had any old English papers, as he was forgetting all his English, as he had been away from England for five years. And a fourth writes, *The great majority of these Italians have been in different parts of America* (this of course is a wild exaggeration!), *they are very delighted to have a chat. In fact I think the Italian people are very sociable. Nearly all the boys can begin to make themselves understood.* These tributes are obviously sincere. They occur in the midst of good-natured grumbles about the heat, and the monotony of macaroni and rice and stew, and of requests for "more fags" and of hopes that "this business will soon be over."

The fact that so many Italians, having lived in England and America, can speak English and know something of us and our ways, accounts for much. For a foreign language is the Great Barrier Reef against the voyages of ordinary people towards international understanding. And the country counts for something, too. Its natural obstacles compel admiration for an Army which has achieved so much in spite of them. And I am sure that no British gunner, however inarticulate, who has served in Italy, and especially those young fellows who, when war broke out, stood only on the threshold of their manhood, with their minds still wide open for new impressions, has not felt some sort of secret thrill at the astounding and incomparable beauty of this country, the very contemplation of which sometimes brings one near to weeping.

I recall, for instance, a tough old Sergeant Major, with twenty-seven years' service with our Artillery all over the world, an utterly unromantic person. He and I were bringing back my working party on the 10th of August from Versa to Rubbia in a lorry. The men were singing loudly, and greeted an Italian sentry on Peteano bridge with cheerful cries of *"Buona sera, Johnny!"* And the Sergeant Major suddenly observed to me that "this must be a fine country in peace-time," and went on to praise the mountains, and the rivers, and the trees, especially the cypresses, and the surface of the roads, and some town behind the lines, Udine I think, which was "very pretty" and "quite all right." The Italians, too, were "all right," which from him was most high praise. And then, as though half ashamed of having said so much, he added, rather hastily, "But there's nothing to touch the old country after all. I think I shall settle down there when this war's over. I've had about enough of foreign parts."

And what do the Italians think of us, I wonder? I only know that they treat us always with great friendliness, and show great interest in our guns and all our doings. So the international gesture has, I think, begun already to succeed. And its success will grow. For those British graves, which we shall leave behind us—some are dug and filled already—will tell their own story to the future. They will be facts, if only tiny facts, both in British and Italian history, and "far on in summers that we shall not see," bathed in the warm brilliance of Italian sunshine, they will bear witness to Anglo-Italian comradeship across the years.

I Join the First British Battery in Italy

On the 15th of August arrived an operation order indicating our targets in the first and second phases of the great Italian offensive, which had been long expected, and also the objectives of the Infantry. The day on which the offensive was to begin was not yet announced. Six more British Siege Batteries, giving us now three British Heavy Artillery Groups, had arrived on the Carso and in the Monfalcone sector about a fortnight before. The French too had sent a number of Heavy Batteries, which were in position on Monte Sabotino and elsewhere north of the Vippacco. But the counsel of wise men had been disregarded, and no French or British Infantry, no complete Allied Army Corps, had been sent to the Italian Front, where a big military success could have been more easily obtained and would have had greater military and political results at this time, than anywhere else.

On this day I walked to and from S. Andrea, returning to the Battery in the evening greatly perspiring but with an enormous appetite. Large numbers of Infantry were going up the Vallone and the Volconiac in the dusk. Italian Infantry march in twos on either side of a road, not in fours on one side as ours do.

The Austrians shelled a good deal this evening, and put a lot of gas shell into Merna.

****

On the 17th I was transferred to another Battery. It was the eve of the offensive, and my new Battery was an officer short, while my old Battery was again at full strength, the officer who had been in hospital wounded, when I arrived in Italy, having now returned. I joined my new Battery about midday. They were in position on the Vippacco, close to the former position of my old Battery. I was destined to stay with them for seventeen months, till after the war was won, and I came to identify myself very completely with them, and to be proud to be one of them.

This had been the first of all the British Batteries to come into action in Italy, and had fired the first British shell against Austria. The Major in command had the reputation of being the most efficient British Battery Commander in Italy, and, so far as my experience of others went, he deserved it. He was a Regular soldier, and had served with a Mountain Battery in India, a service which requires and breeds a power of quick decision, by no means universal among Garrison Gunners of the Regular Army. Personally he was a most delightful man, at his best a very amusing talker, a pleasant companion and an excellent Commanding Officer. Few officers whom I have met took as much thought and trouble as he for the material welfare of his men. From his junior officers he combined a demand for high efficiency with a sometimes wonderful solicitude for their comfort, health and peace of mind. He never asked any of us to do more, or even as much, as he did willingly himself, and if anything went wrong in the Battery, which it seldom did, he never hesitated, in dealing with higher authorities, to take all the blame. He had been twice wounded already, once on the Somme and again in the Italian May offensive. Later on he was wounded a third time.

Captain Jeune, the Second-in-Command, was also a Regular, but very young. In mind and manner he was older than his years, and he knew his work as a military professional extremely well. Some found him truculent, but he never displayed any truculence to me.

176

On my arrival I became Senior Subaltern of the Battery. The three Junior Subalterns, Darrell, Leary and Winterton, provided a variety of companionship. Darrell was a man of business, a most capable officer, a good Mess Secretary, and very easy to get on with. Leary was a dark-haired Irishman, who had originated in the County Limerick. He was a good mathematician, but in conversation was apt to be long-winded, and had a wonderful capacity for making a simple matter appear complex. He had been, by turns, a civil engineer and an actor, and had a fine singing voice. As an officer he was infinitely laborious and conscientious, but with a queer disconcerting streak of Irish unaccountability. One never quite knew what he would do, if left alone in charge of anything.

Winterton was a good-looking boy, who would have gone up to Cambridge in 1915, if there had been no war. Instead he enlisted in the Horse Artillery, became a Corporal, and went to the Dardanelles as a Despatch Rider. Having spent several months in hospital at Malta and nearly died of dysentery, he came back to England and was given an Artillery Commission. He was a gallant youth but just a little casual, with rather a music-hall mind, but good company, if one was not left alone with him too long.

There was also attached to the Battery at this time an Italian Artillery officer, whom I will call Manzoni, a Southerner, small and very dark. He had taught himself to speak excellent English though he had never been in England. He was an intelligent observer and an amusing companion, and we became great friends.

The personnel of the Battery was splendid, and I do not believe that in any other Battery the spirit of the men was better, nor the personal relations between officers and men on a sounder and healthier footing, than with us.

Some Battery Commanders proceed on the principle that even the most experienced N.C.O. cannot be trusted to perform the simplest duty, except under the eye of an officer, however junior. The Battery in this case becomes helplessly dependent on the officers. If they go out of action, so does the whole Battery. Other Battery Commanders, of whom my new Major was one, proceed on the principle that as many N.C.O.'s as possible should be able to do an officer's work, so that the Battery should be able to continue in action without any officers at all if necessary, and also be able to adapt itself readily to a sudden change from stagnant to open warfare. This principle is universally applied in the French Artillery, where, apart from its evident wisdom, it has been necessitated by the great shortage of officers. My own Major used to train all our best N.C.O.'s with this object in view and, when satisfied of their competence, used to give them in normal times considerable responsibilities in the working of the Battery in action. The result was that we had as capable and reliable a set of "Numbers One" and "B.C.A.'s" as could be found anywhere.[1] The men thoroughly appreciated the amount of trust reposed in them and never failed us. Furthermore, when I joined the Battery there was hardly a man who was not a trained specialist, either as a Signaller, Gunlayer or B.C.A.

Seventeen months later, only the Major, Leary and myself, out of the officers in the Battery when I joined, still remained with it, and death, wounds, sickness, promotion and commissions from the ranks had taken from us many of our best N.C.O.'s and men. But through all the varied experiences of those long months, there had been a continuity of tradition and an unchanging spirit. We were still, for me and for many, the First British Battery in Italy.

1: A "Number One" is the Sergeant or other N.C.O. in charge of a gun and its detachment when in action. A "B.C.A." (or Battery Commander's Assistant) assists the officer on duty in the Command Post in locating points on the map, in making numerical calculations, and in other miscellaneous duties.

CHAPTER 16

The Offensive Opens

On the 18th of August I got up at half-past four in the morning. There was a mist in the air, which cleared away as the day grew warmer. The big bombardment in what the journalists called the Twelfth Battle of the Isonzo began at six o'clock and went on continuously all day. Once the thing was started, I had little to do except to change occasionally the rate of fire—*lento*, *normale*, *vivace*, *celere* and *double vivace* by turns. The first part of the day I was in charge of the Right Section of the Battery and sat most of the time on a wooden bench at a table under a tarpaulin among the acacias. By my side sat a telephonist in communication with the Battery Command Post, some four hundred yards away to the left, beyond the Left Section. My only other apparatus was a megaphone, a notebook and pencil, and a pipe. Occasionally I would go and stand by one of the guns, to check the gun-laying and to see that the guns were recoiling and coming up again without undue violence. One had also to guard against a dust cloud being raised by the blast of the guns, thus giving away our position to the enemy. To prevent this, we formed a chain of men every half hour to pass water-buckets from hand to hand, from the river just behind us down the sunken road, to lay the dust in and around the gun pits. But under an Italian August sun the ground soon grew parched and dusty again.

The Austrians did not shell much till the evening, when they nearly hit our Mess and shell-shocked a man of another

Battery in the road close by. But the Italian bombardment all day was very heavy, and our guns and theirs were to go on firing all night. Just before midnight I relieved the Major in the Command Post, and he and the rest of the officers went to bed. So I sat there wakefully among the acacias, awaiting any sudden orders from the Group to switch or lift to new targets, or to vary the rate of fire. Every now and then I took a walk round the Battery to see that all was working correctly, and every hour the N.C.O.'s in charge of each gun brought in their fired tubes to the Command Post and reported how many rounds had been fired in the preceding hour and how many tubes misfired.

****

It was a clear, starlight night, up above the multitudinous flashes of British and Italian guns. At close quarters these flashes were blindingly bright, and flung up showers of red sparks. In the intervals of a few seconds between flashes, if one stood with one's eyes fixed on the guns, the stars seemed blotted out in an utterly black darkness. A long bombardment is one of the most boring things in the world by reason of its intense monotony, and because in a queer half-unconscious way it begins, after many hours, very slightly to fray the nerves. Listening and watching in the small hours, and from time to time directing, I found myself able, with almost discreditable elastic-mindedness, to call up at will any of the aspects of modern war,—its utter and inherent wickedness, its artistic and scientific majesty, its occasional moral justification against the oppressor, its ultimate blank insanity. But I would not have liked to be an Austrian yesterday or this morning. The Italian Infantry attacked on our sector at 5.30 a.m. There was a tremendous crescendo of gunfire at this time. The Major relieved me in the Command Post at 5 o'clock, and urged me to go to bed, but I did not feel inclined to sleep. Instead I went up about 6 o'clock through Pec village to an O.P. on a hillside beyond, to see what could be seen. But all the Front

180

was hidden in a thick mist, made thicker by the smoke, shot through with innumerable momentary flashes. All round us thousands of guns were going off, filling the air with a deafening and continuous roar. A telephonist was with me who had been through a good deal of the Somme fighting, and had found the Italian Front, in times of lull, a little uneventful. But this morning he was full of appreciation. "This is something like it, isn't it, Sir?" he said. Being able to see nothing, I went back to bed for some hours and spent the afternoon at a Battery O.P., which had been specially arranged for this offensive, in an Italian reserve trench just off the Pec-Merna road.

******

The bombardment continued through the 19th and 20th and 21st of August, now with guns firing independently, now with salvos or rounds of Battery fire, now with individual guns being ranged afresh from some O.P., with hardly an hour's interval of silence. How little the individual soldier knows of what is happening at these times! Conflicting rumours of varying credibility came in to us during those three days, rumours of big advances both to the north and to the south. But on our own sector we knew that no permanent advance had been made, for we were still firing a good deal on old "Zone 15," one of our first day's targets, and on that damned Hill 464, the most important of the first objectives of the Infantry.

Before this offensive began I had slept in a hut above ground, but the Major had now insisted that I should sleep in a small dug-out half-way up a steep bank, at the bottom of which our Mess Hut stood in an orchard stretching down to the river bank. The Austrians shelled us intermittently, but without doing any damage. In the small hours of the 21st I was dozing in my dug-out, where I had been reading Lowes Dickinson's *Choice Before Us,* a congenial book at such a time, with nine-tenths of which I was in complete agreement. I then heard a series of Austrian "4.2's" come sailing over my dug-out and burst just at the foot of the bank. They made miserable bursts in the soft earth, so small as to make me suspect gas shells for a moment, but this suspicion did not worry me, for no one was sleeping at the bottom and gas cannot run uphill. Next morning I found a shell hole fifteen yards from the Mess Hut, another on the path and several others among the trees. They were "double events," with a shrapnel and time fuse head and a high explosive and percussion fuse tail, but neither head nor tail had been of much effect. There was very heavy firing that morning, but less in the afternoon. Great gloom prevailed on our sector, where we were back again in most of our first positions. The Infantry were reported to be unable to make headway against machine guns on Hill 464 and the Tamburo. To the south, on the Carso, the ruins of the village of Selo had been taken, but not much else.

But, though we did not know it then, the Italian Army in those first three days had won magnificent successes to the north of us.

CHAPTER 15

We Switch Our Guns Northward

On the 22nd of August we got for the first time definite news of the Italian advance on the Bainsizza Plateau. The day was rather hotter than usual, and on our own sector there was still no appreciable progress. Hill 464 had been won and lost three times since yesterday morning, and, to the south of it, Hill 368 also had been won and lost again. Up there it must be a vain and shocking shambles. It was claimed for Cadorna's communiqués, I think justly, that at this time no others were more moderate and truthful. No point was claimed as won, until it was not merely won but securely held.

The Italian Battery beside us were moving north that night to the Tolmino sector and next day our Left Section was to move out into a position in the open, in order to switch north and shell S. Marco, which we could not reach from our present gun pits. S. Marco, being north of the Vippacco, was in the area of the Italian Second Army, commanded by Capello, which had been performing the great feats of these last days. It was clear that, for the moment, the main Italian effort was being made to the north.

Indeed by the 24th all the British guns of our Group were pointing north-eastward, firing at S. Marco and neighbouring targets. British casualties and those of the Italian Heavy Artillery had been very light, the Austrian having concentrated practically all his Artillery fire, in addition to his machine guns, on the Italian Infantry, amongst whom there had been hideous slaughter.

But in the early morning of the 23rd an Austrian shell killed a Sergeant and two men in one of our Batteries. The Sergeant was torn into several pieces, one of which landed on the top of the Officers' Mess and another in a gun pit 150 yards away. One of his legs could not be found, so they had to bury what they could, an incomplete set of torn fragments. But three or four days later the smell of the lost limb came drifting down a ravine above their guns, and following the scent, they found it, black with flies among the stones.

In my old Battery, too, four hundred cartridges went up with a direct hit, and the Austrians then shelled the smoke with unpleasant effect. A twelve-inch shell also burst very close to the Battery's Mess, killing a number of Italian telephonists next door.

Throughout these days, periods of very heavy firing alternated with periods of comparative quiet.

****

On the 25th a party of nearly thirty British officers and men, a procession of two cars, three side-cars and twelve motor bicycles, went up Podgora Hill. The Italian Second Army, to whom we were strangers, watched us with interest as we went past in a cloud of dust. On the top of Podgora Hill was a series of O.P.'s, known collectively as Maria O.P., hollowed out of the rock, approached through rock passages, and in front a wide rocky platform commanding a splendid panorama. At our feet was a precipitous descent, clothed with acacias, at the bottom Podgora with its gutted factories, then the broad stream of the Isonzo, and Gorizia on the further side. To the left we could see the Isonzo winding down out of the mountains, between Monte Sabotino and Monte Santo, the latter hiding from our sight the Bainsizza Plateau. In the centre of our view rose the great mass of San Gabriele; Italian patrols were out on its southern slopes, clearly visible through field-glasses. Then Santa Catarina and the long low brown hillside of San Marco. Away to the right the flat lands of the Isonzo and Vippacco valleys, and beyond these again the northern ridge of the Carso, from Dosso Faiti to the Stoll, beautifully visible. On the right everything seemed quiet, but there was tremendous Allied shelling of San Gabriele, Santa Catarina and San Marco. French Gunners also were here with fifteen-inch guns firing on San Marco, and two of their officers were at Maria O.P. that day. It was symbolic that from this height, for the first time on the Italian Front, Gunners of the three Western Allies were looking out eastward together toward the Promised Land.

The enemy trenches on San Marco lay out of view behind the crest, and our registration point, a white house on the top of the ridge, was almost completely blown away by a big French shell while we were watching, and waiting our turn to fire. We saw another shell burst in the Isonzo just above Gorizia, causing a huge waterspout. Colonel Canale arrived while we were firing. His white gloves were a little soiled, and he seemed rather worried and more serious than usual. He was disappointed at the stoppage of the offensive on the Carso.

CHAPTER 16

The Fall of Monte Santo

Even when our guns were turned against San Marco, we continued to man Sant' Andrea O.P., for one could get good general observation to the northward from the other side of the ruined house which was the old O.P., and most of the trenches on San Marco were invisible except from aeroplanes. I spent the night there several times during the August offensive, watching by turns with one of our Bombardiers, to whom I explained that wars were made by small groups of wicked men, generally also rich, sitting and planning in secret. I proposed to him the need to shell such groups, while they were yet forming, with the shrapnel of public opinion.

It was also at Sant' Andrea that I met a young Lieutenant of Italian Field Artillery, a Sardinian from Cagliari. He had still the face of a child, and he had, too, that perfect self-possession and that wonderful, soft charm which are so often found together in the Italian youth. I think of him often with affection, and with an eager hope that he passed unharmed through all the vicissitudes which were to follow.

He and I spent many hours together, watching those bloody, memorable hills. I met him first on the 24th of August, and we drank a bottle of Vermouth together, and discussed with enthusiasm many subjects. We even worked out in detail a scheme for the interchange of students, for periods of a year at a time, between Italian and British Universities after the war. We then turned to modern history and I noticed that he did not respond as much as I had expected to the name of Garibaldi. He held the historical theory that, broadly speaking, there are no really great men, but only lucky ones. He put forward in support of this view the distribution of death, wounds and decorations in this war. This theory of history has in it larger elements of wholesomeness and truth than has, for instance, the pernicious bombast of Carlyle. I told my Sardinian friend that I had once heard it said by a most learned man that, if Rousseau had never lived, the world would not look very different to-day, except that probably there would be no negro republic in the island of Haiti. This saying pleased him and he was inclined to think it plausible.

He told me that day that Monte Santo was reported taken, but the news was not yet sure.

****

I saw him again three days later and by then all the world knew that Monte Santo had fallen. For Cadorna in his communiqué of the 25th had cried: "Since yesterday our tricolour has been waving from the summit of Monte Santo!" Already we could see the flashes of Italian Field Guns in action near the summit. All day I was buoyant, exhilarated, and as absorbed in the war as any journalist.

Victory has an intoxicating quality in this bright clear atmosphere, and among these mountains, which it has, perhaps, nowhere else. All day there seemed to be in the air a strange thrill, which at evening seemed to grow into a great throbbing Triumph Song of the Heroes,—incomparable Italians, living and dead. The emotion of it became almost unbearable.

"Our tricolour is waving from the summit of Monte Santo!"

Here on the night of the 26th there occurred a scene wonderfully, almost incredibly, dramatic. The moon was rising. Shells passed whistling overhead, some coming from beyond the Isonzo toward the Ternova Plateau, others in the opposite direction from Ternova. Rifle shots rang out from beneath Monte Santo, along the slopes of San Gabriele, where the

Italian and Austrian lines were very close together, where no word on either side might be spoken above a whisper. Suddenly there crashed out from the gloom the opening bars of the Marcia Reale, played with tremendous *élan* by a military band. The music came from Monte Santo. On the summit of the conquered mountain, the night after its conquest, an Italian band was playing amid the broken ruins of the convent, standing around the firmly planted Italian flag. It was the Divisional Band of the four Regiments which had stormed these heights. On the flanks of the mountain, along the new lines in the valley beneath, along the trenches half-way up San Gabriele, Italian soldiers raised a cry of startled joy. Below the peak an Italian Regiment held the line within forty yards of the enemy, crouching low in the shallow trenches.

Their Colonel leaped to his feet and his voice rang out, "Soldiers, to your feet! Attention!" All along the trench the soldiers, with a swift thrill of emotion, sprang to their feet. Then again the Colonel cried, "My soldiers, let us cry aloud in the face of the enemy, 'Long live Italy! Long live the King! Long live the Infantry!'" Loud and long came the cheers, echoing and re-echoing from the rocks, taken up and repeated by others who heard them, first near at hand, then far away, echoing and spreading through the night, like the swelling waves of a great sea.

The Austrians opened fire on Monte Santo. But the music still went on. The Marcia Reale was finished, but now in turn the Hymn of Garibaldi and the Hymn of Mameli, historic battle songs of Italian liberty, pealed forth to the stars, loud above the bursting of the shells. And many Italian eyes, from which the atrocious sufferings of this war had never yet drawn tears, wept with a proud, triumphant joy. And as the last notes died away upon the night air, a great storm of cheers broke forth afresh from the Italian lines. The moon was now riding high in the heavens, and every mountain top, seen from below, was outlined with a sharp-cut edge against the sky.

Four days after, not far from this same spot, General Capello, the Commander of the Italian Second Army, decorated with the Silver Medal for Valour some of the heroes of the great victory. Among these was a civilian, a man over military age. It was Toscanini, Italy's most famous musical conductor. It was he who, charged with the organisation of concerts for the troops, had found himself in this sector of the Front when Monte Santo fell, and, hearing the news, had demanded and obtained permission to climb the conquered mountain. He reached the summit on the evening of the 26th and, by a strange chance, found his way among the rocks and the ruins of the convent, to the place where the band was playing. His presence had upon the musicians the same effect which the presence of a great General has upon faithful troops. They crowded round him, fired with a wild enthusiasm. Then Toscanini took command of what surely was one of the strangest concerts in the world, played in the moonlight, in an hour of glory, on a mountain top, which to the Italians had become an almost legendary name, to an audience of two contending Armies, amid the rattle of machine guns, the rumble of cannon, and the crashes of exploding shells.

****

"Our tricolour is waving from the summit of Monte Santo!"
If the souls of poets be immortal and know what still passes in this world, be sure that the soul of Swinburne sings again to-day, from hell or heaven, the Song of the Standard.

This is thy banner, thy gonfalon, fair in the front of thy fight.
Red from the hearts that were pierced for thee, white as thy
*   mountains are white,*
Green as the spring of thy soul everlasting, whose life-blood is light.
Take to thy bosom thy banner, a fair bird fit for the nest,
Feathered for flight into sunrise or sunset, for eastward or west,
Fledged for the flight everlasting, but held yet warm to thy breast.
Gather it close to thee, song-bird or storm-bearer, eagle or dove,
Lift it to sunward, a beacon beneath to the beacon above,
Green as our hope in it, white as our faith in it, red as our love.

CHAPTER 17

The Conquest of the
Bainsizza Plateau

The Italian advance on the Middle Isonzo in the early days
of the August offensive reached a depth of six miles on a front
of eleven miles. The Italians had swept across the Bainsizza
Plateau, and had gained observation and command, though
not possession, of the Valley of Chiapovano, the main Austrian
line of communication and supply in this sector. This advance
and the resumption of the war of movement raised, for the
moment, tremendous expectations, which were destined, alas,
to die away without fulfilment.

The passage of the Isonzo, here a deep cleft in the mountains, from Plava to above Canale, had been accomplished
by the combined skill and valour of Infantry, Artillery and
Engineers. The preliminary work of the Engineers in road
making on the western side of the river had been, as always,
worthy of the highest praise. A great mass of bridging material had had to be accumulated in the valley, alongside
camouflaged roads. The Austrians must have been on their
guard, but it seems probable that they did not expect a big
attack to be made here. For they were fully conscious of the
natural strength of their positions.

First to cross the river on the night of the attack were
boats carrying Engineers and detachments of Arditi. As
they crossed, the river gorge was full of mist and they were
not detected. But when the work of bridging began, and

sounds of hammering and the dragging of planks into position could be clearly heard, suddenly all along the further bank the Austrian machine guns began to spit fire, and red rockets went up calling for the Artillery barrage. Many boats were hit and sank, and the Bridging Detachments suffered severe casualties. One bridge, half built, was set on fire, and one could see dark shadows, lit up by the glare amid the darkness, darting forward to extinguish the flames. Fourteen bridges were thrown across under heavy fire, and, as the Infantry began to cross, Platoon after Platoon, the Austrian Machine Gunners fired at the sound of their footsteps, and many Italians fell, especially officers leading their men. But the crossing went on and, when dawn broke, the attackers had a firm footing on the left bank of the river. They swept round the flanks of those machine guns which had not yet been put out of action, and making use of the subterranean passages which the enemy had pierced in the cliffs for sheltered communication between the higher and the lower levels of the mountain, began to pour forth upon the crest of the ridge which overlooks the river. Then, as the advance continued, the Austrian right wing above Canale gave way in confusion and the Italians pressed forward on to the Bainsizza Plateau.

But their difficulties were tremendous. When they left the valley of the Isonzo behind them, they entered a waterless land, without springs for some four miles. In the early stages of the battle all water for the troops had to be brought up by mules, and likewise all food, ammunition and medical supplies, until the Engineers could get to work with road-building on the left bank of the river. The Bainsizza Plateau itself, lying amid a mass of barren mountains, contains woods, pastures, springs, small villages, a few roads and many tracks. The Italians swept over it on the 21st and 22nd of August, but soon found themselves once more in difficult country. In the days that followed the advance was slower and more spasmodic, but it still continued. By the

27th, 25,000 Austrian prisoners had been taken, together with a great quantity of material, and several whole Austrian Divisions had ceased to exist.

It had been a wonderful feat of arms, finely conceived by the Staff, magnificently executed by the rank and file. It opened out a great vista of new possibilities, but, for the moment, it was over. Before any further advance was practicable, the positions won had to be consolidated, roads had to be built, dumps and stores of every kind to be moved forward.

****

In a village on the Bainsizza Plateau, half wrecked by shell fire, two old peasants were sitting outside their house. Austrian shells whistled through the air and burst a few hundred yards away.

"These are not for us," said one of the old men to an Italian soldier, "the shells and the war are for the soldiers, not the civilians."

CHAPTER 18

The Fighting Dies Down

On the 28th of August the offensive was really beginning again. We were firing on San Marco at a slow rate from six a.m. for an hour, then *vivace* from seven till noon, and at noon we lifted and continued *vivace*. San Marco was not rocky, and the trenches there should be bombardable into pulp. In the early morning from Sant' Andrea the hills all round were clearly outlined, except where some long belts of motionless, white, low-lying cloud partly hid the Faiti-Stoll range. Later, with the sun up, a warm haze hid everything. Firing continued heavy till six p.m., and then slowed down. The attack on San Marco had failed.

Next day there was a good deal of shelling and some torrential showers. We set fire to some woods on the lower slopes of San Daniele, with a high wind blowing.

****

The Battery's good luck continued. On the 30th, while my Gun Detachment were at breakfast, a 5.9 burst in their shelter trench, at the moment unoccupied, and covered every one with showers of loose earth. All the breakfast vanished, and our shells were thrown about like driftwood in a storm. But no ammunition was exploded and no one was hurt. Raven, who had been up Sabotino that day, told us that "San Gabriele is tottering." Our offensive seemed to have completely come to an end on the Carso and in the Vippacco Valley. But we were still hammering away at San Marco and San Gabriele, at intervals of a few days at a time. On the 2nd of September San Gabriele was still "tottering," on the morning of the 4th it was reported taken, on the 6th we heard that it had been taken, lost and retaken, the Arno Brigade having distinguished themselves by some wonderful bombing. Cadorna's objective now, it was said, was Lubiana, and not Trieste. The Major and I both agreed that the Entente ought to put every available man and tank on to this Front and go for Vienna. On the 8th Raven told us that the top of San Gabriele was held, but not the lower slopes nor Santa Catarina, which were still precariously supplied from behind San Marco. A few days later we lost the top of San Gabriele, and the attack upon it was not renewed.

Then followed quiet times, except for activity by Austrian Trench Mortars against our trenches on Hill 126. We established direct telephonic communication from the Battery to the Infantry Brigade Headquarters in order to provide rapid retaliation, and we made several reconnaissances to try to locate Trench Mortars in the tangle of broken ground through which the enemy line ran.

On the 17th we were warned to be ready to move at short notice to the neighbourhood of Monfalcone, for a big push against the Hermada in three weeks' time. Battery positions were chosen, but we never went. Instead a rumour began to spread that all British Batteries were leaving Italy and going East. It was said that the War Office had the wind up about the Turks. An international tug of war was going on behind the scenes. On the afternoon of the 28th we were told on high authority that our movements were still undecided, but the Battery was inspected that day by General Capello, the victor of Bainsizza, who looked like an Eastern potentate, and was heard to say that he wanted as many British Batteries as he could get, to increase the gun power of the Second Army. That evening, however, our fate was said to be unofficially decided. We, with the rest of Raven's Group, five Batteries in all, were to stay in Italy, the other two Groups were to go away. It was not till the 3rd of October that we received definite orders on the subject. The other Groups went to Egypt and a couple of Batteries, after three months of doing nothing in Cairo, came back to Italy again. They had at any rate found a little employment for some of our surplus shipping and they had missed some queer experiences in Italy meantime.

It was also announced that we were not moving down to Monfalcone, but were probably remaining in our present positions for the winter. We therefore began systematically to prepare winter quarters. The Italian Corps Commander in a special Order of the Day expressed his satisfaction that our Group was remaining under his command.

****

On the 5th I got up at four o'clock in the morning and carried out a Front Line Reconnaissance with Sergeant Cotes, the No. 1 of my gun, and Avoglia, an Italian Sergeant Major attached to our Battery, rather a sleek person, who had been a *maître-d'hôtel* at Brighton before the war. We went along the front line trenches on Hill 126, recently captured. These trenches ran beside the river and were now in fine condition, great repairs and reconstruction having been carried out during the past three weeks. It was here that Austrian Trench Mortars were active. They were firing when we arrived and caused some casualties. As it grew light, a strong Austrian patrol was seen moving about in No Man's Land, and it was thought that a raid might be coming. The order "Stand to" was given, and the Infantry came swarming out of their dugouts, a crowd of youths, some very handsome, with almost Classical Roman features, and older men, sturdy and bearded. They densely manned the parapet, with fixed bayonets and hand grenades. The machine gun posts were also manned. But nothing happened!

A little later an Austrian was seen to emerge from cover in No Man's Land, about a hundred yards away from us, and run towards our trenches, throwing away his rifle and shouting some unintelligible words. He was sick of the war and wanted to surrender. But a young Italian recruit, in the trenches for the first time, quivering with excitement and eagerness to distinguish himself, not realising the man's motive, fired at him through a peephole. He missed, but the Austrian turned and doubled back like a rabbit to his own lines, where I suppose he was shot, poor brute, by his own people. I was standing quite close to the young recruit when he fired. No one rebuked him, but a Corporal patiently explained things to him. We smiled at one another, and I wished him *auguri* and went on up the hill.

The Austrian snipers were busy, and another Italian standing close to me, looking out slantwise through a peephole, was shot through the jaw. He was bandaged up, profusely bleeding, and went stoically down the hill, supported by a companion, leaving a red trail along the wooden duck-boards that paved the trench.

I went down two saps which the Italians had pushed out, one to within twenty yards, the other to within ten yards, of the Austrian front line. Here every one spoke in a low whisper or by signs. They warned me to keep well down, as the Austrians hated khaki worse even than *grigio-verde*, as one is always apt to hate third parties who butt in against one in what one conceives to be a purely private quarrel.

But I went back armed with some useful information regarding the position of those Austrian Trench Mortars.

CHAPTER 19

A Lull Between Two Storms

From the beginning of October the Battery were hard at work on their winter quarters. We had two large dining and recreation huts for the men, one for the Right Section and one for the Left, fitted up with long wooden tables and benches. These huts were dug into the bank, one on either side of the road leading up from the Battery position to Pec village. The dug-outs were improved and made watertight and the Officers' Mess and sleeping huts were moved up from the river bank into the Battery position itself. Everything was very comfortable and handy.

We maintained close relations with an Italian Battery next door commanded by a certain Captain Romano. His men helped us in putting up our huts, which were of Italian design, and we had frequent exchanges of hospitality. Romano was a Regular officer, about 28 years old, with twinkling brown eyes and a voice like a foghorn even when speaking from a short distance away, but a fine singer. He had a wonderful collection of photographs, was a good Gunner and popular with his men.

****

On the 9th I spent the night in Lecce O.P. on Hill 123, overlooking Hills 126 and 94. It was named after the Lecce Brigade who made it, one of the best Brigades in the Italian Army. When they were in front of us, we saw a good deal of them. Now the Parma Brigade were holding the line and the British officer in the O.P. used to take his meals at the Brigade Headquarters. Things were rather active that evening. At half-past five in the afternoon the enemy opened a heavy bombardment, increasing to a pitch of great fury, on our front and support trenches. Our own lines down below me were blotted out from sight by dense clouds of crashing, flashing smoke. Just before six the Italian Brigadier asked me for a heavy barrage from all the British Batteries. A big counter-bombardment was now working up from our side. I spoke on the telephone to Raven, who told me that all our Batteries were firing *double vivace*. At a quarter past six the Austrians attacked. There was a terrific rattle of Italian machine gun fire, almost drowning the sound of the heavier explosions, and a stream of rockets went up from our front line calling for more barrage. The attack was beaten off by machine guns and hand grenades. A few Austrians reached our parapet, but none got into our trenches.

Firing died down about a quarter to seven, and the Brigadier came up to the O.P., very pleased with the support we had rendered, and asked that a slow rate of fire might be kept up. Later on an Austrian telephone message was overheard, which suggested that the attack was to be renewed just before dawn, after a gas attack. We kept on the alert, but nothing happened. Two of our Batteries went on firing at a slow rate all night. When dawn broke, it was evident that our bombardment had been very destructive. The enemy's trenches were knocked to pieces; uprooted trees, planks, sandbags and dead bodies lay about in confusion. It was thought that owing to our fire some Austrian units, which were to have taken part in the attack, could not, and others would not, do so, in spite of a special issue of rum and other spirits. I saw also, motionless amid the Austrian wire, a figure in Italian uniform, one of a patrol who had gone out four nights before, and had not returned.

On the 12th I went out with a Sergeant, a Signaller and

Corporal Savogna, a Canadian Italian, on a Front Line Reconnaissance on the northern side of the Vippacco, in the Second Army area. The day was wonderfully clear and we could see the everlasting snows beyond Cadore. We went through Rupa to Merna and, being evidently spotted, were shelled with 4.2's and forced to proceed along a muddy communication trench knee deep in water. At Raccogliano Mill we visited the Headquarters of the Bergamo Brigade, which was holding the line. A guide took us along the front line, which had been considerably advanced here in August and September, and again by a successful local attack a few days before. We went down one *caverna* in which, on the occasion of this last attack, a Magyar officer and 25 men surrendered. The Austrian sentry, also a Magyar, had been fastened by the leg to the doorpost outside the entrance to the dug-out. In the Italian bombardment one of his feet was blown away, but his own people had done nothing for him. Now his dead body lay out in the open behind the new Italian front line.

****

On the 14th Jeune went on leave to England, no one having any expectation that anything of importance was likely to happen in the near future. In his absence I acted as Second-in-Command of the Battery.

On the 19th we heard that the Italian High Command was preparing another big offensive from the Bainsizza against the Ternova Plateau, and the same day the Intelligence Report contained the information that a series of German Divisions had been seen detraining at Lubiana since the beginning of October, and that, owing to the Russian collapse, a thousand Austrian guns had been moved across from the Russian to the Isonzo Front since the middle of September. We had noticed a perceptible increase in the enemy's Artillery activity for some time, but this, we thought at the time, was purely defensive. There had also been a week of heavy rains, but the Vippacco, after rising rapidly and threatening to flood us all out, fell eighteen inches in one night. It swept away a number of Italian bridges, however, from Merna and Raccogliano further up stream, and we saw pieces of these rushing past in the swift current.

On the 21st the Major and I motored to Palmanova and bought some winter clothing at the Ordnance. An Austrian twelve-inch howitzer, whom we had christened "Mr Pongo," was shelling all day at intervals, chiefly in the back areas. An unpleasant beast, we agreed, who wanted smothering!

On the 22nd it was evident, from the Austrian shelling, that quite a number of fresh heavy howitzers, both twelve- and fifteen-inch, had appeared behind the Austrian lines. A few, no doubt, of those thousand guns from Russia! Listening to their shells whistling over one's head like express trains, and to their (happily distant) deep crashes on percussion, one realised very vividly the immediate military effects of the Russian collapse. We heard that the Italian offensive was not coming off after all.

On the 23rd we heard that a big Austrian attack was expected last night and might come that night instead. We received orders to clean up and prepare, in case of necessity, the old position at Boschini on San Michele, which the Battery had occupied when they first arrived in Italy. This, I thought, seemed rather panic-stricken. Romano's Battery had similar orders. It would be annoying to leave our present position after all the work put into it to make it habitable for the winter. But I noted that the atmosphere was tinged with apprehension.

CHAPTER 20

The Beginning of the
Enemy Offensive

On the morning of October 24th soon after nine o'clock
the enemy launched a big attack against the Third Army
Front, especially violent between Faiti and the Vippacco, and
renewed it in the afternoon. But he gained no ground. All
through the previous night and all that day till evening the
bombardment on both sides was heavy. We had not fired during the night but began at seven in the morning and went on
throughout the day. A message came in that the enemy would
probably shell Batteries for four hours with gas shell, starting
with irritant gas and going on to poison. He had already employed these tactics up north, as we learned later. Gas alert was
on all night and we were listening strainedly for soft bursts.
Heavy rain came down steadily all day, and everything was
drenched and dripping. The spaces between our huts filled
with water, and needed continual baling out. But when gas
was expected, one welcomed heavy rain[1] and high winds and
loud explosions from bursting shells.

Between nine and ten p.m. I heard a series of soft bursts
just across the river and arranged with Romano's Battery
for mutual alarms if any gas should come too near. An hour
later I was relieved in the Command Post and turned in.
As I was undressing, I heard the wind rising again and the

1: It was not till a later date that gases were employed, the effects of which
were increased by rain.

telephonists next door baling out their dug-out. We were keeping up a desultory fire all night to harass any further attacks that might be attempted. The Major, who had been out on a Front Line Reconnaissance that morning in the neighbourhood of Merna, had come in for some very heavy shelling and returned very weary.

****

The next day, the 25th, was at least fine; it was even rather sunny. We did a little firing, but not much, between seven a.m. and two p.m. Enemy planes came over continually, flying very low, about thirty in the course of the morning. They attacked one of our observation balloons, which descended rapidly as they approached, and I think got down safely. Italian anti-aircraft guns brought down one of them. Whenever we shelled Mandria, a little village up the valley, a plane came over. Evidently they had something there as to which they were sensitive, perhaps a General's Billet!

At half past ten the Italians ditched a lorry full of ammunition just at the top of the road from the Battery position to Pec village, in full view of the enemy on Hill 464. At this time the village was being heavily shelled by 5.9's, and our cookhouse on the outskirts was all but hit, shells bursting all round it in a circle. Showers of bricks and lumps of earth and masonry rose high in the air. One shell hit the Artillery Group Headquarters of Major Borghese and I saw all his office papers going up, a cloud of shreds, shining in the sun. I laughed and said to myself, "There goes a lot of red tape!" I saw Borghese himself later in the day limping along with a stick; a chunk of one of his office walls had fallen on his foot.

The enemy meanwhile had begun to shell the lorry, methodically as their idiotic habit was, with one shell every five minutes. It was too near us to be pleasant, so the Major took out a party and hauled it out of their view under cover of a bank. But this took some time. Leary stood by with a stopwatch calling out the minutes. At the end of every fourth minute, the party ran for cover. Then a few seconds later we heard the next shell coming. The Major was hit on the hand once by a shell splinter which drew blood, but nothing more serious than this happened.

About two o'clock a big bombardment worked up again, and the Volconiac and Faiti became a sea of smoke and flame. This went on till dusk, we firing hard all the time. More enemy planes came over, one even after dark, a most unusual thing, flying very low indeed, under a heavy fire of anti-aircraft Batteries and machine guns from the ground. Our planes had been very scarce all day. They had nearly all gone north. For the time being we had quite lost the command of the air in this sector.

The two British Batteries who were furthest forward had orders to move back that night to reserve positions on San Michele. The Italians were going to horse their guns, for it was said that the majority of the tractors had gone north too. This move looked rather panicky, I thought.

Many red rockets went up in the early evening from Volconiac and Faiti. The enemy were making another attack. Then a little later tricolour rockets, red, white and green, went up. This was the signal that the attack had been beaten off and that the situation was quiet again. The firing died down about seven. We fed and put up for the night an Italian officer, whose Battery used to be here, but had moved north yesterday. He had just come back from a gas course at Palmanova. From a newspaper which he had I saw that a strong offensive had begun on the afternoon of the 23rd to the north of the Bainsizza Plateau. Either the attacks here were only holding attacks, or the attack to the north was a feint and the real thing was to be here. Anyhow, I thought, it is their Last Despairing Great Cry! I turned in just after midnight. The night was still and there was a bright moon and stars. A thick mist lay along the Vippacco, just behind the trees. The air was damp and cold. It seemed pretty quiet for the moment all along the Front.

****

I had a troubled night. In the early morning we were bombarded with gas shell and had to wear respirators from a quarter to three till four o'clock. We were firing from five till six and again steadily from a quarter past seven onwards. We got orders to move back that night to Boschini, on San Michele. I thought this a great mistake. Later in the day our move was cancelled, as the two forward Batteries which pulled out last night would not be in action on San Michele till to-morrow. They had been last heard of stuck fast in a crush of traffic at the bottom of the hill at Peteano. A strong team of horses were straining their guts out in vain attempts to pull an Italian twelve-inch mortar up the hill. It was this which had caused the block. Those two forward Batteries *might* have lost their guns in a quick retreat, I thought, but hardly we. It seemed to be feared, however, that the two bridges across the Vippacco might go.

That day we were shelled heavily with every kind of weapon, from fifteen-inch downwards, especially the Left Section in the afternoon. We had, as usual, marvellously good luck, and only had one casualty, and that a slight wound. The spirit and endurance of the men were wonderful. Enemy planes were over all day; we counted twenty-two between daybreak and four p.m. Some hovered overhead and ranged their guns on us. Several times we put our detachments under cover and ceased fire owing to the shelling. My own gun was half buried by a great shower of earth kicked up by a 9.45, which pitched right on top of the bank in front of us. But Cotes, my Sergeant, and myself, crouching under cover of the girdles, were quite unhurt. The rest of the detachment had been ordered down into their dug-out. Another time the enemy neatly bracketed our Command Post with twelve-inch, and several of us within were uncomfortably awaiting the next round. But luckily for us he switched away to the right.

We had to fire hard most of the day, especially in the afternoon and evening. It had been exhausting and almost sleepless work for the detachments for several days past, for

Darrell and a working party of forty were away preparing the reserve position on San Michele, and we had hardly any reliefs for the guns. The Major, too, looked very tired and frayed, but, whenever our eyes met, he gave me a smile of encouragement and leadership. That evening, during a short break in the firing, he asked me, since he himself could not leave the Command Post, to go round and "buck the men up" and thank them on his behalf for the way in which they had behaved. "So long as the Major's pleased, we're satisfied," said one man. Another, a Bombardier who afterwards got a Commission, and had been with Darrell on a reconnaissance on Faiti a few days before and had nearly been killed on the journey, said, "Well, Sir, we were thinking of the boys in the Front Line today." And well he might, for it had been a hellish bombardment up there. After delivering my message to the men, I walked up and down the road in front of the guns for a few moments in the short silence, realising how the Alliance of Britain and Italy was burning itself more deeply than ever into our hearts in these days of trial.

That night the enemy attacked again, and we lost Faiti and Hill 393, and had to fire on them. I heard afterwards from the Group that Colonel Canale, when he gave the order to fire on 393, was almost weeping on the telephone. Next day we counter-attacked and retook Faiti, but 393 remained in Austrian hands. Rumours and denials of rumours came in from the north. It was said that we had lost Monte Nero and Caporetto, and that German Batteries had kept up a high concentration of gas for four hours on our lines in the Cadore. And we knew that the Italian gas masks were only guaranteed to last for an hour and a half in such conditions, and that each man only carried one.

CHAPTER 21

From the Vippacco to
San Giorgio Di Nogara

On the 27th the rumours became bad. The German advance to the north was said to be considerable and rapid. Orders came that all the British Batteries were to pull out and park that night at Villa Viola, behind Gradisca, "for duty on another part of the Front." Probably, we thought, we were going north. "The gun concentration up there must be awful," said the Major. I told Cotes that we were probably going into the thick of it, and his eyes shone with pride. He was a fine fellow. That day the sun was shining, and the Italian planes in this sector seemed to have regained command of the air. For the moment there was a little lull in the firing, but we felt that some big fate was looming over us. I went away to my hut for five minutes and wrote in my diary, "I here put it on record once more that I am proud to fight in and for Italy. I repeat that dying here is not death, it is flying into the dawn! If I die in and for Italy, I would like to think that my death would do something for Anglo-Italian sympathy and understanding."

In the early afternoon the Major went down to Headquarters. He rang me up from there to say that two guns were to be pulled out at once, and the other two to double their rate of fire. No. 4 gun was now engaging two different targets with alternate rounds and different charges.

When the Major came back, he called all the men together

and said. "I am not going to conceal anything from you. The situation is serious. The Italians have had a bad reverse up north. But there is no need for anyone to get panicky. We shall pull out and go back to-night. That is all I know at present. When I know more, I will tell you more. One gun will remain in action till the last. No. 2 is the easiest to get out, so I have chosen her for the post of honour."

As the men scattered, I heard several saying, "Good old No. 2!"

The Major told me that the Austrians were almost in Cividale, staggering news. Tractors and lorries were to come and take away our guns and stores in the evening. But the number of tractors was very limited and Raven was doubtful if enough would come in time. The whole Third Army was retreating, and three British Batteries, ourselves, the Battery in Pec village and the Battery at Rupa, would be the last three Batteries of Medium or Heavy Calibre left on this part of the Front.

All through the afternoon and evening Italian Infantry and Artillery were retreating through Pec. Some looked stolid, others depressed, others merely puzzled. But a little later a Battalion came along the road the other way, going up to be sacrificed on Nad Logem. They halted to rest by the roadside, full of gaiety and courage. They cheered our men on No. 2 gun, who were pumping out shells as fast as they could. *"Bravi inglesi!"* cried the Italians, and some of our men replied, "Good luck, Johnny!" Unknown Italians were always "Johnny."

As the dark came on, ammunition dumps began to go up everywhere; the Italians were deliberately exploding them, and great flashes of light, brighter than even an Italian noon-day, lit up the whole sky for minutes at a time. Romano's Battery next door to us threw the remains of their ammunition into the river, and pulled out and away about 6.30. They were horse-drawn and did not need to wait for tractors. We wished each other good-bye, and hoped we might meet again some better day. We too got orders to destroy all ammunition we could not fire, as there would be no transport to take it away. So we gave No. 2 a generous ration and heaved the rest into the waters of the Vippacco.

No. 2 went on firing ceaselessly. So did one gun of the Battery in the village, and one gun at Rupa. That Battery, being the furthest forward, was in the greatest danger of the three. About 7 o'clock our first tractor arrived and took away No. 1 gun with Winterton and Manzoni. Enemy bombing planes came over frequently. One came right over us and then turned down the Vallone, and there was a series of heavy explosions, and great clouds of brownish smoke leapt up beneath her track.

Why, I kept asking myself, didn't the fools shell Pec village, where a crowd of men and guns were waiting for transport? Why didn't they put over gas shell? Why didn't they bomb us? Evidently there were no Germans *here!* About a quarter to nine No. 2 finished her ammunition, and we pulled her out. The other three guns had gone now and the other two British Batteries were clear, all but two lorries. Just after nine o'clock our last tractor came along and took off No. 2, with Darrell in charge of her. How the Italians had managed to get all these lorries and tractors for us, I don't know, for, in the Third Army as a whole, they were terribly short of transport. Many made the criticism that we should have kept out in Italy our own transport. But the Italians certainly did us very handsomely, at the cost of losing some bigger guns of their own.

After the last British gun had ceased to fire there was for about five minutes an eerie stillness, as though all our Artillery had gone and theirs was holding its fire. And then an Italian Field Battery opened again on the right of Pec. For over an hour now I had been expecting, minute by minute, to see the enemy Infantry come swarming along the Nad Logem in the dusk, cutting off our retreat, for I knew we had nothing but rear-guards left up there. But they did not come!

Only the Major and I and about forty men were left now, and we had been told that there would be no more transport. So we destroyed everything that we had been unable to get away, and the Major informed Headquarters of the situation and then disconnected the telephone and the men fell in and we marched away. We were just in time to see an Italian Field Battery come into Pec at the gallop, the gunners all cheering, unlimber their guns, take up position and open fire. It was a smart piece of work, done with a real Latin gesture. How infuriating it was to be leaving these wooden huts of ours and these good positions, on which had been spent so many hours of labour, where we could have passed such a comfortable winter, going forth now none knew whither! Old Natale, one of the Italians attached to us, chalked up in German on the entrance to one of the huts, "You German pigs, we shall soon be back again!" But at that moment I did not feel so sure. Natale was afterwards lost in the retreat, and was reported by us as "missing." But one of our men saw him again six months later with an Italian Battery and said he looked several years younger!

We passed Campbell, the Medical Officer, standing outside his dug-out on the road. He was waiting for the last of the other Batteries' parties to get away. He told me afterwards that we were out only just in time. Within half an hour of our going, the Austrians fairly plastered the position with shells of all calibres. They shelled the road a little as we went along, but not too much. As we passed the railway embankment at Rubbia, we saw and spoke to some Italian machine-gunners in position, whose orders were to hold up the enemy till the last possible moment. They were quite calm and determined, those boys, knowing perfectly well that, by the time the enemy came, the Isonzo bridges would have been blown up behind them. I dragged myself on with an aching heart. One who retreats cuts a poor figure beside a rear-guard that stays behind and fights.

We crossed the Isonzo at Peteano, and took a short cut across the fields to Farra. In the crowd and the dark we were jostled by some Italian Infantry. We hailed them and found that they were our old friends, the Lecce Brigade. The Major made our men stand back.

"Pass, Lecce," he said. "Good luck to you!"

We marched on through Farra to Gradisca, both blazing in the night. The towns and villages everywhere in this sector had been deliberately fired by the retreating Italians, in addition to the ammunition dumps. The whole countryside was blazing and exploding. I thought of Russia in 1812, and the Russian retreat before Napoleon, and Tchaikovsky's music.

It began to rain, but that made no difference to the burning. In Gradisca burning petrol was running about the streets. Earlier in the evening there had been a queer scene here. The Headquarters of the British Staff had been at Gradisca, and the Camp Commandant had made a hobby of fattening rabbits for the General's Mess. When the time had come that day to pack up and go, it was found that the lorries provided were fully loaded with office stores, Staff officers' bulky kit and 20,000 cigarettes, which the General was specially proud of having saved from his canteen. There was no room for the Camp Commandant's rabbit hutches, so these were opened and the fat inmates released, to the delight of the civilians and Italian soldiery in Gradisca, who knocked them over or shot them as they ran. I heard this from a gunner, who was officer's servant to one of the Staff and witnessed the scene.

A few miles away, at the Ordnance Depot at Villa Freifeldt, thousands of pounds' worth of gun stores stood ready, packed in crates, to be removed. But no transport came for them, and they were abandoned and fell into Austrian hands. For lack of them, our Batteries were afterwards kept out of action for several weeks. Whoever ordered these things seems to have thought it more important to save the Staff's kit and the General's cigarettes.

Just before we entered Gradisca, we passed a Battalion of the Granatieri, the Italian Grenadiers, all six foot tall, with collar badges of crimson and white, coming up from reserve to fight a rear-guard action. I had seen them a few days before in rest billets and admired their appearance. And in their march that night and in their faces was scorn for fugitives and contempt for death. The Major said to me, as they swung past us, that *that* Battalion could be trusted to fight to the end. And they did. Some of our men met a few of their survivors at Mestre a week later. Nearly the whole Battalion had been killed or wounded, but they had held up the Austrian advance for several hours.

On the further side of Gradisca we passed a great platform, which had been erected a few weeks before for the Duke of Aosta's presentation of medals for the Carso offensive. It was here that the Major had received the Italian Silver Medal for Valour. The platform looked ironical that night, still decked with bunting, limp and drenched now by the rain, and lit up by the flames of the burning town. We reached Villa Viola about 11.30 p.m. It was to have been a rendezvous, but there was no one there. Only the rain still falling. About midnight we entered an empty house, and threw ourselves down upon the floor to sleep.

****

We had slept for less than an hour, when we were hurriedly awakened. The Italians had orders to set fire to the house. Meanwhile Savogna, our Canadian Italian Corporal, had just returned from scouting for us, and reported that parties from the other Batteries were in a house half a mile away. We marched off again through pouring rain, our path lit up by the flames, which in places thrust their long tongues right across the road. The wind blew clouds of smoke in our faces. The air was full of the roaring of the fires, the crackle of blazing woodwork, the crash of houses falling in, the loud explosions of ammunition dumps and petrol stores, which now and again for a few seconds lighted up the whole night sky for miles around with a terrific glare, and then died down again. Far as the eye could reach the night was studded with red and golden fires. Everywhere behind the front of the retreating Third Army a systematic destruction was being carried out. The Third Army was retreating in good order, unbroken and undefeated, retreating only because its northern flank was in danger of being turned. The Third Army was proving to the enemy that its movements were deliberate and governed by a cool purpose. The enemy should advance into a wilderness.

Again I seemed to hear in the air the music of 1812, and the bells of burning Moscow ringing out loud and clear above the triumph song of the invader.

****

Our men marched doggedly on, some looking puzzled and full of wonder, others tired but cheerful, others with expressionless, uncomprehending faces. But in the faces of a few I read a consciousness of the tremendous tragedy of which we formed a tiny part. We found the other Batteries in a house not yet marked down for burning. The house was crowded out already and all the best places taken, such as they were. There were pools of water everywhere on the floor. Officers of the Group were there, knowing nothing, awaiting the appearance of Colonel Raven. All our party got in somehow and lay down to sleep. But half an hour later we were roused again. Raven had come and ordered that all should push on to Palmanova.

Some of our men were sleeping very heavily and were hard to waken. When we started it was still raining. The roads were crowded with traffic, including many guns. Our own went by with the rest, Winterton, Darrell, Leary and Manzoni with them. Each Battery party marched independently, the easier to get through blocks in the traffic. The Square at Palmanova had been fixed as the next rendezvous.

The stream of refugees with their slow-moving wagons drawn by oxen, or their little donkey carts, or trudging on foot carrying bundles, became gradually thicker and more painful. For we were back now in country that yesterday or the day before had fancied itself remote from the battle zone. I remember one elderly peasant woman, tall and erect as a young girl, with white hair and a face like Dante, calm, beautiful and stern. She was alone, tramping along through the mud. And she had the walk of a queen.

At Versa we halted for a few minutes at the Hospital. All the wounded had been evacuated.[1] Campbell was lying on a bed in one of the empty wards, snatching a little rest. He had seen the last British troops away from Pec and had then followed on a motor-bicycle. I went into the old R.A.M.C. Mess to see if any food or drink was left. The question of food was beginning to be serious for the whole retreating Army. Italian troops were clearing out everything. I found a wine bottle half full, and took a deep drink. It was vinegar, but it bucked one up. I handed the bottle to an Italian, and told him it was "good English wine." He drank a little, saw the joke, smiled and passed it on to an unsuspecting companion. I got a little milk which I shared with the Major and some of our men. Then we resumed the march.

We reached Palmanova about 7 a.m. It was now the 28th of October. We met Raven in the Square, where were also collected a British General and his Staff officers. They were standing about, with a half lost look on their faces. There was no evidence of decision or any plan. The General was smiling, as his habit was. The Staff Captain was telling someone, in a hopeless voice, that he had heard that the Italians were going back to the Tagliamento. Just as we arrived, the Italians began to set fire to the town. Dense clouds of black smoke, fanned by a strong wind, began to pour over our heads. Flames were soon roaring round houses, where three months ago I had been a guest. But the inmates had all gone

---

1: One wounded British soldier, who had been in an Italian Field Hospital which was not evacuated in time, was taken prisoner by the Austrians. He told me, when he was released a year later, that the Austrians bayoneted the Italian wounded whom they found in this hospital, but spared the British, and, on the whole, treated them well.

now. Food and drink was being sold in the shops at knock-down prices. The Italian military authorities were requisitioning all bread, and issued some to us. The Major ordered it to be kept in reserve.

I went round the town and into the Railway Station looking for our guns. But there was no sign of them. I came back and slept for an hour amid some rubble under the archway inside one of the town gates. The town was burning furiously. Our men, wet to the skin, sheltered themselves from the smoke and the cold wind in the dry moat outside the walls.

Then the order came to move on. We formed up and started with the rest. Nobody knew whither. Some said Latisana, but no one knew how far off this was. The men had no rations except the bread obtained at Palmanova, and no prospect, apparently, of getting any. The Supply Officers of the A.S.C. might as well have gone to Heaven, for all the use they were to us during those days of retreat. It was raining again and the roads were blocked. We proceeded slowly for a mile or two, and were then turned off the road into a damp, open field, which someone said was a "strategic point." Here a number of different Battery parties collected. We were to wait for the guns. The downpour steadily increased, the field rapidly became a marsh, and there was no shelter anywhere. Raven walked up and down, puffing at this pipe, taking the situation with admirable calm. It was at this time that I personally touched my bedrock of misery, both mental and physical. For there seemed to be nothing to be done, and, what most irked me, there were so many senior officers present that I myself could take no decisions. Then some of our guns arrived, and were halted at the side of the road to wait for the rest. But this made the traffic block worse, and they had to move forward again, and the idea of getting them all together was abandoned.

Raven then gave the order to the rest of us to move on. There were some vacant places in various cars and lorries at this point and some footsore men were put in. The Major insisted, in spite of my protests that I preferred to walk, that I should get into one of the cars, which I shared with Littleton, the Chaplain who had thought that war "might be tremendously worth while" and three junior officers from Raven's Headquarters. I was, in truth, pretty done at this stage, chiefly through want of sleep, compared to which I always found want of food a trifling inconvenience. It was now about 4 p.m. and we could only make very slow progress. A rendezvous had been fixed by Raven at Foglie, where rations were to have been distributed. But there was no one and no rations there, and it seemed that Raven had taken the wrong road. The enemy were said to be advancing from the north at right angles to our only possible line of retreat, and the chances seemed strongly in favour of our all being cut off.

An Italian doctor ran out into the road and stopped our car, almost beside himself with despair. He had been left in charge of a number of severely wounded cases, without any food, medical necessities or transport. But we had no food and could do nothing to help him, except promise to try to have transport sent back to him from San Giorgio di Nogara.

CHAPTER 22

From San Giorgio to the Tagliamento

We reached San Giorgio about 9 p.m. and here I got out of the car, which two of Raven's Staff took on to try and arrange for transport to be sent back for the Italian wounded. Having slept for an hour or two in the car, I felt quite a different being and fit for anything. Stragglers were coming in from the various Batteries' dismounted parties, and I collected nearly a hundred of these men into a hall on the ground floor of an Italian Field Hospital. They lay about on the stone floor, sleeping like logs. Upstairs a panic had spread among the wounded that they would be abandoned. Men were crying with terror and struggling to get out of bed. Campbell, who had now joined us, went up and helped the Italian medical personnel. Soon afterwards ambulances of both the Italian and British Red Cross began to arrive, and the hospital was quickly cleared. From one British Red Cross Driver I got a large box of Cabin biscuits, which I distributed among our men, some of whom were ravenously hungry. I also found a tap of good drinking water in the main street and here we refilled all available water bottles, including those of several men who were too fast asleep to waken.

The question then arose what to do with these stragglers. I went to the station, but found that no more trains were running. Latisana was said to be only "a few kilometres" away. It was in fact more than twenty. I discovered that it was on the Tagliamento and I supposed that, once across the river, we should be momentarily safe from risk of capture, and, if ammunition was forthcoming, our Batteries might once more come into action. Meanwhile we should push on as soon as possible. On the other hand the men were very tired, having been marching for twenty-four hours, with only a few short breaks. A few hours' sleep now might be worth a lot to them later on.

Several civilians came up to me and asked when the Germans would be here. "This is my house," one old man explained, pointing to a small house near the Hospital, "and I shall have to leave everything if I go away. But I cannot stay....," and he began to cry.

In the early hours of the 29th I put some of our most footsore stragglers on to lorries going in the direction of Latisana. The rest marched off under Henderson, one of the officers from Raven's Headquarters, who had come with me in the car to San Giorgio. Meanwhile I was keeping a look-out for our guns in the dense columns of traffic slowly crawling past. I saw guns belonging to other Batteries, and was told that some of ours were further behind. It was just getting light, when a tractor appeared drawing two of our guns and one belonging to another British Battery, which we had picked up on the road a long way back with only three gunners in charge of it, and which would certainly have been lost, if we had not taken it in tow. But, as the result of this additional load, our tractor had been breaking down all the way along, and had fallen almost to the rear of the retreating column. It had a damnable and useless accumulator, but there was no means of changing this. With the tractor and guns were Winterton, Darrell, and Leary, also the Battery Quartermaster Sergeant and two of our lorries. They told me Manzoni was well on ahead with the other two guns and I told them that the Major and the bulk of the dismounted party must also be a good distance ahead, as stragglers from this party had appeared here many hours before.

We were now the last British guns on the road, a post of

honour which we continued to hold. I was delighted to find that I was now entitled, by reason of seniority, to take command. I sent on the two lorries with Winterton and Darrell, to get in touch as soon as possible with the two guns in front and the Major's party. Leary and I remained behind with the tractor and its load. We had about thirty men with us and a small quantity of rations, including a little tea. We moved on slowly and got stuck in a bad block of traffic at San Giorgio cross roads. Here we had to remain stationary for several hours. The dawn was breaking and we made some tea.

About 5 a.m. I got tired of sitting still and walked about half a mile down the road to find out the cause of the block. I began to control and gerrymander the traffic and at first annoyed an Italian officer, who was there with the same object as myself; but I persuasively pointed out to him the benefits to both of us, if we could only succeed in getting a move on, and he then calmed down and began to help me. In the end we both manoeuvred our own transport into a moving stream, and went forward smiling.

We went along at a fine pace for several miles and then our tractor stopped and wouldn't start up again. Whereupon there came to our assistance a young man named Rinaldo Rinaldi, a skilled and resourceful mechanic, who was driving a tractor in rear of us. He patched up our engine and got us going again. But we kept on breaking down after intervals never very long. Time after time Rinaldo Rinaldi came running up, smiling and eager to help. He patched us up and got us going six times. But at last he had to pass us and go on. For he, too, was drawing guns. I shall never forget Rinaldo Rinaldi and the cheerful help he gave us. In the end he left us an accumulator, but it was not much better than our own.

Enemy planes now began to appear in the sky, some scouting only, others dropping bombs. They did more damage to the wretched refugees than to the military. What chances they missed that day! Once or twice, when we were stationary, I

218

gave the order to scatter in the fields to left and right of the road. But they never came very near to hitting us. They flew very high and their marksmanship was atrocious.

Atrocious also was our tractor! Finally, when it broke down and we had no fresh accumulator, we had to unlimber the front gun, attach drag ropes to the tractor, haul vigorously on the ropes until the engine started up, then back the tractor and front limber back to the guns, limber up, cast off the ropes and go ahead again. We did this three or four times in the course of an hour, and enjoyed the sense of triumphing over obstacles. But it was very laborious, and the intervals between successive breakdowns grew ominously shorter and shorter. And the last time the trick didn't work, though we had all heaved and heaved till we were very near exhaustion. We were fairly stuck now, half blocking the road. Great excitement, as was only natural, developed among those behind us.

I sent forward an orderly with a message to the Major, describing our plight and asking that, if possible, another tractor might be sent back from Latisana to pull us. This message never reached the Major, but was opened by another Field officer, who sent back this flatulent reply. "If you are with Major Blinks, you had better ask him whether you may use your own discretion and, if necessary, remove breech blocks and abandon guns." I was not with Major Blinks, and I neither knew nor cared where he might be. Nor had I any intention of abandoning the guns. I determined, without asking anyone's permission, to use my discretion in a different way.

I saw, a little distance in front, an Italian Field Artillery Colonel in a state of wild excitement. He was rushing about with an unopened bottle of red wine in his hand, waving it ferociously at the heads of refugees, and driving them and their carts off the road down a side track. A queer pathetic freight some of these carts carried, marble clocks and blankets, big wine flasks and canaries in cages. The Colonel had driven off the road also a certain Captain Medola, of whom I shall have more to say in a moment, and who was sitting sulkily on his horse among the civilian carts. The Colonel's object, it appeared, was to get a number of Field Batteries through. He had cleared a gap in the blocked traffic and his Field Guns were now streaming past at a sharp trot. But he was an extraordinary spectacle and made me want to laugh. Treading very delicately, I approached this infuriated man, and explained the helpless situation of our guns, pointing out that we were also unwillingly impeding the movements of his own. I asked if he could order any transport to be provided for us. He waved his bottle at me, showed no sign of either civility or comprehension, only screaming at the top of his voice, *"Va via, va via!"*[1]

I gave him up as hopeless, and went back to my guns, intending to wait till he had disappeared and things had quieted down again, and then to look for help elsewhere. But the Latin mind often follows a thread of order through what an Anglo-Saxon is apt to mistake for a mere hurricane of confused commotion. Within five minutes Captain Medola came up to me and said that the Colonel had ordered him to drag our tractor and guns. Medola was in command of a Battery of long guns, and had one of these attached to a powerful tractor on the road in front of us. To this long gun, therefore, we now attached our tractor, useless as a tractor but containing valuable gun stores, and our three guns. It was a tremendous strain for one tractor, however strong, to pull, and we decided a little later to abandon our own tractor and most of its contents.

Medola, having handed over his horse to an orderly, who was to ride on ahead and arrange for a fresh supply of petrol for his tractors, of which there were three, mounted the front of the leading tractor and I got up beside him. He rendered us most invaluable help in a most willing spirit and at considerable risk to himself. For he undoubtedly had to go much more slowly with us in tow than he could have gone if he had been alone.

We saw another Battery of Italian heavy guns going along the road, heavier than either ours or Medola's. They were an

1: "Away with you, away with you!"

ancient type, which we had seen sometimes on the Carso, and not of very high military value. But their gunners took a regimental and affectionate pride in those old guns. They had neither tractors nor horses, but they had dragged their beloved pieces for thirty miles from the rocky heights of the Carso, along good roads and bad, up and down hill, through impossible traffic blocks, down on to the plains as far as Palmanova, with nothing but long ropes and their own strong arms. They had forty men hauling on each gun. At Palmanova new hauling parties had been put on, who dragged the guns another thirty miles to the far side of the Tagliamento at Latisana. And as they hauled, they sang, until they were too tired to go on singing, and could only raise, from time to time, their rhythmical periodic cry of *"Sforza!... Sforza!"*[1]

As we passed through Muzzano, the town and road were heavily bombed. The bell in the campanile jangled wildly and weeping women crowded into the church, as though thinking to find sanctuary there. Others stood gazing helplessly up into the sky. Here I saw some Italian Infantry, mostly young, who were delighted to be retreating. "Forward, you militarists!" they cried to us as we passed. "This is your punishment! How much longer do you think the war is going to last? What about Trieste now?" They spoke with joyful irony, as though the conquest of Trieste had been a slaves' task, imposed upon unwilling Italy by foreign imperialists. They were the only Italian troops I saw during the retreat, who showed any sign of being under the influence of "defeatist" or German propaganda.

The stream of refugees steadily thickened on the roads. More than once I got down and ran on ahead, calling out with monotonous refrain to the drivers of civilian carts to keep well over to the right of the road, so as to let the guns pass. They all did their best to obey, poor brutes, and we gained some useful ground in that endless column.

At nightfall we were still eight or nine kilometres from Latisana. The traffic block grew worse and worse, and there

---

1: "Heave!... Heave!"

were too few Carabinieri to exercise proper control. We stuck for hours at a time, with nothing moving for miles, three motionless lines of traffic abreast on the road, all pointing in the same direction. Tired men slept and wakeful men waited and watched and cursed at the delay. Behind us, far off, we could hear the booming of the guns, which seemed from hour to hour to come a little nearer, and flashes of distant gunfire flickered in the night sky. Back there the rear-guards were still fighting, and brave men were dying to give us time to get away. It seemed just then that their sacrifice might be in vain. What a haul the Austrians would have here!

And behind and around us burning villages were still flaming in the dark, and throwing up the sharp black outlines of the trees.

****

Afterwards I heard of some of the deeds that had been done "back there." I heard of the charges of the Italian Cavalry, of the Novara Lancers and the Genoa Dragoons, crack regiments, full of the best horsemen in Italy, who had been waiting, waiting, all the war through, for their chance to come. Their chance had come at last, the chance to die, charging against overwhelming odds, in order that Italy, or at least the glory of her name, might live for ever. One commanding officer called all his officers around him and said, "The common people of Italy have betrayed our country's honour, and now we, the gentlemen of Italy, are going to save it!" and then he led the charge, and fell leading it. It was a fine, aristocratic gesture, though the prejudices of his class partly blinded him.

Near Cervignano Italian Cavalry charged the massed machine guns of the enemy and, when the horses went down, the men went on, and then the men went down, all but a few, and those few for a moment broke the line and held up the advance, and gave to the mass of the retreating troops just that little space of extra time, which spans the gulf between escape and destruction.

And away up north on Monte Nero, left behind when the rest of the Army retired, Alpini and Bersaglieri resisted for many days, and aeroplanes flew back and dropped food and ammunition from the skies for them. And when their ammunition was all shot away, that garrison came down into the plains, and a few survivors fought their way through with bombs and bayonets back to the Italian lines.

And many other such deeds were surely done that will never be known, because the men that did them died out of sight of any of their comrades who survived.

****

In the small hours of the 30th of October, I left our guns in Leary's charge and determined to walk on to Latisana, to see if I could not find some person in authority and get something done to move things on. I had only gone a little way when I met Bixio, a Captain of Mountain Artillery, attached to Raven's Headquarters. He had come back to see how far behind our rearmost guns were. I saw him several times during the retreat. He did fine work more than once in creating order out of confusion. He looked a magnificent, almost a Mephistophelian, figure, with his dark features, his flashing angry eyes, his air of decision, his sharp gestures, his tall body enveloped in a loose cloak, his Alpino hat, with its long single feather. He told me that all traffic along this road into Latisana had been stopped for the past three hours, in order to let traffic from the north get on, for it was from that direction that the advance of the enemy was most threatening.

I walked on and found a British Red Cross Ambulance stuck in the block. I talked for a few moments to the driver, who gave me a piece of cake and some wine. When I reached Latisana, I found traffic pouring through along the road from the north. I crossed the bridge over the Tagliamento and looked down at the broad swift current, glistening beneath. Hope leapt again within me at the sight. Here, at last, I said to myself, is a fine natural obstacle. We shall turn here and stand at bay, and the invader will come no further.

I had been told that there were some huts on the right hand side, just over the bridge, where our men would be, where the A.S.C. would have delivered rations and the Staff had fixed a rendezvous. I, therefore, expected to find the Major and our dismounted party, or at least someone from another Battery, or some of either Raven's or the General's Staff. But there was nothing there; no British troops, no rations, and no Staff! Only the never ending rain, and a confused stream of Italian troops, chiefly Field Guns, hurrying across the bridge.

There was nothing to do but to go back. The sentries on the bridge tried to stop me, but I insisted that I must see some Artillery officer in authority. They directed me to the Square, where I found Colonel Canale, controlling the movements of Batteries, looking straight before him out of uncomprehending, heavy eyes, like one crushed under a weight of bitter humiliation. He asked where our guns were. I told him they were getting near now, but stuck fast in the traffic. He said it was forbidden to let through traffic on that road at present, but he would do what he could. I asked if there were any new orders. "No," he said, "only forward across the bridge, and then push on as fast as possible to Portogruaro." I left him, and found three of our stragglers from the Major's party, asleep on the floor of a forge. I told them to cross the river and wait on the Portogruaro road for myself and the guns. I asked an Italian Corporal if there was anywhere in Latisana where one could get a drink. He said he thought not, but gave me a bottle full of cold coffee, brandy and sugar in about equal proportions. It was a splendid drink, but a little too sweet.

I walked back along the road towards the guns. Some houses on the outskirts of the town were burning furiously. The traffic was beginning to move forward along our road, very slowly and with frequent halts. I had two overcoats with me when we started from Pec. Both were long ago wet through, and I was wearing over my shoulders at this time a blanket lent to me by Medola. This, too, was thoroughly drenched by now. In the fields on either side of the road Infantry were lying out in the rain, asleep, dreaming, perhaps, of Rome or Sicily or the Bay of Naples. The dawn of another day was breaking, cold, damp and miserable, symbolic of this great weary tragedy.

****

I had not gone far when I met four of our men carrying on a stretcher the dead body of the Battery Staff Sergeant Artificer. He had dropped asleep on one of the guns and, as the tractor moved on, he had fallen forward, head downwards, beneath the gun wheel, which had passed over him, along the whole length of his body, crushing him to death. They said he died before they could get him out. He was a good man and a very skilled worker, full of pluck and spirit. The last thing he had done for me was to get everything ready for rendering the guns unserviceable in case we should have to abandon them. There was no chance of decent burial for him here, but I had his body placed upon an empty trench cart, which was being towed by a lorry of another Battery, and put two of our men in charge of it. They buried him the next day or the day after in a cemetery near Portogruaro.

About 7 a.m., as I was still making my way back through the traffic towards our guns, it was reported that enemy cavalry patrols had been seen to the north of the road, and that shots had been exchanged. For a moment there was some panic and confusion, but a scheme of defence was quickly organised. No one had supposed that they could yet be so near. I found Bixio rallying some Infantrymen, with eloquent words and great gestures, and an Italian Infantry Major, calm and smiling, was putting out a screen of machine gunners and riflemen across the road itself and along a hedge five hundred yards to the north of it. All was in readiness for putting our guns completely out of action. There would be nothing else to do, if the enemy appeared, for we had no gun ammunition, and it was impossible to get on, until the whole traffic block in front of us had been shifted forward. But I told Bixio that I should do nothing to the guns, unless there was some evidence that the enemy was really approaching with a superiority of force over our own.

The enemy, however, did not at that time reappear and the best bit of hustling traffic management that I had yet witnessed during the retreat, now took place. The northern road was at last clear at Latisana, and the authorities turned their attention to us. A breakdown gang appeared and a number of new tractors and lorries with refills of petrol. Civilian carts whose drivers remained, were ordered to drive on, those which had been abandoned were overturned to one side into the ditches, and dead horses and wreckage due to bombing or the brief moments of panic were likewise thrust off the road. Relays of fresh drivers took over all the lorries and tractors which would still go. The rest went into the ditch on top of the dead horses and derelict carts. The heavier loads which single tractors had been pulling were split up between two or more. In a surprisingly short time the whole mass began to move.

Here I parted from Medola, who had been a very good friend to us. Our three guns got a new tractor to themselves and I got up beside the driver. And so at last we entered Latisana. Our new driver was immensely enthusiastic, but very excited. He told me that he had had two brothers killed in the war and had applied, when the retreat began, to be transferred from Mechanical Transport to the Infantry. That morning, he said, he had heard General Pettiti, who was our Army Corps Commander, give the order that all the British Batteries must first be got across the river and only then the Italian. I said that I saw no good reason for this preference, but that anyhow he was driving the last three British guns. This pleased him tremendously. By now I was wrapped up in a new and dry Italian blanket, which I had taken from an abandoned cart by the roadside.

Our tractor, less enthusiastic than its driver, broke down continually. It was rumoured that the bridge had been blown up already, and there were wild screams of despair from a crowd of women, who came running past us. At last we turned the last corner and came in sight of the Tagliamento. The bridge was still intact. Italian Generals were rushing to and fro, gesticulating, giving orders. General Pettiti sent a special orderly to ask me if mine were the last British guns. I told him yes. Our tractor broke down three times on the bridge itself. But at last we were over. One of our party had an Italian flag and waved it and cried *"Viva l'Italia!"* Not long after, the bridge went up, with an explosion that could be heard for miles around.

CHAPTER 23

From the Tagliamento to Treviso

I heard later that the Major and his party had reached Latisana the previous day. Winterton had joined them near Muzzano. They had marched for forty-eight hours practically without food and with only some three hours' rest in stray halts. They had been magnificent, but they were utterly done, and the Major, who had been most done of all, told me afterwards that it had made him cry to watch them hobbling along,—some of them men too old or of too low a medical category to have passed for the Infantry,—and to hear them singing:

What's the use of worrying?
It never was worth while.
So pack up your sorrows in your old kit bag,
And smile, smile, smile!

The spirit of the men in the retreat from Mons was not finer than the spirit of those men of ours.

At Latisana they got on board a train for Treviso. It was about the last train that was running.

****

My party, though they were longer on the road, were at least able to ride a great part of the way on the tractors and guns.

Once across the Tagliamento, our tractor not only continued to break down every few hundred yards, but also developed the unpleasant habit of catching fire. Twice we put the fire out with the squirts and chemicals provided for the purpose, and a third time with mud. I determined not to risk a fourth time, and so pulled on to the side of the road and halted. I sent on the Battery Sergeant Major on a passing lorry to Portogruaro with a note to the Major asking that another tractor might be sent back, and I also sent Avoglia to the nearest Italian Headquarters to see if he could raise a tractor there. We were halted at the top of a hill on the road running along the western bank of the river. We were indeed literally "across," but we should have provided a splendid target for enemy Artillery advancing on the further side. A good system of trenches ran alongside the road, and these were now manned in force by Italian Infantry. Field Guns also had come into position behind them. Our men took advantage of the enforced halt to collect fuel, light fires and make tea. We were still halted here at nightfall.

Soon after dark some Italians came up and told us that we were blocking the road, which was not true, as we were well to the side. However, as neither Avoglia nor the Sergeant Major had yet returned with a new tractor, and as the Italians said that they would pull us on, I cordially agreed to the attempt being made. They attached a tractor with a heavy lorry in tow to our inflammatory tractor and our three guns. They asked that an attempt should be made to start up our tractor also, but I succeeded in persuading them that this was inexpedient. They then started up their own tractor only. To my great surprise, we began to move. It was a magnificent machine, and forged ahead splendidly, contrary to all the laws limiting its capacity, rumbling and backfiring under the unwonted strain, for miles through the gloom.

Then the moon began to rise. The night, for the first time since the retreat began, was fine and clear. We could only go slowly and broke down now and then. But all went pretty well, until we swung our long train a little too sharply round a corner in the road, and the last two guns got ditched. While we were trying to get them out, a British Major, whom I will call Star, appeared on the scene. He came from Portogruaro

229

with the news that five new tractors were on their way back, and that some other British guns were ditched further ahead. I therefore thanked the officer in charge of the Italian tractor and lorry for all he had done for us and advised him now to go on and leave us, as our position was tiresome but no longer critical. This he did.

The moonlight was now bright as day, and one of Star's promised tractors arrived and finally succeeded in getting out our ditched guns.

****

Star had painted a bright picture of Portogruaro. All the British guns, he said, were parked together in the Piazza and there was a large granary close by, full of happy men with plenty of rations and straw. So, it seems, some imaginative person had told him. We reached Portogruaro in the small hours of the 31st of October. The moon had set and it was very dark. Several of us made a most careful search in the Piazza. But there were no British guns there, no granary, no straw, no rations. I halted the guns just outside the gate of the town and told the men to turn in and sleep. Soon after daybreak we all woke feeling very hungry. I issued practically all that remained of our rations, a little bully, a little biscuit and a very little tea.

Wanting a wash and, still more urgently, a shave, I went into a house and asked for the loan of some soap and a towel. A number of terrified old women gathered round me, in doubt whether to fly or to stay. I advised them to stay, for I took for granted at this time that the Tagliamento line would hold. They pressed upon me coffee and bread, and I heard them repeating over and over again to one another my assurances that the enemy was still far away and would never get as far as Portogruaro. It was hard not to cry.

Star arrived during the morning and took charge. There was no need, he said, to hurry on. We had better rest here for a day. He arranged for us all to draw rations from the Italian Comando di Tappa. Treviso was to be our next stopping place. We were disturbed a little during the morning by enemy planes dropping bombs on the town, but none fell very near us.

In the afternoon we moved on and parked our guns near the station along with those of the other British Batteries, which had arrived before us. Bombing raids continued and were more serious that afternoon than in the morning. One bomb fell on a house, which was full of men from one of the other Batteries, and caused a number of casualties. It was only by good luck that a number of my own men were not in that house at the time. Fortunately I had had words, as two tired men will, with one of the officers of the other Battery, about the joint use of the kitchen, and my men, when I asked them, had decided that they preferred, as always, to "run their own show" and not "pig in with other Batteries." To that attitude of independence some of them probably owe their lives.

In the afternoon Raven turned up, and said that he had arranged for us to go on to Treviso by train. We loaded our guns on to trucks, and waited several hours in the station yard for the promised train. It was cold and wet and more bombers came over us. They had bombed the station for the last three nights, I heard. But nothing hit it while we were there. The train left at 9.30 p.m. Leary and another officer and I tried to share one wet blanket. We were too wet and cold to sleep. I walked up and down the carriage trying to get warm. They bombed the railway several times during our journey, and once, when a bomb fell near our train, there was a rumour that the engine driver had gone away and left us standing. But it was quite untrue. We crawled along, with many stops. It seemed a quite interminable journey. But at 8 o'clock next morning, the 1st of November, we came to Treviso.

Chapter 24

Thoughts After the Disaster

We hung about for a while in the station, nobody knowing what was to happen next. Then Leary and I went off to try to find some food. We had been living just lately on ration biscuits and a tin of Australian peach jam. There was not much left at the Buffet, where we found Bixio, but we got a little salami and some eels and wine and coffee. Meanwhile our train had gone on to Mestre, owing to a mistake between two railway officials, and had to return next day. Leary's feet were so bad that he could hardly walk. I got them dressed for him by the Italian Red Cross, but he could walk no better afterwards. The Villa Passi, the British Headquarters, was several miles off. An enemy plane came over and bombed Treviso, when we were in the station square, trying in vain to find a conveyance. But none of the bombs fell very close to us. At last we hailed a British lorry, which took us to Villa Passi, and then on to Carbonera, where odds and ends of Batteries had been turning up for several days past. The Major was very delighted to see us, a rumour having got about that we and the last guns had been left on the wrong side of the Tagliamento, when the bridge went up. He had almost given up hope of seeing us again.

Then I went to bed and slept for hours and hours. Next morning from my window I could see the Alps lying very low on the horizon, like a ball of fluffy snow. The sun was shining and a fountain was playing in the garden. I could hardly realise that we had reached, for a moment at least, a place of peace, where there was no more fighting or retreating. Our men were worn out, most of them, and slept like logs. They had been sorely tried. Their pluck and endurance had been splendid. But they got no message of thanks or praise from the British General who at that time nominally commanded us. This distinguished man I had last seen in the Square at Palmanova, amid the smoke and flames, with his car standing close at hand ready to push off, and he had arrived at Treviso in good time. He was now comfortably installed at the Villa Passi, and the day some of our footsore men limped into Treviso, he was lunching with his Staff, all bright and polished and sleek, in the Hotel Stella d'Oro.

We all expected, for days, that he would call a parade and address the men who had saved what he used to call "his guns," or at least that he would send some message. But he made no sign, except to open a canteen for the sale of the 20,000 cigarettes, which some intelligent subordinate had saved in preference to valuable gun stores now in Austrian hands.

****

The day after my arrival I read a newspaper for the first time for over a week, but the news was very bad and the retreat still continuing. The Austrians were across the Tagliamento in strong force at several points. I tried to reason and make distinctions, but my brain was still too tired to answer the helm, so I left it. We ate hot *polenta* and drank wonderful coffee, having established our Battery Mess in the porter's lodge at the entrance to the Villa Lebreton, and persuaded the porter's wife to cook for us. All the Battery had discovered the *polenta* at the porter's lodge and our men crowded the kitchen at all hours of the day. We all appreciated good food after the short rations of the retreat.

Conversation was intensely depressing when not utterly trivial. I remember walking round and round the vegetable garden at the back of the Villa with an Italian friend of mine, trying both to face the facts and to draw some comfort from them. It was an impossible task. My friend was full of despair and bitterness.

"The fruits of thirty months of war all lost in two days," he said, "and much more lost besides! What will all the mothers think, who have lost sons on San Michele and Monte Santo? It is a common thing in Italy now for families to have lost four or five sons. What will the mothers of Italy think of this? Would not any of them be justified in shooting Cadorna? The Third Army should not have been ordered to retire. They should have counter-attacked instead. But now would it not be better to make peace at once? Is there no man who will rise up and say, 'Stop, stop, stop this bloody business now, before it gets any worse?' Some of our soldiers looked quite pleased to be retreating. Poor children! They thought the war was over and they were going home. There is a frightful danger that the leaders,—the generals and the politicians at Rome,—will say 'fight on!' but the rank and file will go on breaking. 'We are fighting for Trento and Trieste!' they used to say, and now they say 'we are organising the defence of the Piave line!' The Regular soldiers never want the war to end. And soon they will be distributing medals for the retreat. Medals!"

I could find no words worth saying to him in reply.

"What will they be saying about us now in London and Paris?" he went on. "They will be saying,"

I replied, "that help must be sent to you," but my answer I know sounded flat and empty.

"Yes," he said bitterly, "perhaps *now* you will send some of your generals and your troops to Italy. And so you will put us under orders and under obligations to you, and we shall become your slaves. Italians are used to being looked upon as the slaves of other nations."

"No," I said, "all that is over. Those of us who know the facts, know what Italy has done and suffered for the Alliance in this war. It will not be forgotten. Moments of supreme cri-

234

sis such as this test the value and the depth of an Alliance. And ours will stand the test."

But that day he was inconsolable. For Italy was wounded and bleeding, and the dramatic swiftness and horror of the disaster had bent her pride and almost broken it. But, though the future seemed black as a night without stars, the hope of a coming daybreak remained strong in the hearts of a few. But the struggle ahead would be cruelly hard. What had Italy left to offer those who would still fight in her defence? Still, as of old:

Only her bosom to die on,
Only her heart for a home,
And a name with her children to be,
From Calabrian to Adrian Sea,
Mother of cities made free.

Yet this was a rich reward when, a year later, the dawn broke in all its glory.

****

I turned over and over in my mind in the weeks and months that followed, as fresh evidence accumulated, the meaning and the causes of the disaster of Caporetto, and gradually I came to definite and clear cut conclusions. It was the Second Army that had been broken, and in the course of the retreat had almost disappeared. It was a common thing to hear the Second Army spoken of as a whole Army of cowards and "defeatists." Many foreign critics, with minds blankly ignorant of nearly all the facts, seemed to think that the whole business could be accounted for by a few glib phrases about German and Socialist propaganda, or the supposed lack of fighting qualities in the Italian race. Yet it was this same Second Army, which in those now distant days in August had conquered the Bainsizza Plateau, amid the acclamations of all the Allied world. Whole Armies do not change their nature in a night, even when worn out with fighting and heavy casualties. The thing was not so simple as that.

****

In fixing responsibility for Caporetto, one must draw a sharp distinction between responsibility for the original break in a narrow sector of the line, and responsibility for not making good that break, before the situation had got hopelessly out of hand. In the former case the responsibility must rest partly upon the troops and subordinate Staff charged with holding that narrow sector and partly upon the High Command; in the latter case the chief responsibility, and a far graver one, must rest upon the dispositions of the High Command. This was the view apparently taken by the Commission appointed by the Italian Government to investigate the whole question, for the three chief Generals concerned were not only removed from their commands, but given no further employment and placed upon half-pay.

The original break was due to many causes. The great mass of German Divisions and Artillery was concentrated in the Caporetto sector. This fact should have been known to the High Command, and if the Italian troops holding the line at this point were, for various reasons, of poor quality, this also should have been known to the High Command, whose duty it is to know the comparative fighting power of different units. The High Command, when the battle started, claimed that they had known beforehand when and where the blow was coming, that all preparations had been made and that they were fully confident of the result. Such boasts have been made by other High Commands on other Fronts, on the eve of other disasters, and even after them. They greatly deepen the responsibility of those who make them.

The German Batteries on the Italian Front had a much larger supply of ammunition than the Austrians, including a large quantity of "special gas" shell. Many Italian troops, both Infantry and Artillery, subjected to prolonged gas bombardment, found the gas masks provided by the High Command quite inadequate. It was left for General Diaz some months later to order the equipment of the whole Italian Army with the British box respirator.

The number of guns lost by the Second Army was very great. I am told that one reason for this was the fact that the High Command had for some weeks been preparing a further big offensive against the Plateau of Ternova, had concentrated an abnormal number of Batteries on the Second Army Front, and had pushed the majority of the guns much further up than would have been justified, if an enemy offensive had been expected. Then, having made these preparations, the High Command hesitated and began to change its mind. But the disposition of the forward Batteries, thoroughly unsound for defensive purposes, was not appreciably altered, and a quite small enemy advance sufficed to make enormous captures of guns.

When the attack developed, some of the troops in the Caporetto sector unquestionably turned and ran, as troops of every great Army in this war have at times turned and run, under conditions of greater or less provocation. Then the High Command apparently lost its head, and attempted to issue to the world a communiqué of a character unparalleled in the history of this war, naming and cursing, as traitors to their country, certain particular Infantry Brigades. This document was very properly suppressed by the Italian Government.

But where were the reserves which the High Command should have had ready to repair the broken line? And where were the plans for retreating to prepared positions only a short distance behind? It was well known, and indeed it used to be another boast of the High Command, that a local reverse would be of no great importance, seeing that there were no less than twelve prepared lines between the Front, as it then ran, and Udine. I have seen some of those lines with my own eyes. I know what great and patient labour went to the making of them, and I know how strong they were. But, when the moment came to make use of them, no one outside the charmed circle of the High Command was in possession of the plans for their defence, and for falling back upon them in an orderly and systematic manner. It has been said that these plans could not have been made known before-hand to the Subordinate Commands for fear they should fall into the hands of spies. That would have been a small misfortune compared to what actually befell.[1]

When, owing to the omissions of the High Command, the break in the line was swiftly widened and the whole defensive scheme of the Second Army collapsed, it is true that confusion and panic began to spread through the Second Army like fire through dry grass. But it is not within the power of common soldiers, and especially of simple unlettered peasantry, such as most of these soldiers were, to repair the blunders of bad Staff work, and to make for themselves, on the spur of the moment and in face of deadly peril, plans which trained brains should have elaborated long before, at leisure and in safe secluded places. When leadership fails, the best troops fail too. But let one who comes of a nation, none of whose troops have ever acted as those troops of the Italian Second Army acted in those dreadful days, throw the first stone at Italy. That nation will be hard to find. It is not of this world. Those who know the Italian soldier know that no soldier in the world responds more readily to loyal trust, to common kindliness and to efficient and inspiring leadership. British and French officers, who have had opportunities of judging, know this as well as Italians. But the Italian High Command denied these things to the Italian soldier.[2] It is due to him and to the good name

---

1: In fairness to General Capello, the Second Army Commander, who had been highly and deservedly praised for the Bainsizza victory in August, and who was one of the generals removed from his command after Caporetto, it should be stated that on the latter occasion he was away from the Front on leave.

2: Among other charges which may be brought against the High Command at this time are, first, their failure to make adequate provision for the amusement and relaxation of the troops when in rest, such as the Y.M.C.A. and various concert parties provided for British troops, to combat inevitable war-weariness; second, failure to increase the most inadequate scale of rations; and, third, the attempt to apply, with strange disregard of the very different spirit of the Italian people, some of the worst and most brutal traditions of German of Italy, which has been damnably traduced by prejudiced and ignorant men, that the truth should be spoken.

The dark and tragic story of the Italian retreat is lit up by many deeds of heroism, wherein the Italian soldier showed all his accustomed valour. And it was only by the valour of the Italian soldier that the retreat was stayed on the Piave line, which the High Command pronounced to be untenable and wished to abandon, but which the Cabinet at Rome, pinning their faith to the qualities of the Italian soldier rather than to the opinions of the High Command, ordered to be held at all hazards. And the Cabinet at Rome was right. The Italian line stiffened and stood upon the Piave, while the Allied reinforcements were still on the further side of the Alps. If only Lloyd George and Bissolati had had their way, and these reinforcements had been sent a few months earlier, if only we had been able to put a British Army Corps, with its full complement of aircraft, guns and shells, against the Hermada, if only we had had half a dozen tanks to send down the Vippacco Valley, what a different story there would have been to tell!

****

We ourselves were out of the first stages of that great defence. We had no ammunition, and we were terribly short of gun stores, though the bare guns had all been saved. And our men were very short of steel helmets and box respirators, and the boots and clothing of many were in a pitiful condition. But a small supply of ammunition came through from France, and it was decided to send one Section of the Battery into action on the Piave and the remainder back to Ferrara to refit. All gun stores and men's equipment were to be pooled, and those going back were to be stripped for the benefit of those going forward. I remember very vividly our Battery parade on the morning of the 4th of November, when we had to take from some men their greatcoats and even their caps, tunics and boots, in order to make up some sort of equipment for the Right Section which was going forward with the Major. I was put in command of the Left Section, stripped bare for its journey to Ferrara.

The evening before our departure I walked up and down the avenue outside our Villa and talked with Venosta, who had done splendid work in the retreat. He had heard from the survivors of a Cavalry Regiment, who had passed back along the road an hour before, that a Turkish Division was in Udine, and Turkish cavalry in Palmanova. Bulgarians also were said to be on this Front, raping, after Serbs, Greeks and Rumanians, Italians also. It was said that Turks had been on Faiti and Volconiac at the end. I had no sure evidence of this, but, if it was true, the Turks' notorious incapacity for an offensive would help to explain our surprising escape. What we had needed, all through the days of the retreat, was enough rain to swell the rivers and make heavy the roads. What we had got, after the first three days, was brilliant sunshine. The stars in their courses seemed to be fighting against Italy.

"Dio uno ed unno!" said one Italian bitterly.

CHAPTER 25

Ferrara, Arquata and
the Cornice Road

We reached Ferrara at 5 a.m. and drove in lorries from the railway station past the Castello of the d'Estes to the Palestro Barracks, the depot of the 14th Regiment of Italian Field Artillery. Here we were to be lodged by the Italian military authorities.

We were received with every consideration and great hospitality. Our men had excellent quarters in the Barracks. Our officers were invited to have their meals in the Italian Artillery officers' Mess, which was a large and comfortable place and where the food was not only good, but very much cheaper than could have been got outside. The Colonel also offered to put riding horses at the disposal of any of us who should care to ride. I was much struck by the sensible lack of ceremony of this Italian Mess, by comparison with similar Depot Messes in our own Army.

There was no waiting in the anteroom for senior officers who were late, no asking permission of senior officers to leave the table early. Within the hours fixed for meals everyone came in and out as they pleased. There was no special table for the Staff, no rule against bringing evening papers into dinner, no aloofness, no pomposity. The only un-English formalities were the habit of turning and bowing as one left the Mess, if a number of officers were still present, and the universal Italian custom by which a newcomer at his first appearance would walk round and shake hands in turn with all those whom he did not know and introduce himself to them by name.

We were also invited to become members during our stay of the Circolo Negozianti, or Merchants' Club, of Ferrara. This Club had spacious premises in an old Palazzo, and was the warmest place in the town, having a most efficient system of central heating.

Ferrara is spread over a large area relatively to its population; it has broad streets and very few slums. But it has come down in the world since the Renaissance. Degenerate descendants of the d'Estes of that time stripped many of the Palazzi of their artistic beauties and sold them to help pay their debts. Ferrara is a city of old Palazzi, street after street of them, inhabited mainly now by well-to-do peasants, who take a pride in keeping up their exteriors. One of the most interesting sights in the city is the Palazzo Schifanoia, now used as a museum and containing frescoes by Cossa and Cosimo Tura. But what most appealed to me was the superb western façade of the Cathedral.

In peace time Ferrara is prosperous, though a little isolated from the main currents of Italian life. It is the chief centre of food distribution for this part of the country, and is well known for its bakeries. It is also an important centre for the hemp export trade.

After two days at Ferrara I was chosen to go to Arquata Scrivia, a little town on the main line north of Genoa. This had been selected as the Base for the British Forces in Italy, and I was to get in touch with the Ordnance people there, to give them a list of our really urgent requirements and try to hasten their delivery, so as to get us back into action as soon as possible. Siramo, an Italian Artillery officer who was attached to us for *liaison*, accompanied me.

The ordinary passenger train for Bologna was three and a half hours late. Special trains were coming through every ten minutes from Treviso and Venice packed with refugees, going southwards. The organisation of the Italian railways at this time for clearing the refugees from the righting zone was exceedingly good. Siramo thought that, if Venice had to be abandoned, the Germans and Austrians would not damage it. I felt no such security. That night we stopped at Milan. Wild stories of *tradimento* were in the air. It was being said, for instance, that two Generals of the Second Army had been marched through their troops in handcuffs under a guard of Carabinieri. It was also officially announced that Diaz had replaced Cadorna in command of the Italian Armies.

Next day we reached Arquata amid the tumble of the Ligurian Hills, whose sides were clothed with chestnuts and oaks and vine terraces. We found British Staff, Sanitary Sections and Ordnance already in possession. The Ordnance were occupying a large villa just outside the town. My old friend Shield, whom I had known at Palmanova, was there, but most of the others were new arrivals from France. They were surprisingly full of cheerfulness, as *imboscati* are often apt to be, even when things are going badly at the Front. The Italian disaster evidently meant very little to them; they hardly realised it at all. They were the first cheerful people I had seen since the retreat began, and it was no doubt good for Siramo and myself to be cheered up. But it grated on both of us a little.

At my first interview I got the impression that the Ordnance were surprisingly efficient and would be very prompt in giving us what we wanted. But I gradually discovered that they really possessed very little of what they first promised me, and that nothing was known for certain as to when further stores would arrive. I telephoned to Ferrara that the immediate prospects were poor, and was told in reply to wait three or four days and see how much turned up. Having pestered various Ordnance officers to the limit of their endurance, I therefore decided to go away for two days.

Siramo went for two days to his family at Turin and I took the train to Genoa, arriving in the early afternoon. After lunch I set out to walk eastwards along the Cornice Road. It was a relief to my thoughts and feelings to be quite alone. The day was windy and sunless and rather cold, but the warm and audacious colouring of the Villas and the little fishing villages seemed almost to draw sunshine out of the dull sky. I stopped at Sturla and drank two cups of coffee and ate some biscuits, and decided to walk on to Nervi. It was now near the hour of sunset and the sun, having kept invisible all day, half broke through the clouds, turning them first red and then golden. So the sky was when I came to Quarto dei Mille, with its monument looking out to sea, that historic place whence Garibaldi and the Thousand set sail for their great adventure, the liberation of Sicily and Naples, and the unification of Italy, with British warships following them, some say by chance, so that the enemies of Italy dared not interrupt their passage.

Then said I to myself, standing all alone at Quarto, "Italy will not be defeated, nor even mainly saved from defeat by foreign aid. The strongest and best of her children will pull her through, even though they be not all the nation. But the rest will do their share also, and will follow, when the bravest lead. How young, and how uncertain of herself as yet, is Italy! And yet, how lovable, how well worth serving!" The Germans with their "special gas" and with other factors in their favour, counted on breaking, not only the line of the Second Army, but the morale of the Italian people. For a moment they seemed to have succeeded. In the darkest days I talked with many whose stuffing seemed all gone. But then, with the promise of Allied help, with the sight of even a handful of new French and British uniforms, and under the spell of the oratory of their statesmen and their journalists, things began to change and Italian hearts grew brave again.

The Italians are a mercurial people. If they are more easily cast down by defeat than we British, they are more easily encouraged by even the distant prospect of victory, and they react to influences that would leave us unmoved. The coarse insults of the enemy press were everywhere angrily quoted, and the national spirit rose to a red glow of passion. The Socialists Turati and Treves,—the latter the author of the famous

phrase, *"nessuno in trincee quest' inverno,"*[1]—who before Caporetto had criticised the war as aggressive, imperialist and unnecessary, said now that all Italians must unite and fight on to
drive back the invader from Italian soil. And cool brains, such
as Nitti and Einaudi, reinforced all this with logical demonstrations of the economic impossibility of a separate peace,
with the enemy Powers strained to the utmost by the block-
ade and Italy dependent on the Allies for shipping, food and
coal. The Germans would have done far more wisely, if, instead of attacking, they had aimed only at holding the Italian
Army along its old line.

I walked on from Quarto to Nervi and, as it was getting
dark, I decided to take a tram for the last few kilometres. But all
the trams were standing still, the current having been switched
off for several hours. So I stood on the step of a tram and talked
to the conductor about the war, and tried to cheer him up by
telling him that the Germans were on their last legs, and were
making their last great effort, and that the Allies had only to
hold together a little longer, and throw sufficient force against
the enemy here in Italy, in order to see a far bigger and more
precipitate and disastrous retreat than Caporetto, and next time
in the other direction. All this I not only said, but firmly believed (and it all came true within a year). At first he was very
despondent, but he warmed up as I proceeded, and began to
gesticulate again and regain animation and compliment me
on my Italian. And then the current also was restored, and the
tram moved on, and we came to Nervi, where I dined well and
slept at the Albergo Cristoforo Colombo. I am not in general
an admirer of palm trees, but they are sometimes impressive
in the dusk, towering over one's head, as they do at Nervi, in
the long mixed avenue of palms and orange trees which leads
down to the station from the town.

Next morning I got up early and walked back towards
Genoa along the Via Marina. The sun was shining on the sea

1: "No one in the trenches this winter."

and the dark rocks, the stone pines and the great aloes and the brightly coloured villas. There was an exhilaration in the air and I was in the midst of beauty, and, for the first time for many days, I was for a little while really happy. Later on I took a tram back to Genoa, and walked up to the tall lighthouse on the further side of the town, and looked westward at the great curve of the shore, beyond the breakwater and the sands.

In some of the stations along the line were placards, "Long live great old England," "Welcome to the valiant British Army," *"Vive la France,"* *"Vive la victorieuse Armée de Verdun."* The first of the Allied reinforcements were arriving.

At Arquata station I met an advance party of the Northumberland Fusiliers. They told me that they had been quite moved by their wonderful welcome on the way through Italy and by all the hospitality shown to their officers and men at the stations where they had stopped. It gave me a queer thrill to see British Infantrymen again after many months, and this time on Italian soil.

****

After various orders and counter-orders I left Arquata for Ferrara on the 16th, with two truckloads of stores. But this was only a very small proportion of the minimum which we required.

CHAPTER 26

Refitting at Ferrara

I got back to Ferrara on the evening of November 17th, and shared a bedroom with Jeune, who had returned from leave in England, having missed all our most unpleasant experiences. Our brother officers of the Italian Field Artillery were very hospitable and courteous to us through those weeks of waiting. We could do nothing till the Ordnance sent us gun stores from Arquata, and these dribbled in very slowly, a few odds and ends at a time.

I often went out riding on the Piazza d'Arme and along the ramparts and in the country round Ferrara with Italian officers. Days were still very anxious, and the news from the Front not always good, and one rather avoided talking about the war. But one evening at dinner I succeeded in piercing the polite reserve of a little Captain who was sitting next to me.

"Italy should have made it a condition of her intervention," he said, "that the other Allies should have sent troops to the Italian Front. Also more guns and war material. Italy, at the beginning of her war, had many heroes but few guns. The other Allies, equally with Italy, are without statesmen. Your Lloyd George is energetic, but——! The British are not really at war with Austria. They have soft sentiments towards her and don't want her to lose too much. The Jugo-Slav propaganda was at its height, and was being encouraged in Paris and London, at the very moment when Italy was being pressed by the French and British to enter the war.

"We have made too many offensives on our own, unaided. Cadorna should have refused, but he went on and on. He sacrificed thousands of lives uselessly. He demanded too much of his troops. He did not understand them. This last disaster was caused by Croats and Bulgarians, who spoke Italian perfectly, having lived among us and taken degrees at our Universities, getting through our lines in the first confusion, dressed in Italian uniform, and sending false telephone messages and signals in our own cipher, ordering a general retreat.[1] It was men from ——,[2] who first ran away at Rombon and Tolmino. It has been often proved in the history of our country that those men have no courage. Italians have too little unity."

He went on to speak of economic difficulties.

"Italy is poor," he said, "and the Allies are rich. Yet coal costs four times as much in Italy as in France, and shipping is hardly to be had. Our Government has never driven hard enough bargains with the other Allies. After all, Italy came into the war as a volunteer, and not under the conscription of old treaties. But the Allies give her no credit for this. The French, since the war began, have recovered all their old *blague*. They talk incessantly of what they have done, and despise everyone else. But look how unstable they are politically! They change their ministries, as often as some men change their mistresses. The Pope, too, is an enemy of Italy and a friend of Austria. He aims at the restoration of his temporal power. Many of the priests went about, both before and after Caporetto, trying to betray their country. Some told the soldiers that God had sent the disaster of Caporetto to show them the folly and the sinfulness of loving their corruptible country here below in poor earthly Italy, better than the incorruptible country of all good Catholics, God's eternal kingdom in the skies!"

1: I heard this story many times and I believe this was one of the causes of the rapid increase of the first confusion. The Austrians had tried this trick without success against the Third Army on the Carso, as had the Germans against us in France. There must obviously be a certain amount of confusion already existing, if the trick is to have any chance of succeeding.

2: A certain province in Italy, not his own.

He spoke bitterly, as was not unnatural.

I made the acquaintance also in the Mess of a Medical Officer, named Rossi, in peace time a University Professor of Nervous Pathology, who was now in charge of a hospital for *nervosi*, or shell-shock cases, four miles outside the town. One afternoon Jeune and I accepted an invitation to visit this hospital. We drove out to it in a *carrozza*, accompanied by Rossi and a young woman, who went there daily to teach some of the illiterate patients to read and write.

No one can begin to understand what modern war means without some personal acquaintance with shell-shock cases. They are, especially for non-combatants, the most instructive of all the fruits of war, much more instructive than dead bodies or men without limbs. And then, having watched and talked or tried to talk with a variety of these still living creatures, let any man, even a profiteer or a theologian, look into his heart and ask himself whether he really agrees with the Chaplain, whom I have already quoted, that "three or four years of war may be tremendously worth while."

It needs a greater pen than mine to do justice to all we saw that afternoon, for we went through all the wards and saw all the sights there were to see. We saw a young Lieutenant, with large staring eyes, sitting up in bed. When we approached him, he jumped round in his bed very violently, as though his body had been shot out of a gun, and went on staring at us, speechless and with eyes full of wild terror. We saw two soldiers in the corner of a ward, their heads wobbling in perfect rhythm, ceaselessly from side to side, like the pendulum of a clock, with dead expressionless faces.

We saw men cowering beneath their bed clothes, trembling with an endless terror. We saw a man who for months had quite lost his speech, and was now just able to whisper, almost inaudibly, "papa" and "mama," a middle-aged man with a beard. We saw a man with frightened eyes, like a child in a nightmare, with many of the outward signs of having been gassed, struggling for breath, gesticulating feebly, trying to ward off some imaginary blow. He had not been gassed, but wounded in the head. He was alone in a blue ward, where all our faces looked yellow. We saw a youth lying asleep, white as a sheet and with hardly any flesh left on his bones. He had been asleep for two months without ever waking.

We saw a splendid, tall, bearded man, a Cavalry Captain, with a deep voice and a firm handgrip, who could realise the present, but had forgotten all the past. We saw a multitude of minor "tremblers," and men undergoing electrical treatment for paralysis and stiffness of various limbs. One little man, another University Professor, who was almost paralysed in both legs, tried to advance to meet us and nearly fell forward on the ground at our feet.

I spoke also to a young man with a paralysed back and left arm. I said I hoped he would soon be better.

"Yes," he said, "I hope soon to go back to the Front."

For a moment I thought this was irony addressed to a countryman of Mr Lloyd George. But it wasn't. He really meant it. We went into the Convalescents' Mess. There were about twenty present, smiling and very gentle and quiet, like men who were not yet quite sure of the world. One elderly man, a Medical Captain, said to me, very softly, that it was a great pleasure to see visitors from the outside, "especially our Allies." At that moment I could easily have wept. Such sights as I had seen did not physically sicken, nor even much horrify, me. They just tautened all my nerves and made me feel that all my questions were impertinent, and all my good wishes flat and empty, and that I resembled a visitor to a Zoo.

On the way back to Ferrara we talked of literature and Rossi, basing himself chiefly on Wells and Kipling, said that the English, judged by their modern writers, seemed to be a race "logical, but a little isolated."

Two days later the Major and the Right Section of the Battery came to Ferrara, being replaced on the Piave by a section of another Battery. On the 1st of December British Infantry, belonging to the XIVth Corps, moved into the lines for the first time, taking over the Montello sector, to the south of the Italian Fourth Army. This sector was to be held by British troops for four months, but it is worth while again to emphasise the fact that nearly a month had now elapsed since the great Retreat had been brought to an end by the unaided effort of Italian troops. The situation now seemed well in hand, and a further break not at all likely.

There had been a striking scene in the Italian Chamber about this time, when the Prime Minister, Orlando, announced that high military opinion had been opposed to the holding of the Piave line, recommending a further retreat to the line of the Mincio, or the Adige, or even the Po, which would have involved the surrender of Venice, Padua, Vicenza and Verona. But the Cabinet at Rome had rejected these recommendations and ordered that the Piave line should be held at all costs, and the valour of the Italian common soldier had triumphed over the forebodings of the generals.

On the 8th, our re-equipment being at last complete, we were warned to join the XIth British Corps on the arrival of our transport. The end of our stay at Ferrara was now in sight, and our last days were full of partings. The Major told me how one morning a little old man, apparently an artisan, ran after him down the road and, speaking excellent French, said how fine the British soldiers looked, and how splendid the news of the capture of Jerusalem was, and then insisted on his going into a café and drinking a glass of vermouth with him and, on parting, held his hand for several moments, gazing into his eyes with a look of affection and pride.

On the 9th a little ceremony took place in the Artillery Mess, where the British officers presented a silver cup, suitably inscribed, to their brother officers of the Italian Artillery. There was a large gathering. My own Major, who was in command of British troops at Ferrara, made the presentation, and the Italian Commandant made an eloquent reply.

On the 10th I told the page boy at the Circolo that the future of the world was in the hands of himself and the rest of the young, and that they must see to it that there were no more wars. This speech made him open his big brown eyes a bit wider! I had often talked to this boy before, and he was, I think, rather interested in me, thinking me no doubt a queer and unusual sort of person. He used to steal moments to come and enter into conversation with me when none of the older club servants were in sight. If any of them appeared in the distance, he used to pretend that I had called him for the purpose of ordering a drink, and bolt to the bar.

On the 11th another presentation ceremony took place, this time at the Circolo. Those of us who had enjoyed honorary membership here presented to the Club two small silver clocks. The Major again made a short speech and the President of the Club replied, expressing the hope that the hours might be short, which these clocks would record before the hour of final victory. The cordiality of all the members of the Club at this meeting was very memorable. One old gentleman of 76 years of age told me that I was the very image of his son who was serving at the front in the Artillery, and with tears in his eyes kissed me on both cheeks. "Permit this sign of affection," he said, "seeing that here we are in the midst of friends."

That afternoon a few of us had tea for the last time at Finzi's, a favourite haunt of mine between the Castello and the Cathedral. After I had said a few words of farewell, Signor Finzi said to me, in one of those perfectly turned compliments which Italians always pay to foreigners endeavouring to speak their language, *"Lei parla la lingua di Dante,"*[1] and Signora Finzi gave to each of us a small Italian flag.

That night our transport arrived, and our departure was fixed for the following morning. The 12th of December was a day that I shall vividly remember for the rest of my life. We left Ferrara about 1 p.m. after one of the most enthusiastic demonstrations I have ever seen. That morning the town had been placarded far and wide with the following poster:

1: "You speak the language of Dante."

252

Comitato di Preparazione Civile.[1]

Cittadini,

Stamane alle ore undici e trenta (11.30) gli Artiglieri inglesi muoveranno dal Quartiere Palestro diretti alia Stazione Ferroviaria. Essi partono verso il fronte, per difendere cogli eroici soldati d'Italia e di Francia il conteso e sacro suolo della patria, per combattere la barbaria tedesca, che tenta invano di avanzare contro il baluardo offerto dai petti dei soldati di tre nazioni.

Cittadini,

Vi invitiamo ad accorrere ed a portare il vostro saluto ai fedeli e valorosi Alleati. Essi debbono sentire che i vostri cuori palpitano, con loro, di speranza e di fede.

Ferrara. 11-12 Dicembre 1917, Il Presidente Avogli.

By eleven o'clock a large crowd was already gathering outside the Barracks. At half-past we marched out into the street. In front of us went the municipal brass band, gay with cocks' feathers, and school-children carrying four banners on long flagstaffs. There was tumultuous cheering and clapping from a dense crowd. Flowers were showered upon us, and a very handsome girl gave me a bouquet of red roses. The band played impossible march music, so that we weren't able to keep much of a step.

But the enthusiasm was intense. Spectators thronged all the windows overlooking our route, and the cheering

---

1: Committee of Civilian Preparation.
Fellow Citizens,
This morning at 11.30 a.m. the British Gunners will march out from the Palestro Barracks to the Railway Station. They are leaving for the Front, to defend alongside of the heroic soldiers of Italy and France the disputed and sacred soil of our country, and to combat the German barbarians, who strive in vain to advance against the rampart which is formed by the breasts of the soldiers of three nations.
Fellow Citizens,
We invite you to be present and to salute our brave and faithful Allies. They should be made to feel that your hearts, in unison with theirs, throb with hope and faith.

crowd stretched thick and unbroken along both sides of the street all the way. I noticed a specially enthusiastic group on the steps of the Castello, and several busy photographers. In between the efforts of the band our men sang. Outside the station we marched past the Italian General Commanding the District. Then we were halted and the General made a speech. I happened to look round, and found standing beside me, looking up at me, wide-eyed and wondering, the page boy from the Circolo, whom I had harangued on the destiny of the world's youth, and afterwards tipped. The band was playing over and over again, at short intervals, God Save the King, the Marcia Reale, the Marseillaise, the Brabançonne and the Marcia degli Alpini. Whenever any of these national anthems was played, all the troops stood at attention, and we officers at the salute.

Then a little man with a black beard and an eager manner stepped forward and mounted a chair, and on behalf of the Association of Italian Teachers wished us good luck. He spoke in English. He told us that his wife was "an Englishman," and recalled the names of Garibaldi and Gladstone, Palmerston and Cavour. He then presented to the Major an Italian Flag, which was handed to our Battery Sergeant-Major to be carried at the head of the troops as they marched into the station. Many Italian officers were present to say personal good-byes, and an immense crowd was on the platform cheering and singing, and distributing gifts and refreshments to our men.

One gift was a little piece of tricolour ribbon, which an old woman gave to one of us. It had a note pinned to it addressed "to a brave British soldier," saying that she had a son at the Front who always carried just such a little piece of ribbon as a talisman, cut off the same roll, and that it had always kept him safe, and that it would keep the British soldier safe too. The note was signed *"Tua Madrina"* ("your god-mother").

At last it seemed that everyone was aboard, and the train started. But it was then discovered that the Major, Jeune and

Manzoni had been left behind, not expecting the train to start so soon. They had chased it for a hundred yards down the line, but failed to catch it up. So the stationmaster telephoned to Rovigo to stop the train there till the three missing ones arrived, which they ultimately did, riding on an engine specially placed at their disposal. So ended our stay at Ferrara, in a blaze of wild enthusiasm. And I believe that, collectively, we left a very good impression behind us.

CHAPTER 27

In Strategic Reserve

Our train reached Cittadella shortly after dusk. We interviewed a British R.T.O., who had only taken up his duties five minutes' before our arrival, and so not unnaturally knew nothing about us. The Major proposed that the train should be put into a siding and that we should spend the night in it. This was done. We went into Cittadella, but found everything in complete darkness, most of the houses sandbagged, and all shops, cafés and inns closed at dusk by order of the military. We succeeded, however, in getting a meal of sorts, and then went back to the train and turned in early. We were woken up a little after midnight by two British Staff officers, who were very vague and ignorant, but told us to go next morning to San Martino di Lupari, a little village midway between Cittadella and Castelfranco. This we did and found pretty good billets. Monte Grappa loomed over us to the north, deep in snow. I did not go into Cittadella by daylight, but only saw its battlemented outer walls.

Then for a few days nothing happened, except that everyone seemed to have caught a cold. We were now part of the XIth British Corps, who were concentrated in the surrounding district and formed for the moment a strategic reserve, which might be sent anywhere according to the development of the situation. If nothing particular happened, we should probably go into the line south of the XIVth British Corps on the Piave. If, on the other hand, the Italians were driven back in the mountains to the north of us, or were forced to retire down the Brenta Valley,—and this danger had not yet quite passed,—we should move up the mountains and take over part of the Italian line, with the French probably on our right. We received tracings of several possible lines of defence, on the plain itself and on the near side of the mountain crest, described as the "Blue Line," the "Green Line," etc., which we were required to reconnoitre with a view to finding Battery positions and O.P.'s. They were all very awkward lines to defend, as the enemy would have splendid observation and we practically none at all.

On the 15th the Major went out in the car reconnoitring to the east. He met some Alpini on the road to whom he said, *"Fa bel tempo,"*[1] and they replied, *"Le montagne sono sempre belle;"*[2] also an old man who had never seen British soldiers before, and was tremendously excited and pleased, and shouted with joy.

On the 16th the Major went out again with Jeune and myself to look for Battery positions for the defence of the line at the foot of the mountains. We went through Cittadella and Bassano, then southwards along the Brenta to Nove, and then back through Marostica and Bassano. Bassano is a delightful old town, with many frescoes remaining on the outer walls of the houses, and a beautiful covered-in wooden bridge over the Brenta.

Marostica charmed me even more. Its battlemented walls are like those of Cittadella and Castelfranco, but in a better state of preservation and more picturesque, running up a rocky foothill behind the town and coming down again,—a most curious effect. These Alpine foothills for shape and vegetation are very like the Ligurian hills north of Genoa and round Arquata.

At San Trinità, just outside Bassano on the road to Marostica, is a very fine cypress avenue. There was a possible Battery

1: "It's beautiful weather."
2: "The mountains are always beautiful."

position here. I noticed also a row of cypresses standing at intervals of about fifty yards along a hillside, dark and tall amid a mass of grass and rocks and brown fallen leaves. The weather was clear and cold, but the snow had shrunk to subnormal on the foothills. The Weather God was still favouring the enemy. It was very still, though occasionally shells burst over the Grappa. But the hills muffle the sounds beyond them.

On the way back we passed a Battalion of Alpini marching up, many of them very young. I thought of the Duke of Aosta's latest message to the undefeated Third Army: *"A voi veterani del Carso, ed a voi, giovani soldati, fioritura della perenne primavera italica."*[1] Splendid Alpini! They are never false to their regimental motto, *"di qui non si passa!"*[2] They never fail. But nearly all the first Alpini, who went forth to battle in May 1915, are dead now.

On the 20th I went out in a side-car with Winterton to look for positions in the hills above Marostica. Reconnaissances of the back lines were now to be discontinued, a sign, we hoped, of diminishing apprehension and an improving military situation. At San Trinità on the way back we collided with an Italian wagon and had to stop for repairs. A number of Italians gathered round, one of whom I discovered to be a priest, conscribed to serve with the Medical Corps. I bantered this man in a friendly way about secret drinking and the confessional and women and paradise, causing uproarious delight among the bystanders. And the priest took it all in excellent part.

On the 22nd we heard that, irrespective of the movements of the rest of the Corps, a special Group of Heavy Artillery was to be formed, including ourselves, to be lent to the Italian Fourth Army in the mountains. There began to be rumours of an offensive on our part.

On the 23rd we made a reconnaissance up the mountains to look for positions. We started through Bassano, which the

---

1: "To you, veterans of the Carso, and to you, young soldiers, flower of the eternal Italian spring."
2: "No one passes here!"

Austrians had begun to shell the day before with long range guns, starting a trickling, pitiful exodus of terrified civilians. Just before reaching Marostica we struck up a valley running northwards past Vallonara. The road soon began to rise more steeply. It was a war road, broad and of splendid surface, one of those many achievements of the Italian Engineers, which entitles them to rank easily first among the engineers of the great European Armies.[1] Before the war this road had been in parts a mere mule track, in parts non-existent. We went through a number of little Alpine villages, Crosara, Tortima, Fontanelli, Rubbio. We had soon risen more than three thousand feet above the plain, which lay far beneath, spread out gloriously like a richly coloured carpet, green, white and brown, through which ran two broad, twisting, silver threads, the rivers Brenta and Astico. There had been more than a hundred bends in the road up to this point, but the gradient was never uncomfortably steep. Snow lay thick on the higher levels and the pine and fir trees were all snow-crowned. Sometimes the road ran along the edge of rocky gorges, dropping sheer for hundreds of feet below, with a great mountain wall on the other hand rising sheer above us. The air grew perceptibly colder as we mounted higher.

We turned out of view of the plain over undulating snow fields and down a long valley and came out on a small plateau, screened by a gradual ridge from the eyes of the enemy. Here we provisionally chose a Battery position close to a small solitary house, known as Casa Girardi, on the edge of a pine wood. All round Italian guns were firing in the snow. We went on to Col. d'Astiago, which would be our probable O.P. The summit

---

1: I have seen it stated, by an impartial authority, that there has been no roadmaking in war time to compare with that of the Italians on the Alpine and the Isonzo Fronts and in Albania, since the Napoleonic wars. A distinguished British engineer, with great experience of roadmaking in many countries, has also told me that in his opinion the Swedes are the best roadmakers in the world, the Italians a close second, and the rest of the world some way behind.

commanded a wonderful view of the high mountains to the northward, Longara and Fior, Columbara and Meletta di Gallio, and the sheer rock face of the Brenta gorge, and the stream far below, and the great mass of the Grappa rising beyond.

As we came down, lorry loads of Italian troops passed us going up, Alpini, Bersaglieri, Arditi and men of the 152nd Infantry Regiment. They cheered us wildly as they passed, waving their caps and crying, *"Avanti! Avanti! Viva l'Inghilterra! Viva gli Alleati!"* And as the string of lorries turned round and round the spiral curves of the road, now high above us, they were cheering and waving still, until they disappeared from view.

****

The Battery ate their Christmas dinner at San Martino, though the air had been thick with talk of an immediate move. On this, as on other, occasions the Major made an excellent speech, in the course of which he said:

> You will be going very soon into a place where, before this war, no one would have dreamed that Siege Artillery could go. You were the first British Battery to be in action in Italy, and you will probably be the first British Battery to be in action in the Alps. We shall be very uncomfortable, at any rate for a time, but we shall pull through all right, as we always have before. It will be an honour to be proud of, and an experience to remember for the rest of our lives. And I know that whatever happens to us in this coming year, you will all behave as splendidly in the future as you have always done in the past.

The enemy was doing a good deal of night bombing at this period. Treviso and Padua were attacked with great persistency, so much so that the British G.H.Q. decided to move from the latter city to some smaller and more peaceful place. We used to hear the bombing planes coming over nearly every night and explosions more or less distant. They bombed Bassano, Cittadella and Castelfranco, the latter especially because the French had their Headquarters there. But luckily they left San Martino alone, thinking it too small to worry about. There seemed to be no anti-aircraft defences anywhere. But our Air Force soon mitigated the nuisance by raiding their aerodromes, and brought down a number of hostile planes in air fighting.

Our Staff again brought themselves into notice at Christmas by altering our official address from "B.E.F. Italy" to "Italian Expeditionary Force." I heard that the distinguished General, who introduced this reform, estimated that it would hasten victory by several months. But the stupid soldiers and their stupid relatives at home, having got into the habit of using the abbreviation "B.E.F.," shortened the new address to "I.E.F.," and the stupid postal people began to send the letters to India! And then the distinguished General had to issue another order, pointing out that "this abbreviation is unauthorised" and that "this practice must cease."

In the midst of such excitements the New Year began, and the Major was awarded the D.S.O. for work on the Carso. He was as delighted as a child, and I too was very glad. This decoration, even more than most others, has been much too freely dished out during this war among quite undeserving people, who have simply made an art of playing up to their official superiors. The Major, however, had always been something of a thorn in the side of various Headquarters, and seldom hesitated to speak his mind both to, and of, Colonels and Generals and Staff officers generally. For this reason, and also for others, I consider that he deserved a D.S.O. a great deal more than many who received one.

CHAPTER 28

The First British Battery
Up the Mountains

The Major's words were soon to come true, after many of those delays and conflicting orders of which the victims of war time "Staff work" have profuse experience. On the 7th of January we moved up the mountains into the position previously selected near Casa Girardi. We were the first British Battery to go up. Two others and a Brigade Headquarters were to follow, when it had been seen how we got on. When in doubt, try it on the dog!

It began to snow as we came into Marostica, and we had great difficulty with the lorries even on gentle gradients. The roads were frozen hard and in places very slippery. We managed, however, to reach Casa Girardi before nightfall and found that our advance party had put up some wooden huts, and cut some trees for fuel. All that night the snow came down in clouds, but the next day, and the next few following, were very fine. The sun shone all day long from a cold, cloudless sky upon a waste of flashing snow, with here and there trees sticking out of it, and strange red morning lights in the sky behind it, and sweeping winds across it, and in the sunset the white hillsides slowly changed to a mauve pink. It was a scene of wonderful beauty. But the temperature was ten degrees below zero one day at noon, and the next day twenty-four below zero at 9 a.m. and nine above zero at noon.

These conditions were disconcerting to good shooting, the lower temperatures not having been contemplated by those who compiled our range table in England. But we got all four guns satisfactorily registered by the second day, to the evident pleasure of the Italian Colonel under whose command we were temporarily placed. This man had a somewhat ferocious appearance and a reputation for great rudeness, both to his superiors and his subordinates in the military hierarchy. It was said that, but for this, he would long ago have been a General. To us, however, he showed his politer side, patting the Major on the back and repeating several times *"buon sistema, buon sistema!"*

The physical discomfort of those early days was great, but we were full of buoyancy and health. Everything froze hard during the night, one's boots, one's clothing, if damp when taken off, the ink in one's fountain pen. In the morning water poured into a basin froze hard in a couple of minutes and the lather froze on one's face before one had time to shave. The Major, breaking through one of the most fundamental traditions of the British Army, announced that no one need shave more than once in three days. The morning after our arrival we had a discouraging breakfast. No fire could be got to burn and no tea had been made. There was nothing to eat except a few very hard ration biscuits and some eggs boiled hard the night before, and now frozen through and through. One cracked the shell and found icicles beneath, and miserably held fragments of egg in one's mouth until they thawed!

But gradually, by patient work and organisation, these early troubles were surmounted. The whole Battery had been provided with Italian greatcoats and other Italian mountain equipment,—white Alpine boots lined with fur, alpenstocks, spiked snow grips, which could be fastened on to one's boots like skates, and white clothing to put on over the top of everything else, to render us invisible against a snowy background. I used to hear some amusing comments in the Battery on our Alpine situation.

"This is the sort of thing you see pictures of in books, but...!"

"I suppose folks would pay quids in peace time to see this!"

"Why, it's like a blooming Cook's tour!"

Being the first of the British who had been seen in these parts, we were objects of great interest to the Italians, who used to collect in crowds to watch our guns firing. We became great friends with the members of a mixed Mess not far away, consisting of two Anti-aircraft Batteries and the personnel in charge of a large ammunition dump. Between this Mess and our own there were frequent exchanges of hospitality.

One day an Italian General's car skidded into a ditch close to our position. We supplied a party of men to get it out again and the General, thanking us, asked if there was anything we wanted. The Major told him that we should like two or three more huts and two good stoves for cooking. A few days later these were delivered by the Italian authorities. Our own Brigade Commander, who had now followed us up the mountains with his two other Batteries, noticed these things and asked how we had come by them. When we told him, he seemed displeased, and next day we got an official letter to inform us that: "it has come to notice that British units have in some cases recently been approaching the Italian authorities direct.... This practice is irregular and must cease.... Indents must be submitted through the proper channels." We smiled and obeyed. But we kept our huts and stoves which were better than any which we should have been likely to get "through the proper channels."

We were very short of water except snow water, there being only one water point for all troops within several miles. Here there was a long queue waiting most of the day. It is probably not generally known that it takes ten *dixies* full of snow, when melted down, to make one *dixie* full of water. For this and for hygienic reasons snow water was not much use to us. We were not at this time required to fire very much, but we were warned to get acquainted with the surrounding country, as an action of some importance might be coming off before long. This provided the occasion for several reconnaissances.

On January 15th the Major and I went up Monte Costahmga, a few miles to the west. It was a zigzag, scrambling track, and it was thawing enough to make everything rather unpleasant. But we gained some, useful new knowledge.

On the 24th, Jeune, together with an Italian officer, a telephonist and myself made a long day of it. Starting early, we were on the top of Costalunga about 9 o'clock, were given a guide by an Italian Field Battery on the summit and went on, along a mountain road commanding a magnificent view, to Cima Echar. Here was a good O.P. from which I got my first sight of Monte Sisemol and Asiago, of which part of the *campanile* was at that time still standing. But it was brought down by Italian shell fire very soon afterwards. I remember thinking that the whole Asiago Plateau should be easy to retake, if we only brought up enough guns. Later on I began to realise that it would not be as easy as it looked.

It was impossible to get telephonic communication with the Battery from Cima Echar, so we could not, as we had hoped, do from there some registrations on wire and trench junctions on Sisemol, which were among our allotted targets. We therefore went back to Costalunga, where the Italian Field and Mountain Batteries along the crest were firing away with great vigour, and after an excellent lunch, which had been hospitably prepared for us, went down again into the valley and walked several miles further west to Monte Tondo.

I noticed at lunch, as on several other occasions lately, a change in the Italian attitude to good weather. They no longer hoped that it would break and so prevent further Austrian offensives. They hoped it would continue and so permit offensives of their own. Their morale was rapidly rising. We had, indeed, received the previous day the artillery portion of an elaborate offensive plan, but no date had yet been fixed for it.

We climbed up Monte Tondo and down the other side and made our way to an O.P. in a front line trench. For fifty yards of the way there was a break in the trench line and we had to run across the open through knee-deep snow. But the Austrians didn't fire. From this O.P. we had again a fine view of Asiago and the country round it. After delays connected with the telephone, we succeeded in registering two targets. While we were firing, all the woods and houses grew rosy in the sunset. It was dark when we finished. We went back with a Major of the Pisa Brigade, a quiet, spare little man, of great energy and exhausting speed of movement. He gave us coffee and showed us maps at his Brigade Headquarters and then sent us on to the Regimental Headquarters, further down the hill, where they gave us rum punch, believing, as all Italians do, that an Englishman is never happy unless he is drinking alcohol. We got back to the Battery in the moonlight.

On January 27th the long expected action began, and our Brigade lost one of its best officers, who was hit in the head in the front line O.P. on Monte Tondo. His steel helmet and the skill of Italian doctors just saved his life, but he was permanently out of the war. The Italians put their best doctors right forward in the advanced dressing stations. All that day we bombarded enemy Batteries and cross roads and barbed wire. Next morning the Italian Infantry carried Col Valbella and Col d'Echele by assault. The day after they took also Col del Rosso, and beat back very heavy counter-attacks. The Sassari Brigade and a Brigade of Bersaglieri specially distinguished themselves. It was an important and useful success. It considerably improved our line between the Asiago Plateau and Val Brenta, it deprived the enemy of the secure use of the Val Frenzela, and it was the first offensive operation of any importance undertaken by the Italians since the great retreat. Its success went to prove that the Italian Army had been effectively reorganised, and that its morale was again high.

From my sleeping hut and from the Battery Command Post I used to hear for days afterwards the Italian Infantry singing in great choruses, far into the night. There was triumph in their songs, and there was ribaldry and there was longing. I thought I knew what dreams were in their hearts, and, if I was right, those dreams were also mine.

The advance left us a long way behind the new front line, and we expected to move our guns forward; indeed we selected and asked to be allowed to occupy a very good position behind Montagna Nuova. But this was not allowed, and we stayed where we were for another six weeks. It snowed a great deal and we fired very little. But we had plenty to do to keep pathways dug between the guns and the huts; often we had to clear these afresh every hour.

During this time I made the acquaintance of several interesting Italians and Frenchmen. Among these was Colonel Bucci, who had been attached the year before to the Staff of one of the British Armies in France. He was now in command of a Regiment of Field Artillery, including a group of Batteries known as the Garibaldian Batteries, which were always placed at their own request in the most forward positions. I heard that, when he took over this command, he sent for all his officers and said:

"Now here we are, some old men and some young men and two or three boys, and we are all here for the same purpose and I hope we shall all be always the best of good friends. But, as a matter of convenience, someone has got to be in command of the others, and I have been chosen because I am the oldest."

He used to tell an amusing story of an encounter he had in France with a British officer from one of the Dominions, who walked into his bedroom late one night, after a liberal consumption of liquor, and said he "wanted the fire" and asked if Bucci was "that Portuguese." Bucci, having persuasively but vainly asked him to go away, got out of bed and genially taking him by the shoulders—he is a powerful man—ran him out into the passage. Whereat the British officer, surprised and protesting, said:

"You have no business to treat me like that. Don't you see that I am a Major and have three decorations?" pointing to his left breast.

"Yes," said Bucci, "and I am a Colonel, and I have some decorations too, but I don't wear them on my nighty, and I want to go to sleep."

He had been in Gorizia before Caporetto, and had kept, as a melancholy souvenir, the maps showing the line of his own Regiment's retreat.

"I call it the Via Crucis," he said. "I want to go back. I want to see an advance across the Piave with Cavalry and Field Artillery. I want to advance at the gallop. I have applied to be sent down there."

He was a natural leader of men, and I felt that I would willingly follow him anywhere.

We saw a good deal too of the officers of a French Observation Balloon. One of their officers was a tall man, promoted from the ranks, with big upturned moustaches, a delightful smile and twinkling eyes. He smoked more cigars than any man I have ever met. He smoked them, like some men smoke cigarettes, one after another all the evening, with no interval between. He came from Marseilles. Another was from Auvergne, always most elegantly dressed. He never smoked at all, for he was very proud of his white teeth. He spoke Italian and German, but no English. A third was a little blonde Alsatian business man. He was usually rather quiet, but one evening I saw him roused, when someone had said something that displeased him about Alsace. Then he showed us that he could be eloquent when he chose.

They are very implacable, these Frenchmen. Undoubtedly Clemenceau spoke in their name, when he said, "my war aim is victory." Another Frenchman said to me once, "when Clemenceau is speaking, no one dares to interrupt, for they know it is the voice of the soldier at the Front speaking." And one can scarcely wonder that they are implacable.

In Alsace-Lorraine and in the occupied territories of

Northern France, they say that it is known with complete certainty that the daughters and wives and widows of many French officers and men have been compelled to take up their abode in brothels, and there to await at all hours of the day and night the visits of their country's enemies. Is it surprising that certain French Regiments, knowing these things, never take prisoners? And can one fail to admire, even if one does not unconditionally agree with, the soldier who would fight on and on, until everyone has been killed, rather than accept anything less than a complete victory?

It is all but impossible for a foreigner to measure the spiritual effects upon a proudly and self-consciously civilised Frenchman of these unpardonable, brain-rending, heart-stabbing provocations. But the statesman at home who, drawing good pay and living in comfort far behind the Front, is ever ready to declare that his country "shall continue to bleed in her glory" is a less admirable spectacle. It is his business to conceive some subtler and more comprehensive war aim than bare military victory, and to make sure that, when he has died safely in his bed and been forgotten, other men shall not have to do over again the work which he complacently bungled. A fighting soldier, who risks his life daily, may speak brave words, which are indecent on the lips of an *imboscato*, whether military or civilian.

CHAPTER 29

The Asiago Plateau

About the middle of March the British Divisions moved up from the Montello to the Asiago Plateau, and all the British Heavy Artillery was concentrated in the Asiago sector. We, therefore, moved six miles to the west and found ourselves in support of British, and no longer of Italian, Infantry. Our Brigade ceased to be a "trench-punching" and became a "counter-battery" Brigade. Most of our work in future was to be in close co-operation with our own Air Force.

My Battery was destined to remain here, with two short interludes, for seven months. It was in many ways a very interesting sector. The British held the line between the Italians on their left and the French on their right. To the right of the French were more Italians. The move had amusing features. One compared the demeanour of the lorry drivers of different nationalities. The scared faces of some of the British the first time they had to come up the hundred odd corkscrew turns on the mountain roads, taking sidelong glances at bird's eye views of distant towns and rivers on the plain below, were rather comical. Even the self-consciously efficient and outwardly imperturbable French stuck like limpets to the centre of the road, and would not give an inch to Staff cars, hooting their guts out behind them. The Italian drivers, on the other hand, accustomed to the mountains, dashed round sharp corners at full speed, avoiding innumerable collisions by a fraction of an inch, terrifying and infuriating their more cautious Allies. But I only once saw a serious collision here in the course of many months.

The Asiago Plateau is some eight miles long from west to east, with an average breadth of two to three miles from north to south. On it lie a number of villages and small towns, of which the largest is Asiago itself, which lies at the eastern end of the Plateau and before the war had a population of about 8000. Asiago was the terminus of a light railway, running down the mountains to Schio. The chief occupation of the inhabitants of the Plateau had been wood-cutting and pasture. In Asiago were several sawmills and a military barracks. Army manoeuvres used often to take place in this area, which gave special opportunities for the combined practice of mountain fighting and operations on the flat. It was moreover within seven miles of the old Austrian frontier. Asiago was hardly known before the war to foreign tourists, but many Italians used to visit it, especially for winter sports.

Across the Plateau from north to south ran the Val d'Assa, which near the southern edge, having become only a narrow gulley, turned away westwards, the Assa stream flowing finally into the river Astico. The Ghelpac stream, which flowed through the town of Asiago, joined the Assa at its western turn. Apart from these two streams the Plateau was not well watered. In summer, when the snows had melted, water was even scarcer on the surrounding mountains. All our drinking water had to be pumped up through pipes from the plain.

The Plateau was bounded at its eastern end by Monte Sisemol, which stands at the head of the Val Frenzela, which, in turn, runs eastward into the Val Brenta near the little town of Valstagna. Sisemol was of no great height and was not precipitous. It had a rounded brown top, when the snow uncovered it. But it was a maze of wire and trenches, and a very strong point militarily. There had been very bitter fighting for its possession last November and it had remained in Austrian hands.

At the western end the Plateau was bounded by the descent to the Val d'Astico. On the northern side of the Plateau rose a formidable mountain range, the chief heights of which, from west to east, were Monte Campolungo, Monte Erio, Monte Mosciagh and Monte Longara. This range was thickly wooded with pines, among which our guns did great damage. I always more regretted the destruction of trees than of uninhabited houses, for the latter can be the more quickly replaced. This range was pierced by only four valleys, through each of which ran roads vital to the Austrian system of communications, the Val Campomulo, the Val di Nos, the Val d'Assa and the Val di Martello. The Austrians had also a few roads over the top of the mountains, but these were less good and less convenient.

Along the southern side of the Plateau ran another ridge, less mountainous than the ridge to the north, and completely in our possession. This ridge also was thickly wooded, and pierced by only a few valleys and roads. The road we came to know best was the continuation of the wonderful road up from the plain, through Granezza to the cross-roads at Pria dell' Acqua, and on through the Baerenthal Valley to San Sisto. Thence it led through the front line trenches into the town of Asiago itself. At Pria dell' Acqua, a most misleading name, where there was no water, but only a collection of wooden huts, another road branched off westwards, running parallel to the front line, behind the southern ridge of the Plateau.

The Italian Engineers had created a magnificent network of roads in this sector of the Front. Before the war there had been only one road into Asiago from the plain. Now there were half a dozen, all broad and with a fine surface, capable of taking any traffic. And, in addition, there were many trans-verse roads, equally good, joining up and cutting across the main routes at convenient points.

When the British troops took over this sector in March, the whole Plateau, properly so called, was in Austrian hands. It had been taken last November in the mountain offensive which followed Caporetto. At one perilous moment the Aus-trians had held San Sisto and their patrols had passed Pria dell' Acqua, but they had been thrown back by Italian counter-attacks to the line they now held. Our front line ran along the southern edge of the Plateau, and, on the right, along the lower slopes of the southern ridge, just inside the pine woods. On the left, further west, it ran mostly on the flat and more in the open. Where the Val d'Assa turned west, our front line ran on one side of the shallow gulley and the Austrian on the other. The Austrian front line was completely in the open. The first houses of Asiago were only a few hundred yards behind it.

From the defensive point of view our line was very strong, and the trenches, particularly at the eastern end, very good, deeply blasted in the rock. The wooded ridge, running close behind our front line all the way, completely hid from the enemy all movement in our rear. He could get no observation here except by aircraft. Even movements in our front line, owing to the trees, were largely invisible at a distance, and, owing to the lie of the ground, large parts of No Man's Land could be seen from our own trenches, but from nowhere in the enemy's lines, with the result that we were able to post machine guns, trench mortars and even, for a short time, a field battery there, without being detected, until these weapons had served their immediate purpose. Our systems of transport, supply and reliefs of the troops in the line could, therefore, be carried out at any hour of the day or night with almost complete disregard of the enemy. His intermittent shelling of the roads was perfectly blind and haphazard and seldom did us any damage.

He, on the other hand, was in a very undesirable situation. Not only was his front line all the way in full view from our various ground O.P.'s, but a long stretch of flat country several miles broad behind his front line was equally in view. Only a few small folds in the ground were invisible from all points along our ridge. We could see also most of the nearer slopes of the northern ridge, though here the thick woods and breaks in the hillside gave him greater opportunities for concealment. Taking into account, therefore, ground observation only, we had him at a tremendous disadvantage. He dared not move nor show himself in daylight behind his line, and was compelled to carry out all his supply and troop movements at night, or during fogs that might lift at any moment. One French Battery did no other work except sweep up and down his roads throughout the hours of darkness, and it is obvious that the probable damage done in this way was far greater than anything he could hope to do to us.

Taking into account the possibilities of observation from the air, the balance in our favour became even greater. We had a strong superiority in the air, whenever it was worth our while to enforce it, partly because our airmen were individually superior to the Austrians, and partly because we had more and better machines. Our pilots often flew over the northern ridge, both to observe and to bomb, but the enemy seldom crossed the southern ridge. His anti-aircraft Batteries were, however, at least as good as ours, and, in my opinion, better.

Most of our pre-arranged counter-battery shoots were carried out with aeroplane observation against enemy Batteries situated in the thick woods on the slopes of the northern ridge, the airman flying backwards and forwards over the target and sending us his observations by wireless. But it was often necessary to spend more than half of the four hundred rounds allotted to a normal counter-battery shoot in destroying the trees round the target, before the airman could get a good view of it. Flying, however, was always difficult on the Plateau, especially during the winter, and more difficult for our men than for theirs, since there were no feasible landing-places behind our lines. Our nearest aerodromes were down on the plain, and a big expenditure of petrol was required to get the airman up the mountains and actually over the Plateau, and also to get him down again. The time during which he could keep in the air for observation was, therefore, very limited. Weather conditions on the Plateau, moreover, were often very unfavourable for flying even in the spring and summer. The practical importance of our superiority in the air was thus smaller than might have been expected.

From the defensive point of view, then, our position was pretty strong. But the sector was important and might at any time become critical, and much depended upon its successful defence. For the mountain wall that guarded the Italian plain had been worn very thin in this neighbourhood by the Austrian successes of last year. An Austrian advance of another few miles would bring the enemy over the edge of the mountains, with the plain beneath in full view. Further defence would then become extremely difficult and costly, and the whole situation, as regards relative superiority of positions and observation, now so greatly in our favour, would be more than reversed. We were too near the edge to have any elbow room or freedom of manoeuvre. Our present positions were almost the last that we could hope to hold without very grave embarrassment. It would have seemed evident, then, that to obtain more elbow room and security, we should not be content with a defensive policy, but should aim at gaining ground and thickening the mountain wall by means of an early local offensive, even if larger operations were not yet practicable.

But, from the offensive point of view, our position presented great difficulties. To make only a small advance would leave us worse off than now. Merely to go out into the middle of the Plateau, merely to reoccupy the ruins of Asiago, would be futile, except for a very slight and transitory "moral effect." To carry the whole Plateau and establish a line along the lower slopes of the northern ridge would be no better. We should only be taking over the difficulties of the enemy in respect of his exposed positions, while he would escape from these difficulties and obtain an immunity from observation nearly as great as that which we now possessed. No offensive would benefit us which did not give us, at the very least, the whole of the crest of the northern ridge. And to aim at this would be a big and risky undertaking, involving perhaps heavy casualties and large reserves. We had only three British Divisions in Italy at this time, the 7th, 23rd and 48th, two of which were always

275

in the line and one in reserve. The French had now only two Divisions in Italy and the Italians, when the German advance in France became serious, had sent to France more men than there were French and British left in Italy. The large fact remained that, since the military collapse of Russia the previous year, the Austrians had brought practically their whole Army on to the Italian Front and established a large superiority over the Italians, both in numbers and in guns. Considerable Italian reserves had to be kept mobile and ready to meet an Austrian offensive anywhere along the mountain front or on the plain. There was not likely to be much that could be safely spared to back up a Franco-British offensive on the Plateau. None the less, the value of a successful offensive here was recognised to be so great, that it was several times on the point of being attempted in the months that followed. But it did not finally come, until events elsewhere had prepared the way and sapped the enemy's power of resistance.

This, however, is anticipating history. In March, when we first arrived, we moved into a Battery position in the pine woods behind the rear slope of the southern ridge. Our right hand gun was only a hundred yards from the cross-roads at Pria dell' Acqua, disagreeably close, as we afterwards discovered. For the enemy had those cross-roads "absolutely taped," as the expression went. In other respects the Battery position was a good one. Being an old Italian position, it had gun pits already blasted in the rock, though they were not quite suited to our guns and line of fire, and we had to do some more blasting for ourselves. In the course of this, a premature explosion occurred, wounding one of our gunners so severely that he lost one leg and the sight of both his eyes and a few days later, perhaps fortunately, died of other injuries. He was a Cornishman, very young and very popular with every one in the Battery. We missed him greatly. In this same accident Winterton was also injured, and nearly lost an eye. He went to Hospital and thence to England, and saw no more of the war, for the sight of his eye came back to him but slowly.

The Italians had also blasted some good *caverne* in the position, and these we gradually enlarged and multiplied, till we had cover for the whole Battery. Being on the side of a hill, and our guns not constructed to fire at a greater elevation than forty-five degrees (the Italians had fired at "super-elevations" up to eighty), we had to cut down many trees in front of the guns. But this clearance hardly showed in aeroplane photographs, as there were already many bare patches in the woods. We had perfect flash-cover behind the ridge and were, indeed, quite invisible, when the guns were camouflaged, even to an aeroplane flying low and immediately overhead. From our position we could shoot, if necessary, right over the top of the northern ridge, on the other side of the Plateau. And this was good enough for most purposes.

We prepared another position, which was known as the "Forward" or "Battle Position," at San Sisto, about four hundred yards behind the front line. This position we never occupied, but we should have done so, if an offensive had come from our side while we were still on the Plateau. San Sisto, I was told, was once the centre of a leper reservation. There is a little chapel there, but no other buildings. This chapel was used by the R.A.M.C. as a First Aid Post. One day I saw a shell go clean through the roof of it, but there was no one inside at the time.

The Battery O.P. was a glorious place, up a tall pine tree on the summit of Cima del Taglio, a high point to the east of the Granezza—Pria dell'Acqua road. This O.P. had been built by the French. It was reached by a strong pinewood ladder, with a small platform half way up as a resting-place. The O.P. itself consisted of a wooden platform, nailed to cross pieces, supported on two trees. It was about fifteen feet long and four feet broad and some ninety feet above the ground. At one end of the platform a hut had been erected, with a long glass window, opening outward, on the northern side, and a small fixed glass window on the western. The other end of the platform was uncovered. When the weather was bad one could shelter in the hut and imagine oneself out at sea, as the trees swayed in the wind. The O.P. was well hidden from the enemy by the branches of the trees. The view was superb. Immediately below the thick pine forest sloped gradually downwards, the trees still carrying a heavy weight of snow. Among the trees patches of deep snow were visible, hiding rocky ground. Beyond lay the Plateau, studded with villages and isolated houses, with the ruins of Asiago in the centre of the view, and, to the left of it, the light railway line and its raised embankment, along which the Austrian trenches ran. And beyond, more pinewoods on the northern ridge, and beyond, more mountains, one snowy range behind another, up to the horizon. The visibility was often poor and variable from one minute to another. Great clouds used to sweep low over the Plateau, blotting out everything but the nearest trees, and then sweep past, and Asiago would come into sudden view again, and the sun would shine forth once more upon the little clusters of white houses, some utterly wrecked, some mere shells, others as yet hardly touched by the destruction of war. The prosaic name of this O.P. was "Claud."

There was another O.P. called Ascot, which we used sometimes to man at the beginning. It was on, or rather in, Monte Kaberlaba, just behind the front line, approached through a communication trench and then a long tunnel through the rock, named by our troops the Severn Tunnel. This tunnel was full of water and many worse things, and it was impossible to clean it out properly. The unfortunate telephonists off duty had to live and sleep in it. The O.P. was a cramped, little, stinking place at the far end of the tunnel, shared with the Italians, undoubtedly visible and well known to the enemy, and with practically no view. The Major, by his usual skilful diplomacy, soon arranged that we should man Claud permanently, but Ascot never.

My only pleasant recollection of Ascot is that once, about midnight, as we were keeping watch together, a young Italian gunner from the Romagna sang to me.

'Addio, mia bell', addio!'
Cantava nel partir la gioventù,
Mentre gl' imboscati si stavano
Divertire, giornale in mano E la sigaretta.
Per noi l'assalto Alla baionetta!
Come le mosche noi dobbiam morir,
Mentre gl' imboscati si stanno a divertir.[1]

This is one of many front line versions of a patriotic draw-ing-room song. It has an admirable tune. He sang me also another longer song, composed by a friend of his, which is not fit for reproduction.

****

We experienced great variations of weather on the Plateau. When we first arrived in March the snow was in full thaw, and every road a sunlit, rushing torrent. We climbed about at that time in gum boots. Later it snowed again heavily and often. Sometimes for several days running we were enveloped in a thick mist, and then suddenly it would clear away. Once, I remember, it cleared at night, and one saw the full moon rising through the pine trees into an utterly clear, ice-cold sky, and under one's feet the hard snow scrunched and glit-tered in the moonlight. British, French and Italian Batteries were all mixed together in this sector. On our left came first another British Battery, then two French, one in front of the road and one behind it, then another British, then an Italian. On our right, slightly more forward, the Headquarters of an Italian Heavy Artillery Group, in front of them a British and an Italian Battery, one on each side of the road leading past Kaberlaba to the front line. To the right of the Italian Head-

---

1: "Good-bye, my darling, good-bye!"
Sang the young men as they went away,
While the *imboscati* were standing about
To amuse themselves, with a newspaper in their hand And a cigarette.
For us the bayonet charge!
Like flies we must die.
While the *imboscati* stand about to amuse themselves.

quarters, across the San Sisto road, was a French Battery, with two Italian Batteries in front of it. To our own right rear was one Italian Battery and two French, and in rear of them, back along the road to Granezza, our own Brigade Headquarters.

This mixture was a good arrangement, stimulating friendly rivalry and facilitating *liaison* and exchange of ideas. Our relations were specially cordial with the Italian-Group Headquarters and with one of the French Batteries on our left. The Italian Major commanding this Group was a Mantuan and he and I became firm friends. It was in his Mess one night, in reply to the toast of the Allies, that I made my first after-dinner speech in Italian. I do not claim that it was grammatically perfect, but all that I said was, I think, well understood, and I was in no hesitation for words.

Not till the end of May did Spring really climb the mountains, and the snow finally vanish, and then the days, apart from the facts of war, were perfect, blue sky and sunshine all day long among the warm aromatic pines and the freshness of the mountain air. Here and there, in clearings in the forest, were patches of thick, rich grass, making a bright contrast to the dull, dark green of the pines, and in the grass arose many-coloured wild flowers.

The Italians have buried their dead up here in little groups among the trees, and not in great graveyards. There was one such little group on the hillside in the middle of our Battery position, between two of our gun-pits. There was another in the middle of our forward position at San Sisto, and another, where some thirty Bersaglieri and Artillerymen were buried, in the Baerenthal Valley. It was here one day that an Irish Major, newly come to Italy, said to me, "I don't want any better grave than that." Nor did I. It was a place of marvellous and eternal beauty, ever changing with the seasons. It made one's heart ache to be in the midst of it. It was hither that they brought in the months that followed many of the British dead, who fell in this sector, and laid them beside the Italians, at whose graves we had looked that day.

CHAPTER 30

Some Notes on National Characteristics

For a week or two in May an Italian Engineer officer messed with us. He had a sleeping hut on the hill just behind us, and was in charge of a party of men who were working on British Field Artillery positions. His men were on British rations and did not altogether like them. They would have preferred more bread and less meat and jam, and they missed their coffee. Our tea they did not fancy. The first time it was issued to them, they thought it was medicine.

"Why do the English give us *camomila?*" they asked their officer, "We are not ill!"

****

I have had, at one time and another, much gay and delightful intercourse both with Frenchmen and Italians, which has led me to certain speculative comparisons and to many dangerous generalisations, some of which I will venture tentatively to set down here. But it is difficult to find forms of words which are not mere journalism.

Italian humour is more primitive and uproarious than French, and the Italians seem to present fewer barriers to intimacy, but the proportion of rational discussion is larger in the conversation of the French. Both the French and the Italians combine natural and easy good manners with great punctiliousness in small matters of etiquette. Only very arrogant or very boorish people find it difficult to get on well with either.

It is idle for any wide-awake observer to deny that a certain antipathy exists between the French and the Italians. Both, I think, generally prefer the British to their Latin brothers, and I have heard both say unjust and absurdly untrue things about the other. Their antipathy is rooted partly in temperament, partly in history, and partly in that ignorance and lack of understanding which accounts for nine-tenths of all international antipathies. As Charles Lamb said, in an anecdote which President Wilson is fond of quoting, "I cannot hate a man I know."

It is sometimes said that the French and the Italians are too much alike to be in perfect sympathy. The Frenchman has at times an instinct to be what an Englishman would call "theatrical," which instinct the Englishman himself hardly possesses at all. But in the Italian this instinct is even stronger than in the Frenchman, and he gives it freer play. Thus the Frenchman often notices the Italian doing and saying things which he himself dislikes, but which it needs a deliberate effort of self-repression on his part not to imitate. The Englishman has no inclination to do and say such things, and is, therefore, more tolerant of them than the Frenchman, thinking them either charming or merely "queer," according to his temperament.

If the French are the more admirable, the Italians are the more lovable; if the French are the more creative, the Italians are the more receptive. In the French, though not so much in the Italians, one does find that "sheer brutality of the Latin intellect," which, since the French Revolution, has dethroned many previously dominant ideas and institutions. One finds in the French a tradition of limpid precision, of concise and ordered logic, while the Italians are still groping rather turgidly among those great abstract ideas which the French handle so easily. The spirit of France shines with the hard splendour of the noonday sun, of Italy with the soft radiance of the light of early mornings and late afternoons.

The French are proud and sometimes intolerant, the Italians tolerant and often diffident. It has been truly said that in every modern Frenchman there is still something Napoleonic, however subconscious it may have become. One could never be surprised if, in the midst of conversation, a Frenchman should suddenly draw himself up and cry *"Vive la France, monsieur!"* But one does not expect an Italian in like circumstances to cry *"Viva l'Italia!"* In general, the French are the more tenacious and clear-visioned in adversity, but none are more irresistible in success, nor more conscious of its drama, than the Italians.

The low birth-rate of France, as compared with Italy, is a fact of deep and permanent importance. In years to come the French will grow more and more negligible, numerically, in world politics, but the French spirit is immortal and unconquerable. It will penetrate the hearts of the best men for ever, and ideas characteristically and originally French will continue to mould the world's thought and action till the end of time. The Italians on the other hand will play in future history a greater part numerically, and moreover, by a greater intermarriage with other races, will continue to produce fine and generous human types, not wholly Italian. Italians will continue to show a shining example to the world by reason of their gaiety and charm of character, their mental subtlety, which with time will grow less involved and more lucid in expression, by their art of life, even now not much inferior to the French, by their sensitiveness to beauty, by their capacity for enthusiastic appreciation, and by their technical genius in applied science.

Italy is a naturally democratic and peaceable polity, and her present imperfections will diminish rapidly with the increase of her national maturity and stability. She will be a sane and healthy element in the future international order.

In some respects, as in their indifference, sometimes excessive, to foreign opinion, the French resemble the British, just as, in their excessive sensitiveness on this point, the Italians resemble the Americans. This is the contrast between age and youth, between nations with a continuous tradition of centuries behind them and nations born or reborn only yesterday.

There remains the larger contrast between the Latins on the one hand and the Anglo-Saxons on the other. At first sight it is the latter who are the more realistic and the more practical, the former who are the more effusive, idealistic and poetical. But, as Mr Norman Douglas admirably puts it in *South Wind*, "Enclosed within the soft imagination of the *homo Mediterraneus* lies a kernel of hard reason. The Northerner's hardness is on the surface; his core, his inner being, is apt to quaver in a state of fluid irresponsibility." The comparative method of approach to the institution of marriage among Latins and among Anglo-Saxons illustrates this truth. And it serves also, perhaps, for an example that, in the midst of the terrors of war, the dim project of a League of Nations, the only hope of the world, first took shape in the minds of Anglo-Saxon dreamers and not of Latin realists. The Latin often thinks more clearly, but not always more profoundly, than the Anglo-Saxon. The currents on the surface are not always the same as the currents in the deep.

CHAPTER 31

Rome in the Spring

I was at Rome in May. Of the many things and persons I saw there, not much is relevant here. But there is an intoxication and a beauty and a sense of wonder in Rome in the Spring, as great as I have found at any time elsewhere. Rome grew upon me, rapidly and ceaselessly, during the few days that I spent there, and sent me back to the mountains, clothed with their pinewoods and their graves of much brave youth, uplifted in heart and purified in spirit.

****

Early one afternoon in the Piazza Venezia I fell in with two Italian officers, an Alpino and an Engineer, both wounded and not yet fit to go back to the Front. We rapidly made friends, and, having drunk beer together, we took a *carrozza* and drove to the Villa Borghese Gardens, where we walked and sat for several hours. Then we went back to the Piazza Venezia, and walked in the neighbourhood and contemplated the monuments. My friends said that Rome was the capital city of the world, and praised also the giant memorial to Italian Unity and Victor Emmanuel II., which, still unfinished, dominates the Piazza, and indeed a large part of the city. This memorial is, I believe, condemned by the greater part of foreign aesthetic opinion, the Germans alone conspicuously dissenting. Personally I like it in the fading light from close at hand, and in a bright light from a distance, as one sees it, for instance, from the Pincio.

We spoke a little, but not much, of the war. They were both for fighting on till final victory, whatever the cost, and both spoke with admiration of the inflexible and stubborn spirit of the British nation. Very wonderful too is the spirit which animates the Alpini. My Alpino friend had been wounded in the leg last August at Rombon, and still walked lame. He told me of incidents which he had witnessed, of Alpini charging across and through uncut enemy wire, with the wounded and the dying crying to their comrades, *"Ciao![1] Ciao! Avanti!"*

He sang me also certain songs of the Alpini, in one of which they sing that in the Italian tricolour the green stands for the Alpini,[2] the white for the snow on their mountains and the red for their blood. O these *"fiamme verdi,"* who can talk and sing themselves into such transfigured ecstasies, as to turn, death and pain almost into easy glories!

The three of us dined at a little restaurant near the Pantheon, and my friends wrote their names and a greeting to my wife on a post card, and an old man at the next table ordered a bottle of wine, in which we all drank the health of the Allies, and a party at another table began to sing, and went on singing for nearly an hour. We stayed in that restaurant talking till eleven p.m., when the lights were turned out, and then my friends demanded that we should make another *giro artistico*, which terminated beneath Trajan's Column, where in the warm air we sat and talked for half an hour more, and separated about midnight, I having had eight hours of continuous practice in the use of the second person singular of Italian verbs.

****

Next day I lunched with my friends the Marinis, at their charming Villa on Monte Parioli, and in the afternoon Signor Marini offered to act as my guide to places of interest. We took the tram to the Piazza del Popolo, which was laid out in 1810 under the French Empire, perfectly circu-

---

1: *Ciao* is a colloquialism, much the same as our own "so long," or "good-bye and good luck!" It is an intimate word, used only between friends at parting.
2: The regimental colours of the Alpini are plain green, worn on the collar.

lar and symmetrical, thus differing from the more Italian of Roman Piazzas, such as the elongated and quite unsymmetrical Piazza di Spagna. We passed along the broad embankment beside the Tiber and through the Square of St Peter's. Just outside the gates of the Vatican, my guide pointed out to me the little shabby building occupied by the Giordano Bruno Society, symbolic of the brave defiance thrown out, all down the ages, by poverty and the spirit of freedom and intellectual honesty, in the face of wealth and power and oppression, intellectual bondage and the dead weight of tradition.

My guide thought that, out of the wreck of her material defeat and disaster, Russia would perhaps give a new spiritual religion to the western world, to take the place of old forms now dead, and historic organisations which, having lacked the audacity and the wisdom to remain poor when riches were within easy reach, had now become visibly and irremediably detached from the life of the people. He did not fear, as some did for France, a clerical revival in Italy after the war. For the Italian branch of clerical power had shown itself in the hour of Italy's deadly peril to be largely lacking in Italian patriotism, and to have been scheming for the maintenance, if not the expansion, of Austrian dominion, and, perhaps, for the re-establishment by the aid of Austrian and German bayonets, or Turkish, if it had been necessary to solicit them, of the Temporal Power of the Papacy over Italian citizens and Italian soil. I saw one of the Swiss mercenaries of the Papacy gazing forth a little contemptuously through a door of the Vatican upon the secular outer world.

From St Peter's we drove up the Janiculum, stopping on the way at the convent of S. Onofrio, where Tasso passed the last three weeks of his life and where a Tasso Museum has been accumulated. Very admirable is the equestrian statue of Garibaldi on the Janiculum, both as sculpture and for its details of intention, such as that sideways turning of his head, looking down hill at the Vatican, as though saying, *"Non ti di-*

mentico,"—"I do not forget you, my old enemy." The view of Rome from this point is magnificent, the best that I have seen, though the view from the Pincio only just falls short of it.

Thence, passing outside the old city walls through the Porta San Pancrazio, we stood on ground made memorable by Garibaldi's defence of the Roman Republic in 1849, and went down, past the. Pope's monument to the French who died fighting to defend his Temporal Power against the Garibaldini, into the beautiful garden of the Villa Pamfili. *"Attendono il finale risorgimento,"*[1] says the Pope's Italian version on the monument. It is an ironical phrase in view of the history of the next twenty years.

"They did not have long to wait," I said, "a bird in the hand is worth two in the bush." And my guide said, I thought well, of the French that they are a people of great gifts and of most generous mind, but that their rulers have often showed *"un po' di volubilità, un po' di fantasia."*

We visited last of all the depot of the Bersaglieri in Trastevere, where is also the famous Bersagliere Museum. Here we were received and shown round with great courtesy by the Colonel commanding the depot, a handsome man with most sad eyes, but full of great regimental pride in this creation, intimately and characteristically Italian, of General La Marmora.

In the Museum, among much that was trivial, I found much that was interesting and even deeply moving: the relics of Enrico Toti, an artist who, having only one leg, joined the Bersaglieri Ciclisti as a volunteer at the beginning of the war, and rode up mountain tracks on a bicycle with a single pedal, and died, after acts of the greatest heroism and after sustaining for many hours grave wounds, crying with his last breath *"Avanti Savoia!"*, upon whose dead body and brave departed spirit was conferred the most rare Gold Medal for Valour; photographs of all the Bersaglieri, who since the foundation of the Regiment have won the Gold Medal, some twenty of

---

1: "They await the final resurrection." But *risorgimento* to most Italians suggests modern history more than theology.

them, hanging together on one wall, all dead now; the steel helmet of a Bersagliere Major, killed on the Carso, while leading his men; this is all that they found of him, but it has three holes through the front, sufficient proof, said the Colonel, that he was not going backward when he died; a menu card, signed by all the officers of a Bersagliere Battalion, who dined together on the eve of the victorious action of Col Valbella last January, in which they played a worthy part.

The Colonel told me that his own son was killed and is buried beyond the Isonzo, near Cervignano. It had been suggested to him that he should have the body brought home, but he preferred to leave it where it fell. *"C'è un' idea che è morta lì,"* he said, "It is an idea which has died there. Some day, if I live, I shall make a pilgrimage thither, but the Austrians may, by now, have destroyed the grave."

Outside in the courtyard, where the Colonel took leave of us, I saw many young Bersaglieri, the latest batches of recruits, mere boys. "They are splendid material," he said, with a military pride, not without a half-regretful tenderness, "one can make anything out of them."

They were, indeed, incomparable human stuff, whether for the purposes of peace or war. They seemed to have the joy of the spring in their eyes, just as that middle-aged Regular soldier had in his the sadness of autumn. And amid all the beauty of Rome in the spring, I was haunted by the grim refrain, *"Nella primavera si combatte e si muore, o soldato,"*—"In the springtide men fight and die, young soldier."

****

I went away from Rome strengthened in my previous judgment that the Italians are not a militarist nation. There was no sign of the militarist, as distinct from the military, spirit at the Bersagliere Depot. The relations of the Colonel and Signer Marini illustrated this. They had never met, nor, I think, heard of one another before. Yet this little civilian seemed to find it quite natural to march into a military barracks without any preliminary inquiries, to walk upstairs and straight into the Commanding Officer's office and, not finding the Commanding Officer there, to send a message into the Officer's Mess, and, the Commanding Officer having come out, to present his card, without any appearance of servility or undue deference, and to ask to be taken round. And the Colonel seemed to see nothing odd in these proceedings, but placed himself at once at our disposal and showed us everything and talked without aloofness and without reserve to both of us. I could not help thinking that things would not have happened quite like this at the depot of a crack regiment in most other European capitals.

CHAPTER 32

The Fifteenth of June, 1918

I happened to be the officer on duty in the Battery Command Post on the night of June 14th-15th. There had been a thick fog for several days and not much firing. No one expected anything unusual. The Battery was much below strength owing to the ravages of what the doctors in the mountains called "mountain fever" and the doctors on the plain called influenza. We had, if I remember rightly, about forty men in Hospital owing to this cause alone. I myself had a touch of it, but, thinking I could probably count on a quiet night, I refused the offer of a brother officer to take my place, coldly calculating that a few nights later, when it would be my turn to take his duty, I might have more to do. But my hopes of much sleep were soon dispersed.

Orders came in from Brigade for an elaborate counter-battery shoot with gas shell, in two parts, one between 11 p.m. and midnight, the other between 2 and 3 a.m. We had never fired gas shell from six-inch howitzers before, though we had been warned that we should soon be required to do so. We had no gas shell in the Battery, but we were informed by Brigade that a sufficient quantity would arrive by the time the shoot was to begin. In fact, however, the first consignment of gas shell was not delivered in time to enable us to take part in the first part of the bombardment, and I was told not to fire high explosive instead, as that would tend to disperse the gas which other Batteries would be simultaneously firing on the same targets.

The method adopted on this and later occasions, when gas was used, was that a number of our own Batteries should concentrate for, say, five minutes at the fastest rate of fire possible on a particular enemy Battery, then all switch together to another enemy Battery, and so on, all coming back together on to the first enemy Battery after an interval sufficient to lull the human elements forming part of the target into a delusive sense of security and a return to slumber without their masks, or, alternatively, to make them wear their masks continuously for prolonged hours of expectation, thus subjecting them to much discomfort, depriving them of sleep, lowering their morale, and making them likelier victims for fresh forms of devilment in the morning. War is a filthy thing, and must be stamped out ruthlessly. The facts of gas will have helped to drive this simple conviction into many a thick, egotistical, insensitive head. But, as has been wisely said, you cannot half make a war of the modern sort, you cannot let a faint savour of regret hang about all your actions, and enervate your will. And, in plain, brutal truth, our employment of gas was a big factor in determining and hastening the end. Of the military efficiency of our gas tactics we had much evidence later on.

We joined in the second part of the gas bombardment in the early hours of the 15th of June, and, when this was nearly over, I got orders to fire at my leisure ten rounds of high explosive at "Archibald," which was our code name for a certain Austrian searchlight, which used to sweep round the country from the summit of Monte Mosciagh on the far side of the Plateau. So I fired the ten rounds, and the officer at one of the O.P.'s, whom I had previously warned of my intention, reported that Archibald had gone out after the fourth round, and that, judged by the flashes of their explosions, all the rounds had seemed pretty near. It was now nearly half-past three, and, conscious that I had a high and rising temperature, I determined to lie down and get a few hours' sleep. Some of the gas shell which had been intended for the first part of the bombardment, but had arrived about four hours too late, was still being unloaded from lorries on the road outside. But I asked a Corporal to look after this, and send the unloading party to bed as soon as they had finished.

I had just fallen asleep when the Corporal awakened me. Were the men, he asked, to go on unloading the shell? Still half asleep, I asked why not? He said that the road was being shelled. I pulled myself together and went to the door of the Command Post. Not only the road, but the whole Battery position and apparently the whole area for some distance round, was being bombarded very violently. So I ordered every one to take cover. It was just 3.45 a.m.

I thought for a moment that this was merely Austrian retaliation for our first use of gas and for the shots at Archibald. In fact, it was the beginning of the big Austrian offensive, which had long been prearranged. During the last few days the Austrians had brought up a large number of new guns to our sector, and had placed a number of them right out in the open. And owing to the thick fog our airmen had been able to see nothing. The bombardment continued with great fury for several hours, with guns of all calibres, but fortunately mostly small, with shrapnel, high explosive, and gas, chiefly lacrimatory, but mixed with a certain quantity of lethal. Luckily we had pretty good cover, mainly *caverne* blasted in the rock. The Command Post itself was proof against anything less than a direct hit from a pretty heavy shell. It was also supposed to be gas proof, but was not. I collected about half a dozen men in it who had nowhere else to go, including two A.S.C. lorry drivers.

Early on, a young Bombardier was hit rather badly in the leg just outside. We brought him into the Command Post, bandaged his wound and laid him on the camp bed, on which I had been hoping to get some sleep, and there left him till the shelling should abate and it should be reasonably safe to carry him to the dressing-station a quarter of a mile away. He lay there, I remember, looking like a little tired cherub, and another Bombardier sat beside him and tried to persuade him to go to sleep.

They were very great friends, those two boys, both signallers, and inseparable both on and off duty. The one who was not wounded went out that same morning and spent hours repairing telephone lines under very heavy fire, for which act he won the Military Medal. The other, months later, when his wound was healed and he had returned to the Battery, also won the Military Medal for gallantry on the Piave.

The conduct of the two lorry drivers afforded a strong contrast in psychology. One, a man of middle age, was superbly cheerful. "They can't keep this up much longer," he said several times with a placid smile, "they haven't the stuff to do it." The other, though younger, was a bunch of visible nerves. A shell exploded just behind the Command Post and violently shook the whole structure and a storm of stones hit the log framework. He collapsed on the floor, and was convinced for a couple of minutes that he had been hit, and for some time after that he was suffering from shell shock.

Such illusions come easily at such times. A gas shell made a direct hit on one of our smaller dug-outs. A Sergeant inside was badly gassed. They put him for the moment in a gas-proof shelter, higher up the hill, and several hours later I saw him being carried away on a stretcher, apparently lifeless. But he finally pulled through. A gunner who was with him in the dug-out came running into the Command Post crying out that he also was gassed. I made him lie flat on the floor, and told him to keep as quiet as he could. And then I watched his breathing. It was clear after a minute or two that, if he had had a breath of gas at all, it was only of the slightest. But, when I told him this, he was very unwilling to believe me. Another man was hit just outside, and lay on the ground screaming like an animal in pain. Him, too, we carried into the Command Post, and, later, on a stretcher to the dressing station.

Meanwhile all the telephone lines had gone owing to the shelling, cutting us off from Brigade, other Batteries and O.P.'s. But intermittent communication was maintained by runners, and signallers were out, hour after hour, mending breaks in the line and showing their invariable gallantry. Till about six o'clock our orders were to lie low, to keep under cover and not to open fire. The rain of shells continued without slackening. We were wonderfully lucky to get off as lightly as we did. It is one of the most extraordinary phenomena of war, how many shells can fall in a position of no great size, and yet do very little damage. It was estimated, and I think quite soberly, that at least two thousand rounds were pumped into our Battery position that morning.

It was soon after six that we got orders, passed along from the next Battery up the road, to open fire on our "counter-preparation target." This was a sign that the advance of the Austrian Infantry had either begun, or was thought to be imminent. They attacked, in fact, about a quarter to seven on our sector. Their synchronising was faulty, as between the different sectors attacked. Some went forward earlier and others later than had been intended. They were all newly equipped and were carrying full packs and blankets on their backs. They had been told by their officers that this was to be the last great offensive of the war, that they were going to drive us headlong down the mountain side, that after two days they would be in Verona, and after ten days in Rome. They were not told that they had British troops in front of them. They came forward bravely and with great determination, in five successive waves.

On the British left Divisional Front, to the west of us, they gained a large initial success, and pushed us back well behind our first line of guns. Here for some time the situation looked serious. But next day strong counter-attacks by British and Italian troops restored the line, our lost guns were retaken and the retreating Austrians suffered great slaughter and demoralisation.

On the British right Divisional Front, in support of which our Brigade was operating, the British 23rd Division fought a fight worthy of their high reputation. Forced back for a while from their front line trenches, after a prolonged and intense bombardment and by an overwhelming superiority of numbers, they never even fell back to their support line. But, turning on the enemy who was advancing along and astride the San Sisto road, they drove him back and re-established their own front line within six hours of the first attack. It was here that a boy Colonel, a Sherwood Forester scarcely twenty-one years old, won the V.C. and fell severely wounded. When things looked black, he had organised the defence and the subsequent counter-attack, collecting together British Infantrymen of several Battalions, together with British Artillerymen and Italian Machine-Gunners and Engineers, welding them into a coherent force and making swift, yet well thought out, dispositions which did much to save the situation.

On the right of the British, the French Infantry, though furiously assaulted, never, I believe, budged an inch. On the right of the French, the Italians were momentarily driven from Col Valbella, Col del Rosso and Col d'Echele, which they had won in January, but retook all three a few days later.

But we in the Battery knew nothing of all this at the time. We knew only that we had to open fire on our counter-preparation target. The gun-pit of our No. 1 gun near the cross-roads was in low-lying ground, now so full of gas that one could hardly see one's hand before one's face. Fortunately we could achieve the rate of fire required by using three guns only, so we left No. 1 out of action for the time. The enemy's bombardment, as far as we were concerned, was beginning to slacken a little, but was still heavy. The Major, out on the road with a signaller mending wire, was hit in the face with shrapnel. It turned out, happily, not a serious wound, but at the time it looked less hopeful. He went down the mountains in the same Field Ambulance with the young Colonel of the Sherwood Foresters, of whom I have already spoken.

There was an abandoned Field Ambulance in the road, half in the ditch, with the engine still running. The driver had found the shelling too hot to stay. There was no one inside it, but we got a couple of stretchers from it. And we had need of them. No. 4 gun, my own gun, which was nearest to the road, suffered most severely. Seven of the detachment on this gun were hit, not all at once but, what is apt to be much more demoralising, at intervals of a few minutes. A Bombardier was in charge of the gun that day, no senior N.C.O.'s being available. He showed a very wonderful coolness and courage. Shells were bursting all round the gun-pit, and sometimes in the gun-pit itself. But the rate of fire never slackened. Every now and again the cry was heard "another casualty on No. 4!" and stretcher bearers would start down the road from the Command Post. But, each time, almost before they had started, came the deep report of another round fired. No casualties and no shelling could silence her. At one time this Bombardier had only two other men to help him work the gun. And both of them were as undismayed as he. He won the Military Medal for his gallantry that day, and I was very proud of him and of No. 4.

The Brigade Chaplain appeared in the course of the morning and gave a hand in carrying the wounded away on stretchers. It was outside his official work and I give him all credit and respect for the help he gave us. But one N.C.O. in the Battery, with the plain speaking that comes naturally in the face of common danger, said to him, "Well, Sir, we never thought much of you before, either as a man or as a preacher, but we're glad to see you here to-day doing your bit."

The Austrian gunners had a fine sense of discrimination in their targets. The wooden hut, in which I and two of my brother officers used to sleep, had been hit two or three times that day, and much of our kit had been destroyed. So had both volumes of Morley's *Rousseau*, which were on a shelf over my bed, leaving behind only a few torn and scattered pages. Much damage had also been done to a collection of Pompeian photographs of great historical interest. But Baedeker's *Northern Italy*, which lay alongside, had not been touched!

****

The God of Battles also discriminates delicately. He takes the best and leaves the worst behind. There died that day, struck by a shell at the foot of our tree O.P. on Cima del Taglio, one of the finest personalities in the Battery, a signalling Bombardier who had worked for some years on a railway in America and, just before the war, as a railway clerk in the Midlands. He was the father of a young family, thoughtful and capable, and loyal without subservience to those of higher military rank, in so far as he judged them to be worthy of his loyalty. I remember one night at the beginning of the year, when we were keeping watch together among the snows at Col d'Astiago, with the sky cold and clear and full of stars, and when he and I talked in complete understanding and agreement of the waste of war and the deeper purposes of life and the need to build up a better world. Now he is buried in the beautiful Baerenthal Valley, along which runs the road from Pria dell'Acqua to San Sisto and Asiago.

As that day ended, which the Italians always afterwards spoke of as *"il giorno quindici"* (the fifteenth day), the firing on both sides in our sector slackened, though our guns were seldom silent for more than an hour at a time, and the Austrians still carried out sudden bursts of vicious fire in our neighbourhood. But that night, and the next day and the next, we began to get through information of what had been happening all along the line. And when, a week later, the whole tale could be told, it was evident that no great offensive on any Front during this war, prepared with so great elaboration and carried out with so great resources, had ever quite so blankly failed, as the great Austrian offensive from the Astico to the Sea. And the effect upon the self-confidence and morale of the Italian Army and of the Allied contingents was correspondingly great. For, to speak frankly, this offensive had been awaited with much apprehension and anxiety, with the memory of Caporetto not yet faded and in view of the success of the German offensive in France.

CHAPTER 33

In the Trentino

The Austrian offensive on the mountain sector, from the Astico to Monte Grappa, had been obviously and decisively broken by the 18th of June. But there was still danger on the plain, particularly in the Montello sector, where the Austrians were established in strong force west of the Piave. A flying Brigade of British Heavy Artillery was hurriedly formed and sent down the mountains. Of this Brigade my own Battery formed part. Our general function was to reinforce the Italian Artillery in what was at the moment the most critical sector of the whole Front, our particular function to destroy by shell fire the Piave bridges behind the Austrian troops. But when we arrived we found that the emergency had already passed. The bridges had already been destroyed by airmen and Italian Artillery, and the Austrian forces had either been driven back across or into the river by Italian counter-attacks, or had been cut off and compelled to surrender. We, therefore, came back to the Plateau without firing a round.

But we did not remain there long. The idea of a mobile Artillery of manoeuvre was much talked of at this time, and early in July a Brigade consisting of three British Siege Batteries, my own included, was moved westwards up into the Trentino. We travelled all the way by road, through Verona up to Brescia, "the eagle that looks over Lombardy," and thence beside Lake Idro, up the Val Chiese, past Storo into the Val D'Ampola.

All this last stretch of country is famous in Italian history as the scene of Garibaldi's campaign of 1866, which, had it not been interrupted by the course of events elsewhere, would probably have hastened the liberation of Trento by more than half a century, and greatly modified the problems of Italian policy in recent years. The story is well known of the recall of Garibaldi, which reached him at the moment of victory at Bezzecca, and of his famous reply, a model of laconic self-discipline, in the one word *ubbidisco*—"I obey." The little town of Bezzecca lay this July behind the Italian lines, but in full view and easy range of the Austrians. A company of Arditi was billeted here, with whom I lunched one day, returning from a front line reconnaissance. The Piazza had been renamed by the Italians Piazza Ubbidisco, and under cover of darkness they set up one night on the mountain side just above the town a memorial stone to Garibaldi and his volunteers of 1866, a provocative target for Austrian gunners.

No other British troops, except these three Batteries of ours, ever fought in the Trentino. It was a proud distinction and a very memorable experience. The natural scenery was superb, a series of great mountain ranges, uneven lines of jagged peaks, enclosing deep cut valleys, the lower slopes of the mountains densely wooded, the higher levels bare precipitous rock. The Austrian front line ran along one ridge of peaks and ours along another; between ran a deep valley, all No Man's Land, into which patrols used to climb down at night, often with the aid of ropes. One mountain mass, a continuation of Cima d'Oro, was partly in our possession and partly in theirs, and up there by night among the rocks patrols grappled for the mastery, poised high above the world, and in these struggles men sometimes slipped, or were thrown, to crash to death thousands of feet below in the Val di Ledro.

This country was Austrian before the war, though inhabited wholly by Italians, and Italian troops had conquered it with extraordinary feats of endurance and daring in their first great onrush all along their old frontiers in the spring of 1915.

But now a big advance here by either side, in the face of carefully prepared opposition, seemed almost inconceivable, except as the result of some wide turning movement, hinging on some point many miles away.

The special military problems presented by warfare in such country were numerous and difficult. Our guns had to be dragged into position up a rough mountain track, which at some points was too narrow and at others too weak to allow the passage of a six-inch howitzer without much preliminary blasting and building up. Our first gun to go up took twenty-four hours of continuous labour between the time of starting up the track and the time of arriving in position, a distance of only about two miles of zigzag. No tractor or other power engine could be used here. The only force available was that of men hauling on drag ropes, and a party of sixty Italian gunners reinforced our men.

What may be called the problems of pure gunnery were still more difficult. British Heavy guns had never fired under such conditions before and, for the benefit of such of my readers as may be practical Artillerymen, it may be interesting to remark that for one of our targets the angle of sight, properly so called, worked out at more than twenty degrees, while the map-range elevation was only about fifteen. The devising of an accurate formula for correction of elevation for a large *dislivello*, as the Italians shortly call it, which in English means a large "difference of level" between a gun and its target, is one of the most intricate problems of theoretical gunnery, or, for that matter, of theoretical mechanics, involving, among other factors, the various shapes and sizes of projectiles, their comparative steadiness during flight, the resistance of the air, and the effect of other atmospheric conditions and of the force of gravity.

There was a splendid opportunity for systematically testing various rival formulae in the Trentino, but it was allowed to slip. Among gunners, as among other classes, and especially among Regular Army gunners, the so-called practical man sees little value in scientific experiments, which do not produce large, obvious and quick returns. We fired many hundred rounds in the Trentino and I have no doubt that they were tolerably effective. But most of them were fired at night, with no observation possible, and we were often restricted in our registrations by daylight to four rounds a section per target, from which no really reliable conclusions could be drawn.[1]

****

We were billeted in the village of Tiarno di Sotto, where the Mayor under the Austrian regime, an Italian by race, was still carrying on his duties.

"But I shall have to disappear, if the Austrians ever come back," he said with a smile.

It was a tremendous climb from our billets to get anywhere, the least tremendous being to our Battery position, straight up the nearest mountain side. A very active and energetic man could get up in a quarter of an hour. It used to take me twenty minutes. The weather, moreover, was hot, though considerably cooler than on the plains.

Some Czecho-Slovaks were billeted in the next house to ours, but, owing to lack of a common language, we were unfortunately unable to talk to them. They were well-built fellows, and gave one an impression of great tenacity and intelligence. And I know that they were fine fighters. But they had not the gaiety of the Italians, partly perhaps because they were exiles in a strange land, and must so remain till the day of final victory, which might then have seemed still infinitely remote. An amusing incident happened one evening. Four officers had deserted from the Austrian lines and surrendered to the Czecho-Slovaks; it was one of their military functions to induce surrenders. Two of these officers were themselves Czecho-Slovaks, the third a Jugo-Slav and the fourth an Italian from Istria. They were very hun-

---

1: We could get no help from Italian range tables, which were not merely for different guns and ammunition, but were drawn up on different principles from our own.

gry and were in the midst of a good meal, in the presence of a Czecho-Slovak guard, when a Corporal and two gunners from our Battery, passing outside the house and hearing some language being spoken within, which they recognised to be neither English not Italian, rightly thought it their duty to enter and investigate the matter. The deserters were astonished to see these unfamiliar looking persons, speaking a strange tongue and wearing a uniform which they had never seen before. But they were still more astonished to learn that they were British. They seemed hardly to be aware that the British were at war with Austria, much less that any British troops had been within hundreds of miles of them. The incident closed in much mirth and friendliness.

In the village were also billeted many Italian troops, who used to fill the night with song, long after most of us had gone to bed, *"'Addio, mia bell', addio!' Cantava nel partir la gioventù,"* which is never very far from the lips of any Italian soldier, and those endless *stornelli*, which to an invariable tune they multiply from day to day. *"Il General Cadorna Mangiava la bifstecca; Ai poveri soldati Si dava castagna secca,"*[1] or *"Il Re dal fronte Giulio Ha scritto alla Regina, 'Arrivato a Trieste Ti manderò una cartolina,'"*[2] with its sardonic variant or sequel, *"Il General Cadorna Ha scritto alla Regina 'Se vuoi veder Trieste, Compra una cartolina.'"*[3]

Many of the others are for various reasons unprintable, though many are extremely witty and amusing. Even those which I have quoted were nominally forbidden by the High Command to be sung, but the prohibition was not very rigorously enforced. And General Cadorna, after all, had now passed into history. Of his successor I never heard any evil

---

1: "General Cadorna used to eat beefsteak. To the poor soldiers they gave dried chestnuts."

2: "The King has written to the Queen from the Julian Front 'when I get to Trieste, I will send you a picture post card.'"

3: "General Cadorna has written to the Queen, 'if you want to see Trieste, buy a picture post card.'"

sung, though I remember once hearing a great crowd of soldiers and civilians at Genoa shouting monotonously—"*Viva, viva il Generale Dia!*"

The refrain of the *stornelli* was onomatopoeic, and was intended to represent the sound of gunfire. *"Bim Bim Bom, Bim Bim Bom, Al rombo del cannon."*

****

What a theatrical country Italy is! I remember being out in the streets of Tiarno one evening with a stream of song issuing from almost every house, and looking up at the full moon riding high over the towering peaks that locked in our valley and all but shut out the night sky. I could hardly believe that it was neither a stage setting nor a dream.

I remember another day, when I did a great climb above Bezzecca to carry out a front line reconnaissance, and arrived limp and perspiring to lunch at the Headquarters of an Italian Artillery Group, high, high up, looking out upon a glorious and astounding view. And in the afternoon I took my first ride on a *teleferica*, or aerial railway, slung along a steel rope across the deeps, seated on a sort of large wooden tea tray, some six feet long and two and a half across, with a metal rim some six inches high running round the edge. I was quite prepared to be sick or at least giddy. But I was pleasantly disappointed. My journey took about a quarter of an hour; walking it would have taken about three hours of very stiff climbing. The motion is quite steady, except for a slight jolt as one passes each standard, and, provided one sits still and doesn't shift one's centre of gravity from side to side, there is no wobbling of the tea tray. And looking down from time to time I saw tree tops far below me, and men and mules on mountain tracks as black specks walking.

****

There were various theories to account for our being sent to the Trentino. One was that an Austrian attack was feared there, another that an Italian attack was intended, but that the intention was afterwards abandoned, a third that the whole thing was a feint to puzzle the Austrians. But in any case we did not remain there long. By the beginning of August we were back on the Plateau. On the return journey, which was again by road all the way, we were given three days' rest at Desenzano and I was able to spend half a day in Verona.

CHAPTER 34

Sirmione and Solferino

"Leave is a privilege and not a right," according to a hack quotation from the King's Regulations. This quotation has done good service in the mouth of more than one Under Secretary of State for War, heading off tiresome questioners in the British House of Commons. Leave was a very rare privilege for the British Forces in Italy. In France, taking a rough average of all ranks and periods, British troops got leave once a year. In my Battery in Italy, the majority were without leave home for nineteen months. How much longer they would have had to wait, if the war had not conveniently come to an end in the nineteenth month of their Italian service, I do not know. Even in Italy, of course, the privilege was extended somewhat more freely to junior regimental officers and much more freely to Staff officers and Lieutenant-Colonels, in view of the danger of brain fag and nervous strain following upon their greater mental exertions and their abnormal exposure to shell fire and the weather. The former class went home about every eleventh, the latter about every third month.

The French Parliament fairly early in the war, with that gross lack of discrimination and of military understanding habitual to politicians, insisted on the granting of leave every three months to all ranks in all theatres of war. The Italian Parliament pedantically laid down a uniform period of six months. The British Parliament, with the sure political instinct of our race, preferred to leave the whole matter in the hands of the War Office. The interference in purely military affairs of unpractical sentimentalists was strongly discouraged at Westminster.

Why no leave to England could be granted except in special cases, was cogently explained from time to time during the summer in circulars written by Staff officers of high rank, who had frequent opportunities of informing themselves of the realities of the situation, while visiting London. These circulars were read out on parade and treated with the respect which they deserved. To allay possible, though quite unreasonable, unrest, it was determined to open a British Club, or Rest Camp, at Sirmione, which, as every reader of Tennyson knows, stands on the tip of a long promontory at the southern end of Lake Garda. Here a week's holiday was granted to a large proportion of the officers and a small proportion of the rank and file. Many officers went there more than once. Two large hotels were hired, which had been chiefly frequented before the war by corpulent and diseased Teutons, for whom a special course of medical treatment, including sulphur baths, used to be prescribed.

One of these hotels was now set apart for British officers, the other for men. A funny little person in red tabs was put in charge; there were various speculations as to his past activities, but all agreed that he had got into a good job now, and wasn't going to lose it, if tact could prevent it. This little man used to stand outside the hotel gates as each week's guests arrived from the steamer, and always had a cheery smile of welcome for every Field officer; to General officers he showed special attentions. He took his meals in the same room as the rest of us, but at what was known as "the Staff table," where he invited to join him any officers of high rank, who might be staying at the hotel, or, if there were none such available, certain of his private friends. The food supplied to ordinary people like myself was good, wholesome, reasonably plentiful and cheap. At "the Staff table" special delicacies were provided and additional courses, with no increase of charge. The profits, he used to say, were made entirely on the drinks and smokes.

A series of rules was drawn up, that none of us might be led into any avoidable temptation. All towns within reach—Milan, Verona, Mantua, Brescia, Peschiera—were placed out of bounds. So, too, were some of the larger villages on the shores of the Lake. The hours during which alcoholic liquor might be obtained, either in the Hotels or in the Cafes of Sirmione, were narrowly limited. Beer was strictly rationed. Carefully regulated excursions on the Lake, by steamer or launch, were permitted and even encouraged. Likewise bathing.

I spent a week here, from August 14th to 21st, in gloriously fine, hot weather. Some said that the damp heat was relaxing and depressing, but I, in my second Italian summer, was getting acclimatised. The place was wonderfully beautiful. The end of the promontory is covered with olive trees, the ground thickly carpeted with wild mint and thyme, surrounded on three sides by the deep blue water of the Lake, along the shores of which lie little white villages, backed by groups of straight, dark cypresses, with mountain ranges rising in the background, range behind range, and overhead the hot Italian sun, shining from a cloudless sky. Here, at the point, were the ruins of what are called, upon what evidence I know not, the Villa, the Baths and the Grotto of Catullus. Here, too, was an Italian Anti-Aircraft Battery, and the Grotto of Catullus was filled with their ammunition.

The Austrians still held the upper end of the Lake, including the town of Riva. But only Italian motor boats now survived on the Lake, occasionally raiding Riva. The Austrian boats had all been sunk early in the war.

****

On the 15th I went round the lower end of the Lake in a steamer and, passing along the shores of the beautiful Isola di Garda, on which stands the less beautiful Villa Borghese, landed at Maderno, famous for its lemon groves. Here a church was being used as a ration store. It had fine carving on the door. The French had established Artillery and Machine Gun Schools close to the Lake and several of their officers were on the steamer.

On the 16th I went with a young officer from a Yorkshire Battalion, a most agreeable companion, to Desenzano, which was out of bounds. We played billiards and lunched, and in the afternoon went to sleep on the grass in the shade beside the Lake. We were driven back in a *carrozza* along the promontory by an old Garibaldino, a Capuan by birth, who in 1860 at the age of eleven joined Garibaldi, when he crossed from Sicily to the mainland, and held older people's horses at the Battle of the Volturno. He served with the Fifth Garibaldini in the Trentino campaign of 1866 and knew intimately the country where I had lately been, the Val d'Ampola and Storo, Tiarno and Bezzecca. He then joined the Italian Regular Army, and in 1870 was a Corporal in the Pavia Brigade. He was present at the taking of Rome and claimed that, although an Infantry-man, he helped to load one of the guns which breached the Porta Pia. If this claim be true, there must have been either a lack of gunners on this famous occasion, or a certain degree of enthusiastic confusion. Having entered Rome, he got very drunk and absented himself from his Regiment without leave for three days. As a punishment he was made to march on foot, carrying a full pack, from Rome to Padua. He showed us his old military pay-book, his medals and other souvenirs. Next year he will be seventy years old and will begin to draw a pension. Having returned to Sirmione, we arranged with him to drive us next day to the neighbouring battlefields of 1859, San Martino and Solferino. Much delighted, he assured me, quite without necessity, that next day he would put on his best clothes, would wash and shave, and give his horse an extra bit of grooming.

Accordingly next morning at ten o'clock we started off again in the *carrozza*. We visited first San Martino della Batt-aglia, only a few miles from the southern end of the Lake. This was the northern extremity of the battlefield of Solferino. It was here that the Sardinians and Piedmontese, forming the left wing of the Franco-Italian Army, attacked and drove back the Austrian right wing. A memorial tower has been erected here,

250 feet high, with great avenues of cypresses radiating out-wards from it. The custodian is a handsome boy, who lost a leg at the taking of Gorizia two years ago. There is no stair-case within the tower; one goes up by a spiral inclined plane. At successive stages, as one ascends, are large and detailed paint-ings, running right round the inner circumference of the tower, representing the battles of the Italian Wars of Liberation from 1848 to 1870. As works of art they are not of the first class, but they convey here and there a vivid sense of life and movement, an advance of the Bersaglieri with their cocks' feathers waving in the wind, Garibaldini in their red shirts rushing Bomba's gunners on the Volturno, Italian cavalry charging a Battalion of brown-coated Croats at Custozza, the defence of a fort in the Venetian lagoons against Austrian warships.

On a fine day the view from the top is very good, but that day it was hazy in the great heat. Close by is an Ossario, con-taining the skulls and bones of seven thousand dead collected in the neighbourhood, washed clean with white wine and set out in neat rows, the majority Italian. A good warning, one would think, against war, and more compact and less wasteful of space than a conventional graveyard.

Thence we drove on to Solferino, a little remote village with a single street paved with cobble stones, seldom visited by foreign tourists. The plaster on the walls of the farmhous-es hereabouts still bears many bullet marks. As we drove, the Garibaldino pointed out to us some of the positions where Napoleon III.'s Generals had sited their Batteries. We were the first British officers seen here during the war, and had an enthusiastic reception. I was surprised to find that none of our Regulars had come over from Sirmione, as a matter of professional interest and duty, to study the tactics of 1859 upon the ground.

We lunched well at a small *albergo*. There were four good-looking daughters of the house, who came and sat with us in turn and watched us eat. They had the naturalness and simple charm of dwellers in remote places.

"Four good cows," said the Garibaldino, with the frank realism of the South, "but all the local proprietors are too old."

After lunch my companion remained in the village, and I climbed the ridge from which the French drove the Austrians, a very strong natural position even now. I went up La Rocca, at its south-eastern extremity, on which stands an old square tower, also converted into a battle memorial. Here again there are no steps within, but an ascending spiral plane. The slopes at this end of the ridge are thickly planted with young cypresses, and the place will grow in beauty year by year. Even now it is well wooded, with larger trees just below the tower. The village lies at the foot of the slope. Just outside it, off the road on slightly rising ground at the end of an avenue, is another and larger Ossario, containing twenty thousand skulls and sets of bones, French and Austrian. The building is full of banners and wreaths and memorial tablets, including one lately sent by the French troops now fighting on the Italian Front.

Ceux de la grande guerre A ses glorieux anciens. 1859-1918.

A few skeletons have been preserved intact, including one said to have been an Austrian bandmaster, a giant eight feet tall. The nationality of some of the skulls can be determined by bullets, French or Austrian, found in the head and now attached by a string.

I stepped forth from this well-ordered tomb into the outer sunshine with a sense of personal oppression and of human ineffectiveness. How slowly and how clumsily do the feet of History slouch along! And yet, if Napoleon III. had kept faith with Cavour, the fighting here might have liberated Venetia without the necessity for another war a few years later. How quiet and silent lie these battlefields of yesterday! Even so, one day, will lie the pine woods round Asiago, shell-torn and tormented now, and populous with the soldiers of many nations, yet of a wondrous beauty in the full moonlight and the fresh night air. I shall be back up there in three days' time!

****

We drove back in the warm evening, by the road through Pozzolengo toward Peschiera, along which many of the defeated Austrians fled in 1859. The roadside was dusty, but along all the hedges the acacias still showed a most delicate and tender green.

CHAPTER 35

The Asiago Plateau Once More

During August and September we were kept pretty busy on the Plateau. Concentrations on enemy trenches and wire and special counter-battery shoots by day and counter-battery support of Infantry raids by night were continually required of us. We fired high explosive by day and chiefly gas shell at night. Our own Infantry and the French on our right raided the enemy's front and support lines very frequently, bringing back many prisoners. The French constantly penetrated and reconnoitred the enemy's defensive system on Mount Sisemol. Many of us were inclined to think that the casualties, sometimes heavy, which were incurred in these raids, and the great quantity of ammunition shot away, were largely wasted. We saw no sufficient return for them, beyond a certain amount of information obtained from prisoners, much of which was of small and doubtful value. But in view of what happened later, I think it must be agreed that these continual raids and bombardments did their share in gradually wearing down the morale and power of resistance of the Austrian Army.

There was a persistent rumour that the enemy was on the point of retiring to a line, on which he was known to be working hard, along the lower slopes of Monte Interrotto and Monte Catz on the far side of the Plateau. This line, we learned from prisoners, was commonly referred to as the *winterstellung* (winter position). It would have been stronger, defensively, than his existing line, and would have had the great advantage of being able largely to be supplied and munitioned during daylight, as there was much good cover and roads hidden in the pine woods leading down immediately behind it. It would have involved the moral disadvantage of evacuating the ruins of Asiago. But, with the snow down on the Plateau, every Austrian track and foot-mark would have been visible from our O.P.'s, and the Austrian situation, bad as it already was from this point of view, would have become quite intolerable. If, on the other hand, we had followed up an Austrian retreat to their *winterstellung* by the occupation of Asiago and the throwing forward of our line across the Plateau, the relative situation would have been reversed. Our Infantry and many of our Batteries would then be out in the open, in view from the Austrian O.P.'s, unable to light a fire by day, and only able to send up supplies by night; and our general situation would be so much the worse with heavy snow increasing our discomfort and the visibility of any work we might undertake and of our every movement.

For this reason, as has been explained in an earlier chapter, it was taken for granted that a small advance from our present excellent line would be worse than useless, and that only an advance at least to the crest of the first mountain range beyond the Plateau would be of any military value. The possibility of such an advance being attempted was evidently still in the minds of the Staff, for our forward or Battle Position at San Sisto had to be kept in constant readiness for occupation, and it was suggested by some that the occasion for a big attack would be the moment when the enemy was in the act of retiring voluntarily to his *winterstellung*, necessarily a somewhat difficult and risky operation.

Meanwhile the enemy guns were not silent. They were indeed unpleasantly active, constantly sweeping the road just behind our Battery, putting down violent, though brief, concentrations on the cross roads at Pria dell' Acqua, less than a hundred yards to our right, and apparently also endeavouring to carry out occasional counter-battery shoots after our own pattern. The British Batteries in this sector suffered a number of casualties during this period, and one in particular, not my own, was frequently shelled with great precision by twelve-inch howitzers, most disagreeable weapons, firing at extreme ranges from the cover of some distant valley. Many efforts were made to locate these particular guns, but I am not confident that any of them were successful. Among the victims in this Battery was Preece, a young officer who had served under me in a Training Battery in England. He was the only son of a widowed mother, and, had he lived, might have become a world-famous chemist. His grave, too, is in the Baerenthal Valley.

Our own officers' Mess had several narrow escapes, especially on one occasion when the impact of an enemy shell was broken by a trench cart and a box of tools, only seven or eight yards away. None of the tools were ever found again and portions of the trench cart were seen next morning hanging on the telephone wires beside the road. Only a few splinters came into the Mess and did no harm, all the occupants, myself included, warned by the sound of the approaching shell, having flung ourselves face downwards on the floor. Another frequent exercise of the enemy at this time was night bombing, which during the full moon became somewhat serious. But a big raid by our own airmen on the enemy aerodrome at Borgo in the Val Sugana put an end to this source of trouble.

I was able now and then to make short expeditions down the mountains in the Battery car to Thiene, and sometimes even to Vicenza, for the ostensible purpose of buying canteen and mess stores and drawing the Battery pay. Thiene is the ugliest and dullest little town in Italy. But Vicenza, with its exquisite Olympian theatre, and other fine Palladian architecture, varied by many smaller buildings which are beautiful examples of the Venetian Gothic style, with its busy and animated Piazza, centring round the ever-crowded Café Garibaldi, and with the wooded slope of the famous Monte Berico, rich with historic memorials, rising behind the town, never failed to lift my mind out of the dreary monotony of war into an atmosphere of cleaner and more enduring things. I remember, too, the strange thrill I had one day, when, having passed the sawmills and dumps of stores and shells and the huddle of Headquarter offices at Granezza, I came out on the last edge of the mountain wall, into sudden full view of the great plain below, full of rivers and cities, and saw, for the first time from up here, the sunlight flashing on a strip of distant golden sea. It was the lagoons round Venice.

I spent also many interesting days about this time at our tree O.P. on Cima del Taglio. The Italians had an O.P. in a neighbouring tree, which they called Osservatorio Battisti. The British Field Artillery occupied a third tree, and the French a fourth. The pine trees on that summit were, literally, full of eyes. But the enemy never discovered any of us, though he sometimes dropped a few stray shells in our neighbourhood. Our own O.P. was not generally manned at night, unless some prearranged operation was taking place, but the officer on duty had to remain within call and slept in a log hut near the foot of the tree, in telephonic communication with Battery and Brigade. The French and Italians also had huts close by, and I spent several evenings playing chess with them, or talking, or listening to the mandolin and the singing of Italian *stornelli*. One young Italian, in particular, I remember with some affection, a certain Lieutenant Prato, a mandolin player of great skill and a very charming personality.

One day in September, when the news from the French Front was getting better and better, I remember talking, on our tree top, to the Italian officer, who was at that time acting as *liaison* officer to our Brigade, a member of a family well known in Milan. He knew every inch of those mountains, now in Austrian hands, along the old Italian frontier. His Battery had fought there in the early part of the war. He knew, too, Gorizia and the Carso battlefields. And he was sick at heart, as every Italian always silently was, at the memory of the retreat of last autumn. And I remember saying that what was now happening in the Somme country would happen soon in Italy. There, I reminded him, was a stretch of country which we had once conquered, inch by inch, with terrible losses and infinite heroism and insufficient Artillery, just as Italy had conquered those positions on the Carso and on Monte Santo. And all those gains of ours had been wiped out in a few disastrous hours last March, as Italy's had been wiped out last October, and now we were advancing again over that same country and beyond it, far more rapidly and with far smaller losses than in those bloody days two years ago. And so, I prophesied to him, would it be on this Front too. The day was coming when Italy would win back all she had lost, and far more than she had ever won before, far more swiftly and cheaply than in her early brave offensives, and Austria, like Germany, would be broken in hopeless, irretrievable defeat. He said to me then that he hoped it might come true, but that he was less certain of the future than I. But, two months later, when I had proved to be a true prophet, he reminded me of that conversation of ours.

CHAPTER 36

The Move to the Piave

The second week in October we moved down from the Plateau and lay for a week at Mestre, within sight of Venice. One clear afternoon it looked as though one could throw a stone across the intervening water. Every one took for granted that a big Italian offensive was imminent. The rumour was that it would be timed to begin, as near as possible, on the anniversary of the defeat of Caporetto. In Italy more weight is attached to anniversaries than with us. One felt expectation everywhere in the air.

****

It was during these days that I fell in with the Rumanian Legion. I had been in Padua and saw a group of them standing on the platform at the railway station. They were obviously not Italians. Their uniform was similar to that of the Italian Infantry, but their collars were red, yellow and blue, and they wore a cockade of the same three colours on their hats. They wore Sam Browne belts, too, and carried a *pugnale* like the Italian Arditi. I asked a Carabiniere on duty who they were. He smiled but did not know.

"Perhaps Yugo-Slavs," he suggested.

One of them overheard our conversation and came up to me saying, *"Siamo Rumeni, Legione Rumena."*

Then followed a tremendous fraternisation. We shook hands all round and began to talk. We talked Italian, which, being very like their own language, they all understood. Indeed, for an Italian Rumanian is much easier to understand than many of the Italian local dialects.

They were attractive people, of all ages and very friendly, rather like Italians, but with a queer indescribable racial difference. They were natives, mostly, of Transylvania and had much to say of the oppression of their nationality by the Magyars. Most of them had been conscribed to fight in the Austro-Hungarian Army, but had crossed over to the Italian lines at the first opportunity.

One said, "There are four millions of us in Austria and Hungary." Then, with an air of restrained fury, "Is that not enough?"

Another said, "But after the war there will be a Great Rumania—great and beautiful."

And another said, "We Rumanians must be very grateful to Guglielmone.[1] If he had not made this war, we should not have seen the Greater Rumania in our lifetime. But now, if it was not certain before, the blunders of Carluccio[2] have put it beyond all doubt."

And another told me that his father wrote and spoke English very well, having lived for twelve years in America at St Louis. And another explained to me how the Rumanians had retained, more than any other modern nation, the speech and customs and dress and traditions of the ancient Romans, which things they had originally derived from the legionaries of the Emperor Trajan.[3]

When we parted I said, "May we all meet again on the field of victory beyond the Piave. Long live the Greater Rumania!" And they all cried, "Long live England! Long live victory!"

1: "Big William."

2: "Wretched little Charles."

3: This common boast of the Rumanians is quite true. It is partly to be accounted for by the fact that they were able to retreat before successive invading hordes of barbarians into the inaccessible valleys of the Carpathians, and come down again on to the plains when the danger had passed by.

And so I was going away, when one of them, a little fellow, with a rather sad, earnest face, who had apparently missed a parting handshake, ran after me about twenty yards, and seized me by the hand and cried again, "Long live victory!"

******

From Mestre we moved up through Treviso to a Battery position, on which an advance party had been at work for several days. It grew more and more certain that the offensive was coming at last. Troops of all arms were moving forward in unending streams along every road leading toward the Piave. Prominent among them were many Italian Engineers and bridging detachments with great numbers of pontoons. Beyond Treviso all troop movements took place at night, and our defensive (and offensive) measures against aircraft were apparently sufficient to prevent the enemy from getting any clear idea of what was going on. It seems that he expected an attack in the mountains, but not on the plain. The Italian High Command, on the other hand, considered that the relative strength and morale of the opposing Armies was now such that we could attack on the plain without fear of a successful counter-attack in the mountains, and that, the attack on the plain once well under way, we could pass to the offensive in the mountains also. This view of things was justified by the events which followed. Two British Divisions were moved down to the plain, and one was left in the mountains. The Heavy Artillery was divided proportionately and, of my own Brigade, one Battery was left in the mountains but the rest moved down.

Our new Battery position lay between the ruined village of Lovadina and the river Piave, about three-quarters of a mile from the nearer bank. There was a farmhouse, not much knocked about, close to the gun pits and, with the aid of a few tents erected out of sight along a shallow ditch, the whole Battery was very tolerably billeted. Another British Battery was less than a hundred yards in rear of us, and two others not far

away on our right flank. We were once more in a land of aca-
cia hedges, beginning now to take on their autumn tints. For
miles round us the country was dead flat. Beyond the river we
could see, on a little rise, what was left of Susegana Castle, near
to Conegliano, and on a higher, longer ridge further away the
white *campanile* of San Daniele del Friuli, above Udine. It was
there that, almost a year ago, in the first newspaper I saw after
the retreat, I had read that Italian rearguards were still fighting.
In the far distance rose great mountain masses. Up there were
Feltre and Belluno, and behind, just visible when the light was
very bright, the peaks of Carnia and the Cadore.

It was an unaccustomed feeling, after months of comparative immunity from observation behind mountain ridges,
to be in flat country again. At first we all felt a queer sense
of insecurity whenever we walked about, even when thick
hedges manifestly screened us from enemy eyes. But the road
from Lovadina to the river bank at Palazzon, which ran right
through our position and within a few yards of our billet,
was in full view, and no movement along it was permitted during daylight. When we first arrived we found a deep
sense of gloom prevailing amongst our advanced party. They
were convinced that our position had been spotted already,
for the Austrians that morning had put down a five minutes'
concentration all round the place. Nothing much heavier
than Field Guns had been firing, but it had been lively while
it lasted. It seemed probable, however, on further inquiry,
that this outburst had been caused by the fact that an idiotic officer belonging to the Battery immediately in rear of
us had marched a working party up the road in fours, then
halted them and allowed the men to stand about in groups
on the road for several minutes. It was at these groups that
the Austrians had apparently been firing. A vigorous protest
extracted from our neighbours a promise that more common sense should be used in future.

We were to remain a silent Battery until the start of the offensive, and this was to be dependent on the height of the river,

which at that time was in full flood owing to heavy rains in the mountains. Our guns were well camouflaged and the chances of our detection seemed small. But one day we had a lucky escape. It was very clear and there had been great activity in the air on both sides all the morning. All seemed quiet again, however, and we had the camouflage off one of our guns, and two small parties working in the open on shelter trenches behind. A plane was seen approaching, but the air sentry, whose duty it was to keep a sharp look out through glasses and signal the approach of enemy aircraft by two blasts of a whistle, gave no warning. He had been deceived by the marking on the plane, a very thin black cross instead of the thick one usually found on enemy aircraft. Not till it was right upon us did he blow the whistle, and then it was too late. The plane flew very low over us. We could see the pilot looking calmly down at our uncovered gun, and our men trying, ineffectually and belatedly, to take cover. He certainly took it all in and marked us down on his map. The position was 'very easy to identify owing to the solitary farmhouse and the road close by. A few rifle shots were fired, but they did him no harm, and he sailed away toward the river and his own lines.

We had certainly been spotted. And then we suddenly saw another plane, this time an Italian, coming from the left, flying high, hard in pursuit. The Austrian began to rise, but the Italian outpaced him and got right above him, and pressed him gradually down towards the ground. We heard the wooden-sounding *clack-clack-clack* of machine gun fire. And then we saw the Austrian evidently go out of control, diving toward the ground, more and more rapidly, and the Italian circling downwards above him; and then the Austrian went out of sight behind the acacias and a few moments later a column of smoke began to rise. He had crashed in flames, just this side of the river, and his valuable information with him. The Italian flew back over us, triumphantly and very low this time, and waved his hand to us. And we gave him a grateful cheer.

CHAPTER 37

The Beginning of the Last Battle

By the night of October 24th the river had fallen a few inches, and British Infantry crossed in small boats to the Grave di Papadopoli, a long island of sand in the middle of the stream. On the right a Battalion of the Gordons crossed, rowed over by Venetian boatmen. I met one of their officers afterwards.

"Everyone of those boatmen deserved a decoration," he said. "They were all as cool under heavy shell fire as if they had been rowing on the Grand Canal."

Our Infantry held their preliminary positions here for two days, in spite of considerable Austrian bombardment and counter-attacks. British aeroplanes flew over the island and dropped rations in sandbags. Throughout the fighting of these two days, we were standing by ready to open fire, if orders should come. But no orders came and we remained a silent Battery.

But on the night of October 26th, half an hour before midnight, the big bombardment opened and our guns spoke again. It was to be their last great oration. It was, of its kind, a fine, thunderous performance, and the Austrian reply, in our own neighbourhood, was feeble. Evidently they had not spotted our position, thanks to that Italian airman. Our targets were enemy Batteries and Brigade Headquarters. We fired gas shells continuously for many hours, switching from one target to another, until a strong wind got up, rendering gas shelling comparatively ineffective. Then we got orders to change to high explosive. The gun detachments worked splendidly, as always. We were below strength and could not furnish complete reliefs, but no one spared himself or grumbled.

On the morning of the 27th, just before 7 o'clock, our Infantry attacked, crossing from the island to the further bank of the river. There were no bridges, and the water was breast high in some places. In places it came right over the heads of the smaller men, but their taller comrades pulled them through. Where the current was strongest, cables were thrown across and firmly secured, and to these men held on, as they forced their passage through the water.

About ten o'clock I went forward from the Battery position to the river bank at Palazzon to ascertain the situation. A little man named Sergeant Barini, half an Italian and half an Englishman, but serving in the English Army and attached to our Battery, accompanied me. At Palazzon the river was broad and, under fire, unbridgeable, and we went half a mile down stream along what up to this morning had been our front line trench, to the bridgehead at Lido Island. The islands in mid stream were crowded with prisoners and wounded coming back and fresh troops going forward, and dead bodies lay about, British and Austrian together, of men who had fought their last fight, and two crashed aeroplanes. The Austrians had put up elaborate barbed-wire defences on the island, but these had been pretty well broken up by our fire.

Some enemy guns of big calibre were still shelling the crossings and causing casualties among a Battalion of the Northumberland Fusiliers, who were in reserve, waiting on the bank for the order to cross. I tried to locate as accurately as possible the direction of these guns and reported them by telephone to our Brigade Headquarters. I saw an Infantry Brigadier, who said that things were going well, but asked for some additional Artillery support for his left flank on the other side, and, if possible, for an enemy Battery, which he thought was near Susegana Castle, to be knocked out. I looked across the river and saw the dense white smoke screen which our Field Guns were putting up to cover the advance.

These Italian rivers of the Venetian Plain, fed by the melting Alpine snows, are not at all like the Thames. Where I was, there were about nine successive channels, varying in breadth and depth, and in between, stones and sand and rough vegetation on islands varying in size and shape and number with the height of the river. And it was no uncommon thing for the river to rise or fall several feet in a night, for whole islands to be submerged, or for whole channels to run dry. The difficulty here of carrying out military operations according to a time table arranged several days in advance was very great.

Over the main channels pontoons had been thrown, over others light plank bridges, less strongly supported, through others everybody was wading. Large bodies of Engineers, mostly Italian, were ceaselessly working at these river crossings, and working magnificently. For not only was it necessary to be constantly strengthening and multiplying the bridges already made, to take the ever-increasing volume of traffic that would be required to supply the troops across the river, but the enemy's guns were still firing with terrible accuracy at the crossings, and swarms of enemy planes were constantly appearing, bombing the bridges and the islands in a last desperate effort to hold up our advance. Our planes, too, were never far away, and succeeded in driving off or driving down many of these attackers. But others got through and were constantly undoing the work of the Engineers.

When we had got all the information we could, Barini and I went back to the Battery and reported what we had heard and seen. On the way I let myself go and spouted much cheap rhetoric, I am afraid, at the little man. And he laughed rather nervously and thought me, I expect, a queer companion in rather unpleasant surroundings. For several shells kicked up great clouds of earth and stones pretty close to us. But he too, I know, smelt victory in the air that day.

CHAPTER 38

Across the River

Next day I went over the river and right on, one of the two F.O.O.'s (forward observation officers) from my Brigade who were to establish and maintain contact with the advancing Infantry. Three signallers and a runner came with me, carrying rifles, bayonets and ammunition, a day's rations and much signalling gear. The other officer had his own party. We soon subdivided our work and separated.

The twenty-four hours of my duty do not lend themselves to a sustained description. I passed and identified from the map one of the targets of my Battery in the preliminary bombardment, an Austrian Battery position, which we had bombarded for many hours with gas and high explosive alternately. Our shooting had been accurate and deadly. The position was a mass of shell holes. One of the guns had been blown up, a second badly damaged. A third had been pulled out of its pit and half way up a bank by a team of horses. The enemy had made a desperate effort to get it away. But horses and men and fragments of men lay dead around it. It was a well prepared position, and well concealed by trees. But Italian airmen had spotted it, and marked it down with precision on the map, marked it down for destruction. The enemy had done much work here. There were fine, deep dug-outs, well timbered and weatherproof, comfortable dwelling places in quiet times and strong enough to resist shell splinters and even direct hits by guns of small calibre. But we had got a direct hit on one dug-out and killed half a dozen occupants. And the others had not been proof against our gas. They were full of corpses, mostly victims of gas. Some were wearing their gas masks, but our gas had gone through them. Some had apparently been gassed outside, some with masks on and some without, and had crawled, dying, into the dug-outs in the vain hope of finding protection there. However hardened one may grow, by usage, to the common facts of war, few can look on such a sight as this, without feeling a queer thrill of very mixed emotion. My men looked with solemn faces at the work they had helped to do. One said, "poor chaps, *they* were pretty well done in!" And then we turned and went on.

****

It was a very rapidly moving warfare that day. One Infantry Brigade Headquarters, with whom I kept in intermittent touch, occupied four successive positions, miles apart, in the course of twelve hours. About noon I came to a ruined village, Tezze. I went on to reconnoitre it with one signaller. In a half wrecked house we heard the voices of Italian peasant women and saw through an open door an ugly, little, dirty child, probably about a year old, crawling among rubbish and refuse. The village was only just ours. On the far side of it men of the Manchester Regiment were lining a ditch, under cover of a hedge, waiting the order to charge. They warned me to go no further along the road which, they said, was under enemy machine gun fire. Every few minutes enemy shells whistled over our heads and burst in the fields and houses behind us. A wet wind blew down the road. There was no fixed, clearly marked line. Everything was in movement and rather uncertain. . . .

Enemy guns, captured with their ammunition, swung round and firing at the enemy, big guns and little guns. . . .

On the British left the Como Brigade were advancing rapidly in spite of pretty strong opposition. For a while our left flank had been perilously in the air, but the danger was past now. . . .

All the roads were thick with Austrian equipment thrown away in the confusion of departure, rifles, steel helmets (grotesquely shaped, like high-crowned bowler hats), ammunition, coats, packs (handsomely got up, with furry exteriors), mail bags, maps, office stores, tin despatch boxes, photographs of blonde girls, bayonets, hand bombs, ... everything dead thrust into the ditches, both men and horses, the latter smelling earlier and stronger than the former. (The more I look at dead bodies, the more childish and improbable does the old idea of personal immortality appear to me!) . . . .

At one cross-roads a huge pool of blood, mingling with and overwhelming the mud. Here a whole transport team of heavy grey horses with wagons had been hit and blown up. Close by, in a ditch, two British wounded lay on stretchers, covered with blankets. One, only lightly wounded, gave us information and directions. The other was very near to death. His face was growing pale already, as only the faces of the dead are pale. He was shifting feebly and ineffectually, with the vain instinct to escape from pain. He was past speech, but he looked at us out of wide open half-frightened eyes that seemed to question the world despairingly, like an animal, broken helplessly in a trap. . . .

There were some civilians wandering on the roads, liberated now but uncertain whither to go or what place was safe, their possessions on carts. But soon the storm of battle will have passed well beyond them and they will be able to return to what is left of their homes. One old woman in black, walking lame, asked me if the Austrians would come back, and began to cry. I heard some of our soldiers saying in wonder to each other, "did you see those civies going along the road just now?" Queer, irrelevant creatures in the battle zone!. . . .

Others, more fixed, liberated in their own villages, were eager to talk and to welcome us, but a little lost with the British and their unfamiliar ways and language, full of tales of the lack of food under the Austrian occupation, and the robbery of all their livestock and metal and many other things. But the retreat hereabouts had been too rapid and involuntary for deliberate burning or destruction or trap-setting on an appreciable scale. . . .

That night I made my headquarters in a wrecked church, from the tower of which I sent back signals in the Morse code by means of a lamp. I slept for an hour or two under an Austrian blanket, none too clean as it afterwards appeared, and drank Austrian coffee and ate Austrian biscuits. . . .

All through that day and night and the day following the cannonading continued, but with very variable intensity at different points and times. Sometimes a tremendous affair, heavies, field guns and trench mortars all pounding away together, creeping barrage, smoke screens and the rest of it. Elsewhere and at other times, nothing, Infantry well ahead of the guns, going forward almost into the blue, with nothing heavier than machine guns to support them.

British Cavalry went through in the dawn, spectral, artistically perfect, aiming at ambitious, distant objectives, Northamptonshire Yeomanry who had come from France to Italy a year ago and had been kept behind the lines all through the war and were having their first show at last. The next day they suffered many casualties, but they did fine work. Their reconnaissance officer came into the church soon after midnight and asked me if the Austrians still held any part of the village. I told him no, not since yesterday morning.

Later on in the morning great masses of Infantry moved up through the village; British Infantry with a look of evident satisfaction in their faces, but unemotional; Italian Infantry, looking usually even less expressive, but ready to burst into electrical enthusiasm at a touch, at a word, at a sign. . . . A British General, all smiles, rode past on his horse and stopped to ask me a question or two. He tapped me playfully on the helmet with his riding crop. "When will you get your guns across the river?" he asked. "As soon, Sir, as the Sappers can build a bridge that will carry them," I replied. . . .

Now and again Italian planes going on, or coming back from, raids and reconnaissances, flying very low over our heads, the pilots waving their hands over the side and cheering, the troops on the roads cheering back and upwards in return....

When I was relieved, I tramped back to the Piave, many miles now, and wading those of the channels that were still unbridged returned, tired and footsore but with a song in my heart, to my Battery.

****

Not till later did we come to comprehend the vast sweep and the triumphantly executed plan of this Last Great Battle.[1]

At dawn on the 24th, the same day that the British Divisions had crossed to the Grave di Papadopoli, the Italian Fourth Army had attacked in the Grappa sector, where fighting was desperate and progress slow for several days. On the evening of the 26th the Piave was bridged in three sectors, and on the 27th three bridgeheads were in being; the first on the Upper Piave, in the hands of Alpini and French Infantry of the Italian Twelfth Army; the second on the Middle Piave, in the hands of Arditi and other troops of the Italian Eighth Army; the third further downstream, in the hands of our two British Divisions and the Italian Eleventh Corps. For a while the situation had been critical owing to the gap between the second and third bridgeheads. But by the 28th fresh Divisions had crossed the river at all three bridgeheads, and spread out fanwise, linking up the gaps in the line. The same day on the Asiago Plateau the enemy at last fell hurriedly back to his *winterstellung*, and British troops occupied the ruins of Asiago itself. During the next two days the advancing troops on the plain swept steadily eastwards. On the 31st the enemy's line in the Grappa Sector completely collapsed, with great losses of men and guns. On the 1st of November an attack was

---

1: For a full and lucid account see the official *Report by the Comando Supremo on the Battle of Vittorio Veneto, 24th October—2nd November 1918.*

launched along the whole of the Italian Front, from the sea to the heights of the Stelvio, amid the glaciers and the eternal snows on the Swiss frontier, and on this day Italian, British and French troops carried at last, after strong resistance, the whole northern ridge of the Asiago Plateau, at which we had gazed with eyes of desire for many long months.

CHAPTER 39

Liberatori

On November the 1st a reconnaissance by car was ordered, to test the practicability and the need of accelerating the forward movement of our guns. Leary and I and two others started early in a car, adequately armed and carrying a day's rations and a flask in which rum had been mixed accidentally with *florio* (marsala). This most original mixture, which we christened *florium*, was excellent, more thirst-quenching than rum, more sustaining to the spirit than *florio*.

That day we travelled 76 miles at the least, in a great curve, through liberated country. We had everywhere an astounding reception, never to be forgotten. Everywhere we passed, we were wildly, deliriously, cheered by the civilian population. Old men ran up to us waving their hats, old women clapped their hands, young girls waved and threw flowers at us, little boys ran shouting after us, all crying *"Evviva! Evviva! Liberatori! Viva al' Inglesi!"*

The radiant joy of them, and their smiles, never far from tears, were the manifestation of a form of human emotion, singularly pure and indescribably moving. Every town and village was hung with the Italian flag, and at one place an arch of flowers ran from tree to tree above the road. Everywhere crowds with smiling, wondering faces, stood watching the Allied troops moving up along the roads, wave upon wave upon wave, triumphant, unendingly. Here a few days ago the foreign invader had ruled, perhaps only yesterday, perhaps only a few hours ago: Now he had vanished, like a bad dream from which one suddenly awakes, leaving behind him only his dead, and certain grim marks of his occupation, and vivid memories of many brutal and cruel and thoughtless acts, to prove that he was worse and more real than a dream.

****

We crossed the Piave at Spresiano, on a series of wooden bridges and pontoons, similar to those further down the stream at Palazzon and Lido Island. On the further bank we came first to Conegliano. Here just a year ago some of von Below's German troops, who broke the line at Caporetto, had been billeted, and later a Bulgarian Governor and staff had been installed, for the encouragement and flattery of the wavering minor allies of the enemy powers. On the same principle a Turkish Governor had been appointed at Feltre. The troops of occupation had been guilty of wicked excesses at Conegliano. The little town had been ruthlessly ravaged and set on fire and the majority of the houses had been completely burnt out, only the charred shells of them remaining.

Hence we turned northwards up into the Alpine foothills, through country of exceptional beauty, and along the shores of a piece of long blue water, to the village of Revine Lago. Here were many captured and abandoned Austrian guns. Some, in the last desperate moments of departure, had been thrown down a steep cliff which overhangs the lake, and lay below us, for the time being out of reach. Here I met again several officers of the Italian Field Artillery, whom I met above Val Brenta in January, including the Neapolitan Adjutant of Colonel Bucci. Also General Clerici of the Bersaglieri, who for the moment had his Headquarters here, a friend of one of my companions. They all substantiated the rumour that last night, or the night before, Austrian envoys had appeared with a white flag in the Val Lagarina and had been taken to Diaz's Headquarters.

We parted from our friends and sped on to Vittorio Vene-to, which gives its name to this last great battle, being the point on which those Italian forces moved, whose purpose and whose successful achievement it was to cut the Austrian Armies in two, separating the Armies in the mountains from the Armies in the plain. Vittorio stands on and around the summit of a little hill, itself one of the foothills, the older part of the town picturesque with little winding streets, the newer part well laid out with broad roads, shaded with avenues of trees. Here the Austrian flight had been more rapid and the damage smaller. But we were still many miles behind the ever advancing battle line. We determined, therefore, to turn sharply eastward and make for Pordenone, in the hope of coming up with the fighting thereabouts. For last night, we heard, the Austrians were still defending themselves on the near side of that town.

The road from Vittorio to Sacile grew thicker with advancing troops, at first all Italian, then, as we approached Sacile, mixed Italian and British, much Italian Cavalry and Artillery, then British Infantry and some Batteries of Field Guns. In Sacile itself, which British troops had liberated, the crush of troops was dense, and held us up for more than half an hour. Union Jacks hung out from many houses, side by side with the Italian tricolour. As we waited for a chance to go forward, a Battalion of the Bisagno Brigade went past along the side of the road, two deep, at a steady double. Several officers I recognised, whom I had met at dinner at a little restaurant at Marostica many months before, and again near Casa Girardi on the Plateau. We waved to one another and cheered as they passed. When at last we moved on again, we found the road from Sacile to Pordenone pretty clear for several miles and were able to get up speed. But what a sight this road presented! Along it a confused mass of Austrian transport was moving yesterday in headlong retreat. They were bombarded by Artillery, ceaselessly bombed and machine-gunned from the air. The slaughter here had been great, the ditches were full of dead men and horses, and the loss in wrecked and abandoned material of every kind had been immense. And the civilians, who had been practically without food for many days, had been cutting up and eating the dead horses.

"*Poverini!*" said an Italian officer to whom we gave a lift into Pordenone, "they are all starving and we have little chance yet to bring them food."

Pordenone was ours. It had fallen in the early hours of this morning, but the departing Austrians had burnt and wrecked it. The streets were full of the debris and furniture which they had thrown out of the houses and shops in the last mad search for loot. We pushed on, and came up with British Infantry advancing, and the transport wagons and the steaming field cookers of two Battalions, and some cyclist companies of Bersaglieri. But the transport was at a standstill and the dismounted men only going forward slowly. We soon discovered the cause. The wooden bridge over the Meduna river was on fire, pouring forth clouds of smoke. The Austrians had been here only four hours before and had blown up two spans as they retreated and soaked the rest with paraffin and set it alight. The bridge was effectually destroyed. Italian Cavalry, we heard, had gone through the water in pursuit, and likewise some British Infantry patrols, swimming and wading and making use of various ingenious, improvised devices. But the Austrian had a good three hours start, and was running fast and travelling light, it was thought.

But we, being unable to get our car across, turned northward along the river bank and drove furiously and, after a mile or two, outran the foremost Infantry patrols (I think, of the Royal Warwicks), who were pushing cautiously forward, searching the woods and farmhouses for lurking rearguards. And so it was that, first of all the Allied troops, we four entered the little village of Nogaredo. And, as we came in, we sang, very loudly and perhaps somewhat out of tune, the chorus of *La Campana di San Giusto*, the forbidden song which to the Italian Irredentists stands for somewhat the same officially repressed but inextinguishable emotions, as that once forbidden song

The Wearing of the Green stood for to the Nationalist Irishmen of a now vanished generation.

Le ragazze di Trieste Cantan tutte con ardore,
'O Italia, O Italia del mio core, Tu ci vieni a liberar!'[1]

So to that village *we* were the visible liberators. All the villagers came running towards us, crowding around our car, weeping and cheering, pouring out their stories, touching and holding and kissing us. It is seldom that things happen with such dramatic perfection.

The last Austrians, they said, had been gone only half an hour. We pressed on along a narrow road, but it was late afternoon, and the light was failing. The road grew worse, and the mud thicker. Much retreating traffic had only lately traversed it. At last we stuck deep in two muddy ruts. The wheels skidded round helplessly. We could go neither forward nor backward. Three of us got out and shoved with all our strength. There was a crackle of rifle shots not far away. We were prepared for an encounter. But nothing came of it. We got the car out at last, but the road was too bad for further progress and it was almost dark. We turned and drank up the remains of our *florium* and came back. But that day had been unforgettable.

1: All the maidens of Trieste sing with passion,
"O Italy, O Italy of my heart, thou comest to set us free!"

CHAPTER 40

The Completeness of Victory

The end was almost come. On November 3rd we received
the official announcement that an armistice had been signed,
and that at 3 p.m. on November 4th hostilities on the Ital-
ian-Austrian Front would cease. That same day Trento, Trieste
and Udine fell. One began to be aware of the completeness
of victory. On this day and the days that followed the communiqués of Diaz were decisive and historical.

November 4th. Noon. The war against Austria-Hungary which . . . . the Italian Army, inferior in numbers and
resources, undertook on the 24th of May, 1915, and with
unconquerable faith and stubborn valour conducted un-
interruptedly and bitterly for 41 months, has been won.
The great battle begun on the 24th October, in which
there took part 51 Italian Divisions, 3 British, 1 French,
1 Czecho-Slovak and 1 American Regiment against 73
Austrian Divisions, is finished. . . . The Austrian Army is
annihilated. It has suffered very heavy losses in the fierce
resistance of the first days of the struggle and in the pursuit; it has lost immense quantities of material of every
kind and almost all its magazines and depots; it has left
in our hands, up to the present, about 300,000 prisoners
with complete staffs and not less than 5000 guns.[1] The
remnants of what was once one of the most powerful

1: These figures increased later to more than 430,000 prisoners and 6800 guns.

337

Armies in the world are now flowing back in disorder and without hope up the mountain valleys down which they came with proud self-assurance.

November 4th, 4 p.m. According to the conditions of the armistice . . . . hostilities by land, sea and air on all the fronts of Austria-Hungary have been suspended at 3 p.m. to-day.

November 6th. At 3 p.m. on the 4th of November our troops had reached Sluderno in the Val Venosta, the Pass of Mendola and the Defile of Salomo in the Val d'Adige, Cembra in the Val d'Avisio, Levico in the Val Sugana, Fiera di Primiero, Pontebba, Plezzo, Tolmino, Gorizia, Cervignano, Aquileia and Grado.

Some of these names filled me with memories of a year, and more than a year, ago. Old Natale's message to the enemy chalked on our hut at Pec had come true. We had soon come back.

****

The fighting was over! That night of the 4th of November all the sky was lit up with bonfires and the firing of coloured rockets and white Véry lights. One could hear bells ringing in the distance, back toward Treviso, and singing and cheering everywhere. It was an hour of perfection, and of accomplishment; it was the ending of a story. An epic cycle of history was finished, the cycle of the wars of Italy against Austria. The task of completing Italian unity was finished, so far as a series of wars could finish it.

The fight is done, but the banner won;
Thy comrades of old have borne it hence,
Have borne it in triumph hence.
Then the soldier spake from the deep, dark grave:
'I am content.'

The soldier had done his duty, now let the statesman do no less. Let wisdom and imagination make sure the fruits of valour.

****

The old Austria is dead, and from her grave, which Italian hands have dug, are rising up new nations, the future comrades of the old nations and of Italy, who in these bloody years has grown from youth to full manhood. It has been said that a nation is a friendship, and the common life of nations in the future must also be a friendship, necessarily less intimate but in no way less real. The youth of the world must never be called to swim again, with old age on its back, through seas of needless death to the steep and distant cliffs of military victory. There must be no more secret plots, nor seeming justification of plots, by little groups of elderly men against the lives and happiness of young men everywhere. The world must be made safe for justice and for youth.

****

Youth was rejoicing that night in Italy, when the war against Austria ended. And not youth only, nor Italians only. The British troops loudly and healthily and almost riotously sang also, all the temporary soldiers and nearly all the regulars. Yet here and there were gloom, and drab, wet blankets, trying to make smoulder those raging fires of joy. In a few officers' Messes, especially among the more exalted units, men of forty years and more croaked like ravens over their impending loss of pay and rank, Brigadier Generals who would soon be Colonels again, and Colonels who would soon be Majors. To have been, through long uneventful unmental years, a peace-time soldier puts the imagination in jeopardy and is apt to breed a self-centred fatuity, which the inexperienced may easily mistake for deliberate naughtiness. Yet these brave men, who hate peace and despise civilians, have many human qualities. They are generally polite to women, and they are kind to animals and to those of their inferiors who show them proper deference and salute them briskly. It is not always easy to judge them fairly. And that night one did not try. They jarred intolerably. They seemed a portent, though in truth they were something less. They found themselves left alone to their private griefs, ruminating regretfully over the golden age that had suddenly ended, gazing into the blackness of a future without hope.

In the Euganean Hills

November 12th, 1918. It is all over. For a few days it seemed possible that we might be sent northward, through redeemed Trento and over the Brenner and the crest of the Alps and down through Innsbruck, to open a new front against Germany along the frontier of Bavaria. But that will not be necessary now. It is all over.

Our Battery is living partly in a little terra-cotta Villa and partly in a barn close by. We are among the Euganean Hills, a group of little humps, shaped like sugar loaves, which rise out of the dead level of the Venetian Plain, south-west of Padua. Here Shelley wrote a famous and beautiful poem, and Venice, on a clear day, is visible in the distance from a monastery perched among trees upon one of the loftiest humps. Our guns, which will never fire any more, sit in a neat row, "dressed by the right," along the garden path outside the Villa, their noses pointing across a grass lawn. Their names, which are the Battery's Italian history, are painted on their muzzles and their trails in large white letters, picked out with red upon a dark green ground: *Carso, Piave, Altipiano and Trentino. Trentino* is my gun. They look very ornamental in their new coats of paint, and with a high polish on their unpainted metal parts.

It is an hour of anticlimax. There is nothing to do, and one has to "make work" in a hundred silly, ingenious ways. Next week some of the men who have been out of England for 19 months will go on leave. Then, after a fortnight in England, unless something tremendous and unexpected happens, they will all come back again. And there will still be nothing to do. Was it Wordsworth who said that poetry is "emotion remembered in tranquillity"? Wordsworth would undoubtedly have written much poetry here. Our chief delight is Leary's musical voice. He sings to us in the evenings after dinner, *La Campana di San Ginsto* and *Addio, mia bell', addio* and choice *stornetti*, and *Come to Ferrara with me*, a cheerful song of his own composing, set to a music-hall tune which was famous three years ago, and *We'll all go a-hunting to-day*, an old song with a superb chorus. And so the days pass, one very like another.

I dreamed last night that a regular soldier of high degree and uncertain nationality appeared to me and said:

"Do you not see now, young man, that peace is degeneracy, and that war is an ennobling discipline?"

And I, chancing my luck, replied, "Yes, the great von Moltke himself said that peace is a dream, and not even a beautiful dream."

Whereupon my visitor changed into a white owl and vanished with a hoot. And I awoke, and found that I had overslept myself and that the nine o'clock parade, which I was due to attend, was already falling in outside.

Then said I to myself bitterly, "At any rate we here have all survived, and, therefore, since war is the greatest of all biological tests, we must all be very fit to have survived, especially that most fit young man, who came out to the Battery from England a day or two before the armistice was signed, after three years at Shoeburyness, and the fittest of all must be those whose survival, apart from such dangers as influenza and air raids, has never been in doubt, the valuable people who have been kept in England, because they were members of concert parties or football teams at the depots, or officers' servants to influential *imboscati*, or influential *imboscati* themselves."

And then, with a great and well-disciplined effort, I pulled my thoughts together, and said to myself, "Enough of these musings of the peace-time soldier!"

CHAPTER 42

Last Thoughts on Leaving Italy

On the 3rd of December I passed out of Italy, after eighteen months spent as a soldier within her borders. These eighteen months will always be lit up for me by the memory of a great comradeship between men of Allied nations. We have lived together through the dark days and the sunshine, through sorrow and joy, through uncertainty and defeat to final victory.

I have been very fortunate in my personal relations in Italy. I have found always among Italians, both civilian and military, and from simple soldier to General, the most open friendliness, the most unsparing kindliness, the most happy spirit of good fellowship. And on my journey home I closed my eyes and imagined myself back once more at Venice in full Summer, and at Milan, and at hospitable Ferrara, and at Rome in the Spring, and on the shores of the Bay of Naples, and out on Capri, and in the wonder world of Sicily,—and always among friends. And then my steps went back in fancy to the battlefields, where our guns had been in action. I saw again the great peaks and the precipitous valleys of the Trentino. I saw the wreck of liberated Asiago, ringed round with mountains whose sides were clothed with shattered pine trees, heavy with snow, and I went down once more by that astounding mountain road from Granezza to Marostica, with the Venetian Plain and all its cities spread out beneath my feet, and Venice herself on the far horizon, amid the shimmer of sunshine on the distant sea. I stood again on the bridge at Bassano, look-

343

ing up the Val Brenta, with Monte Grappa towering above me on my right hand, and then turning south-eastward across the level plain I heard again the rushing waters of the Piave and, crossing to the farther side, passed through Conegliano, burnt out and ravaged, and Vittorio Veneto, a name that will resound for ever, to the broken bridge over the Meduna, east of Pordenone, and the village of Nogaredo, whither I came as one of its first liberators. And, as in a dream, I saw Udine, unspoilt and radiant as she was fifteen months ago, before Caporetto, and poor little Palmanova, as I last saw her, wreathed in the black smoke of her own burning, and the cypresses and the great church of Aquileia and the lagoons of Grado.

Then the flying feet of memory carried me beyond the Isonzo, up the wooded slopes of San Michele, where the dead lie thicker, and along the Vippacco, running swiftly between banks thick with acacias, and among the ruined suburbs of Gorizia, up towards those desolate lands, which for future generations of Italians will be, I think, the holiest ground of all— the bare summit of Monte Santo, and the mountain-locked tableland of Bainsizza, and the rocky, inexorable Carso.

These rocks have, perhaps, been more deeply soaked with blood than any other part of the entire Allied line on any continent. Here died many thousands of the bravest and the best of the youth of Italy. *"Nella primavera si combatte e si muore, o soldato."* How many great lovers, fathers, thinkers, poets, statesmen, that might have been, but never were, lie here! These lands will ever be more thickly peopled with the cemeteries of the dead than with the villages of the living, lands desolate and barren, yet strange and beautiful.

Clear and clean is the beauty of those graves in the noonday brightness, delicate and tremulous in the early dawn and in the soft light of a fading day, and for us, who think of those dead with a proud and tender emotion, that beauty is, in some sort, a frail consolation. The dust of strong men from the great mountains is buried here, and of men from the historic cities and the small unknown towns and the little white villages of

Italy, and of peasants from the wide plains, and of brave men from the islands, and a handful of Frenchmen and Englishmen along with them, and very many of those tragic soldiers, drawn from many races, who died in the service of the Austro-Hungarian State, fighting against their own freedom. I see again, as vividly as though it were yesterday, those high-hearted legions of Italy, sturdy men and fresh-faced boys, going forward with a frenzied courage, supported by an Artillery preparation which elsewhere would have been thought utterly insignificant, to assault positions which elsewhere would have been declared impregnable.

"The world," said Lincoln at Gettysburg, "will little note nor long remember what we say here, but it can never forget what they did here. It is for us, the living, rather to be dedicated here to the unfinished work which they who fought here have thus far so nobly advanced; that from these honoured dead we take increased devotion to that cause for which they gave the last full measure of devotion; that we here highly resolve that these dead shall not have died in vain."

So may it be!

They died for the dream of a greater, a free and a secure Italy, and, the more reflective of them, for a better, more coherent world and no more war. A part of their dream is already come true, but part is a dream still, a debt to them that only we can pay. It will need to be a far better world, with a progress sustained and ever growing through centuries to come, if this tremendous sum of wasted youth, of broken hearts, of embittered souls, of moral degradation, of wounds that cannot be healed until all this ill-fated generation has passed away, if this great sum of past and present evil is to be cancelled by future good in the cold balance of historic reality. Of the dead we may say, their task is over, their warfare is accomplished. But not of the living. The future is theirs, to make or mar.

LEONAUR

ALSO FROM LEONAUR

AVAILABLE IN SOFTCOVER OR HARDCOVER WITH DUST JACKET

THE COMPLEAT RIFLEMAN HARRIS *by Benjamin Harris as told to & transcribed by Captain Henry Curling*—The adventures of a soldier of the 95th (Rifles) during the Peninsular Campaign of the Napoleonic Wars

WITH WELLINGTON'S LIGHT CAVALRY *by William Tomkinson*—The Experiences of an officer of the 16th Light Dragoons in the Peninsular and Waterloo campaigns of the Napoleonic Wars.

SERGEANT BOURGOGNE *by Adrien Bourgogne*—With Napoleon's Imperial Guard in the Russian Campaign and on the Retreat from Moscow 1812 - 13.

SWORDS OF HONOUR *by Henry Newbolt & Stanley L. Wood*—The Careers of Six Outstanding Officers from the Napoleonic Wars, the Wars for India and the American Civil War, with dozens of illustrations by Stanley L. Wood.

SURTEES OF THE RIFLES *by William Surtees*—A Soldier of the 95th (Rifles) in the Peninsular campaign of the Napoleonic Wars.

ENSIGN BELL IN THE PENINSULAR WAR *by George Bell*—The Experiences of a young British Soldier of the 34th Regiment 'The Cumberland Gentlemen' in the Napoleonic wars.

HUSSAR IN WINTER *by Alexander Gordon*—A British Cavalry Officer during the retreat to Corunna in the Peninsular campaign of the Napoleonic Wars.

NAPOLEONIC WAR STORIES *by Sir Arthur Quiller-Couch*—Tales of soldiers, spies, battles & sieges from the Peninsular & Waterloo campaingns.

JOURNALS OF ROBERT ROGERS OF THE RANGERS *by Robert Rogers*—The exploits of Rogers & the Rangers in his own words during 1755-1761 in the French & Indian War.

KERSHAW'S BRIGADE VOLUME 1 *by D. Augustus Dickert*—Manassas, Seven Pines, Sharpsburg (Antietam), Fredricksburg, Chancellorsville, Gettysburg, Chickamauga, Chattanooga, Fort Sanders & Bean Station..

KERSHAW'S BRIGADE VOLUME 2 *by D. Augustus Dickert*—At the wilderness, Cold Harbour, Petersburg, The Shenandoah Valley and Cedar Creek.

A TIGER ON HORSEBACK *by L. March Phillips*—The Experiences of a Trooper & Officer of Rimington's Guides - The Tigers - during the Anglo-Boer war 1899 - 1902.

Printed in the United Kingdom
by Lightning Source UK Ltd.
124061UK00001B/340/A